The Girls in the Gang

ANNE CAMPBELL

Second Edition

Basil Blackwell

First published 1984
Reprinted in the USA 1984
Reprinted and first published in paperback 1986

Second edition published 1991

Basil Blackwell, Inc.
3 Cambridge Center
Cambridge, Massachusetts 02142, USA

Basil Blackwell Ltd
108 Cowley Road, Oxford, OX4 1JF, UK

Library of Congress Cataloging in Publication Data
Campbell, Anne, 1951–
   The girls in the gang/Anne Campbell.–2nd ed.
     p.   cm.
Includes bibliographical references (p.   ) and index.
ISBN 1-55786-120-X (pbk.)
1. Gangs–New York (N.Y.)–Case studies.   2. Delinquent girls–New
York (N.Y.)–Case studies.   3. Female offenders–New York (N.Y.)–
–Case studies.   I. Title.
HV6439.U5C37   1991
302.3'4–dc20   90–1216
                                                              CIP

British Library Cataloguing in Publication Data
A CIP catalogue record for this book is available from the British Library

Typeset in 11 on 12pt Baskerville
by Freeman Graphic, Tonbridge
Printed in Great Britain by Billing and Sons Ltd., Worcester

Contents

Introduction to the Second Edition

This is a book about young women by a woman. That's important because most of the writing on gangs – and most of social science – is about men and by men. Gender affects both the researcher and the researched. The traditional way of collecting data in social science is by maintaining a healthy and objective distance between the two. In fact, if researchers can avoid actually meeting their subjects, so much the better. Many academics succeed at this. There are nationally available databases containing survey material and government information on thousands of people, which mean that researchers can write entire books on white-collar crime, domestic violence, victimization, or gun use without ever meeting a criminal or a victim. They simply take the data, code it into categories, put it into a computer program for statistical analysis, and out comes a concise list of the ten variables which best predict rape or robbery or anything else they want to understand.

So what's wrong with that? To many people, including most women, that doesn't constitute understanding. It certainly constitutes knowledge, but understanding demands that one knows not only what variables matter but how they have their impact. Take gender as an example. Men join gangs far and away more than women. If one wanted to explain gang membership using a statistical package, gender would probably show up as the single most important correlate. Does that mean we understand the relationship between gender and gang membership? Not to me it doesn't. What is it about being male that makes the gang so attractive? Is it testosterone, or the demands of machismo, or the way we raise boys as opposed to girls, or the economic pressures of male unemployment? The list of possible explanations could go on and on. The way we understand as opposed to know a phenomenon is to vicariously experience its lived reality – to sense what it would be like to be that other person, to see the world through his or her eyes.

The trouble is that if this is the goal, the only route is to talk to the people you want to understand. And that takes time, a determination to give up one's own perspective in favor of someone else's, and a messy involvement in the social and emotional demands that accompany a relationship between researcher and subject. Now this kind of work is not the sole terrain of women. Elliot Liebow's *Tally's Corner*[1] is a vivid account of streetcorner men in Washington, D.C., and Oscar Lewis's *La Vida*[2] is a wonderful documentation of Puerto Rican life. But the place that they are most referred to is in textbooks on methodology, where they are dragged out as the token examples of "qualitative research" – an arcane means of data collection which is of dubious validity and reliability. But times are changing in social science and the increasing involvement of women in the process is in part responsible for a movement toward greater insight into lived experience.

It was just such insight that I sought when I arrived in New York in 1979 to study girls in gangs. There were around four hundred gangs in the city at that time. For the first six months I concentrated on learning about the types of gangs, differences among gangs from each of the five boroughs of New York, changes in gang crime patterns, and gang philosophies. Some time was spent in libraries but most was used to visit city agencies and facilities, police precincts with gang problems, and gang members and ex-members. I was introduced to members primarily through John Galea and Nazim Fatah. Galea, a police officer in the Gang Intelligence Unit in Brooklyn, patiently drove me around the boroughs introducing me to members. The curiously friendly relationship he had developed with them is worth a book in its own right. He listened to their problems, tried to effect reconciliations with other clubs, played softball with them. They pumped him for gossip on other clubs' activities, expected him to get criminal charges against them dropped, even demanded that he visit them in prison or write them job references. Nazim Fatah, an ex-gang member in charge of the Inner City Roundtable of Youth, introduced me to the gangs who were working with him to stop inter-gang feuds and develop job skills. I edited their newsletter, interviewed members, and through a snowballing process gained access to less public-spirited groups.

It became clear that if I was to represent female members as whole people with their own biographies and attitudes and relationships to the community, I would have to restrict my scope. I selected three gangs who represented the diversity of gang life: a street gang, a biker gang, and a religio-cultural gang. One was racially mixed, one was Puerto Rican, and one black. Two were from Brooklyn and one from Manhattan. The age of members ranged from fifteen to thirty. I spent six months with each gang and in each focused on an individual girl.

I've often been asked how I got the girls to talk to me and I'm still not sure that I know how to answer the question. When I met them I explained that I was going to write a book about girls in gangs and that the only way I could do it was by hanging out with them. They were flattered and interested to find themselves on the receiving end of outside interest. Gangs are not insensitive to the media. Members clipped out any newspaper report that appeared with their name in and some even had scrapbooks. Visibility seemed to them preferable to obscurity, and even if they were castigated as hoodlums it was better than being altogether invisible as they were most of the time. The girls found it hard to believe that I really wanted to talk to them rather than the boys, who were usually the focus of attention. Reassured that I did, they asked permission from the male gang members to go ahead. The boys consented, confident that there was nothing of any real criminal significance that I could learn from the girls. (I think they regretted that assumption later.)

That's how it began. I would arrive at one of the girls' homes at different times of the day and spend the next few hours with her and her friends. I kept as low a profile as possible. I tried to let conversations take their natural course and to be an appreciative audience. As the girls got used to me, they asked about my life – not about my work, but about my marriage and its curious absence of children. (As a mother now, I have a new respect for these girls' struggles to feed and raise their children, often without a partner to offer economic or emotional support.) They accepted me, but not as one of them.

They were quite right, of course: I wasn't. The gulf that divided us was not, oddly enough, money – as a postgraduate fellow I was living on not much more than they were. But I had a way out and they didn't. I went home to an all-white neighborhood with a low crime rate. I had friends in professional jobs and universities. I had a publisher waiting for a book. Sometimes I acted as their representative to middle-class authority, speaking on their behalf to their children's teachers, the building superintendent, the welfare people, or the police. I babysat for their kids and bought my share of beer. They talked to me as individuals on rainy afternoons and as part of the group on humid summer nights in front of the projects or on their stoops. After a while they let me use the tape recorder so that I could get their story right and tell it in their own words rather than mine.

The most obvious danger of this approach, however, is that members can lie to you. But by remaining with a group for a period of time it is quite difficult for either researcher or subject to sustain false impressions. It is hard to maintain a systematic deceit or an alien persona for six months and members of the gang or the community are apt to give the game away. But there were, I do not doubt, facts that were hidden from me. Often accounts of criminal activities were oddly inconsistent over time: I suspect that on occasion members feared they had said too much and made attempts to cover themselves. More often, girls talked freely about more incriminating matters if, upon request, I did not use the tape recorder. The real issue, however, is related to the meaning of "truth" in social life.[3] Ample research in the study of memory generally and eyewitness testimony particularly indicates that errors frequently occur in the rehearsal of "facts." We often fill in details by inference from the information we have. This "filling in" may be only one part of a general process of self-presentation. Social interaction is a creative process in which we select to present ourselves as a particular type of person and then offer accounts of our actions which support that view of ourselves. When we are asked why we did a particular thing, we can offer many explanations of our action. But which account is the *true* reason? All of them. The one chosen for presentation is probably a function of the relationship between the questioner and ourselves. So the accounts the girls give are likely to be a function of their conception of themselves and the person they wanted to present to me. In that sense, everything they say is true. Sometimes, however, the facts may have been altered.

This book differs from other reports of gangs not only in the obvious sense of focusing on girls but in setting out their stories as biographies and as accounts of relationships. This is quite different from traditional reports, which are cross-sectional in design, either using the hit-and-run questionnaire technique or offering a qualitative account spanning the year or two during which the researcher was present to observe events. The reconstruction of the girls' lives came naturally to me and equally naturally to the girls themselves. I don't mean that they sat down one day and decided to pour it all out. Rather they talked about the present and future in terms of events in the past. Difficulties with their children today were linked with recollections of their own childhood and with the anticipation of the time ahead when they would be free from their role as mothers. Matters of honor and dignity in defending their reputations provoked memories of the passive indignity of their mothers' lives. Accusations of being a "whore" reminded one girl of her father's girlfriend – a prostitute – who placed a curse on her to follow in her footsteps. As the old maxim says "We live life forwards but make sense of it backwards."

This is true not only for the girls themselves but for us as the audience to their stories. Joining a gang is an act that, from an outside observer's stance, appears to be one of social self-destruction. It can only make sense in the context of the members' previous experiences. It is only by seeing their history of rejection, anchorless wandering, and interpersonal mistrust that an outsider can understand how the camaraderie they see in the gang holds any real attraction. It seemed obvious to me that, to see the gang as the girl sees it, I had to put it in the context of the long trajectory of the past. We are who we are today because of the cumulative events which have shaped us into these people. The past is expressed in the choices that we make today, just as those choices will constrain the future that has yet to arrive.

The second theme of the book – the importance of the relationships and social network in which the individual is located – also seemed to emerge unbidden. It would in fact have been impossible to recreate these girls' day-to-day lives without mentioning the neighbor from whom they borrowed food, the mother who took the kids for the day, or the girls waiting on the corner for them. Yet in many accounts of male gangs, the reader is left with the eerie feeling that these boys have no family, neighbors, siblings, or teachers. They seem to exist solely in and for the gang.

I understand more clearly now than I did when I began the research why both the girls themselves and I talked so much about relationships. Recent feminist writing in social science has identified the central role of expressive relationships in women's lives, compared with the instrumental relationships of males.[4] Women's lives are intimately involved with others as daughters, wives, and mothers. Concern with the maintenance of reciprocity and mutuality is paramount in their thinking. Issues of abstract rights and wrongs are alien to a woman's view of the world; good and bad have meaning only in the context of people. Held for longer in the confines of the family, bound (however ambivalently) to her mother in the continuity of their shared gender, she knows that the children she bears will look to her for protection and care. To provide this she must learn to relinquish her own needs for sleep, freedom, and material goods. She knows just as surely that she must teach them how to cast her off and find their own place in the world. These relationships structure her life as she reaches not only down to the next generation but across to her peers who face the same day-to-day struggles; the struggles to love without engulfing and to maintain a sense of self while being immersed in the lives of others.

Men, by contrast, distance themselves from the mother early and move quickly into the world beyond. Mutuality is exchanged for competition and a wary distance between competitors. They move about in an essentially male world, subject to male agents of control; the boss, the police, the father. They aspire to be free agents, priding themselves on their autonomy, on the fact that they "don't need anybody." Independence has a price, of course; fear of dependency and vulnerability. The girls in this book fear their own vulnerability too, but for them loneliness is too high a price to pay. They remain enmeshed in the relationships that provide a route to human contact.

When the book first appeared, many people liked it and some didn't. One critic objected that it was too much about talk and not enough about behavior. It seems to me that there is a behavioral hegemony in social science. Nothing really matters except what we do. Attitudes only matter if they predict behavior, emotions only matter if they correlate with action. The assumption seems to be that "real" life is the piling up of one behavior on top of another. But if you think of your daily life, it's not usually the behavior that is important. Indeed, most days are the humdrum repetition of routines and chores, and this is true for gang members too. What constitutes the real fabric of daily life is talk, reflection, and ideas – that is where we construct ourselves and those around us. (And surely academics of all people would accept this as true of their own lives.) By retelling war stories, "bitching" about our enemies, complaining about our partners, comparing our lives with those of others (in the neighborhood and on television), we creatively make ourselves into people with a definite sense of identity and location in the world. All of this matters as much as, if not more than, what we do.

Another critic charged that the book portrayed gang members as too much like other girls from the same ethnic background and community. What lurks behind this viewpoint is the desire to stigmatize gang girls as different – to turn them into "folk devils" whom we can distance from our own respectable lives. It is the old social science need to find the "significant differences" between them and us. But the fact is that gang girls are not nearly as different as academics would like them to be. In letting the girls talk about their own relationships with others both in the gang and beyond it, it became clear that they are connected to, not separated from, the neighborhood and culture around them. Traditionally male researchers have attempted to isolate the gang, to tear it away from the community in which it lives, to give it an abstract sociological existence as a social enigma to be explained. It is possible to do this by refusing to listen when the members talk of their parents, siblings, lovers, and friends, and to demand instead that they place a checkmark in the appropriate box. These kinds of studies not only do violence to the human beings they seek to understand but consistently fail to produce the "significant differences" that researchers are looking for.

At a broader level, these two criticisms (that behavior matters more than lived experience and that gang members are different to the rest of us) spring from the same orientation which has been on the ascendant in the Reagan–Bush years. It is the desire to isolate and control without benefit of understanding. Never mind their poverty, their struggles to raise children, their victimization by fathers and lovers, their need to belong and be accepted. We don't want to hear their problems – they *are* the problem. Count up their crimes and show us how to spot them early.

Criticism also came from the other end of the political spectrum. I was accused of having failed to provide a fully socialist analysis of girl gang members. In stressing their conservatism, their consumerism, their adherence to the romantic vision of finding the right man, I had not told many radical criminologists what they wanted to hear. Ideally they wanted to be told that gang girls were naive revolutionaries, that their crimes were acts of "slow rioting." Of course, left-wing criminologists knew from bitter experience that this wasn't the case, so instead I was supposed to discuss the state of false consciousness in which the gang girls lived. I was meant to explain how the soft machine of capitalism had fooled them into being poverty class republicans; how, powerless and passive, they had been sold a bill of goods by American society. I couldn't oblige. To do that I would have had to do one of two things that were unacceptable to me. I would have had to misrepresent what the gang girls were telling me by omitting any mention of their love affair with conventional society, or I would have had to set myself up as having some direct line to the truth that they themselves were unable to see.

What I hope I have done is to open a door, on the other side of which are Connie, Weeza, and Sun-Africa constructing their lives in communities that we drive through but don't stop in. Their stories are told in their own words. There are many more of the gang girls out there, if anyone wants to listen to what they have to say. If we listen to their voices, we can learn what the gang means to them, and perhaps why they were unable to fulfill their needs elsewhere.

Acknowledgments

My first debt of gratitude must be to Connie, Weeza, and Sun-Africa, who allowed me to share a part of their lives. Their friendship and patience with me made a lasting impression and I hope I have done justice to their experiences. Thanks also to members and ex-members of the following gangs who participated in the work: Angels of the Night, Chingalings, Crazy Homicides, Devil's Rebels, Five Percent Nation, Flames, Montauk Chestbreakers, Sandman Ladies and Sandman, Savage Riders, Sex Girls and Boys, Together Brothers, Turban Queens and Saints, Wheels of Soul, Youths of Hell.

Special thanks must go to John Galea of the New York City Police Department who informed and morally supported the work and introduced me to gangs. Those from agencies and youth projects who also cooperated are Marilyn Masick and Larry Klein (Division for Youth, New York State), Barrie Mason (District Three, Brooklyn) and Terry Henry (Subpalace, Brooklyn). Nazim Fatah (Inner City Roundtable of Youth, Manhattan) went out of his way to introduce me to gang members and to encourage my work. The photographs were taken by Kingsley Bishop (pp. 51, 55, 86, 90, 104, 133, 177), John Galea (pp. 111, 113, 161, 195, 225) and Pete Marsh (p. 108).

My research was supported by a Harkness Fellowship from the Commonwealth Fund and by the Daniel and Florence Guggenheim Foundation through the enthusiasm of Dr. Jamison Doig of Princeton University. The School of Criminal Justice at Rutgers University kindly provided a postdoctoral place and a supportive social environment in which to try out ideas. Dr. Freda Adler was responsible for initiating this hospitality, and her concern went far beyond the call of duty.

In articulating and synthesizing the ideas in this book, I owe a particular debt of thanks to Dr. Steven Muncer. He is my major critic and most loyal supporter. Many of the themes are an extension of work on which we have cooperated in the past. However, as tradition demands, I take full responsibility for the ideas as they are finally expressed. The manuscript was typed by Touraine M. Coleman.

For Erdwin Morales (1963–81)

Chapter 1

The Praised and the Damned

Cops bust up gang rumble on IND tracks
by Philip Messing

A bloody subway rumble involving three notorious Manhattan youth gangs – armed with a sawed-off rifle, baseball bats, metal-studded bracelets and chains – was narrowly averted last night on the tracks of a Manhattan train station.

Ten well-armed members of The Renegades and The Chosen Ones jumped over turnstiles at the IND's 168th St. downtown subway station to chase three members of The Sandmen [sic], a rival gang police said.

"If they had been caught, they would have definitely been hurt badly," said plainclothes Transit Officer Noel Negron.

Negron and his partner, Officer Lenko Kaica, who were standing on the platform, joined in the chase, which continued in the southbound subway tunnel and ended in a nearby park.

Police searched the area and found a sawed-off rifle, leather bracelet with metal studs, leather belts, a baseball bat and a bandolier with several empty bullet casings.

Four youths – including Samuel (Sinbad) Gonzalez, president of The Chosen Ones – were arrested and charged with illegal weapons possession, defacing a firearm, criminal trespass and theft of services.

The rest of the gang members escaped.

Police said The Renegades and Chosen Ones had joined forces after The Sandmen beat up a member of The Chosen Ones and looted an apartment of the rival gang's president.

(*New York Post*, Thursday, October 9, 1980)

Connie is the leader of the the Sandman Ladies, a female affiliate of the Sandman based in Manhattan's Upper West Side. On October 9, 1980, we were sitting together outside the city-owned apartment block in which she lived. Concrete benches and tables had thoughtfully been provided for the leisure hours of the residents, which, given the unemployment rate of the occupants, tended to be many. The seats had been taken over that day by the

4

gang members, who shifted uneasily between surveying Broadway and Amsterdam avenues and returning to smoke, drink, and talk at our table. Between Connie and I lay a brown paper bag, which might have been taken for a beer can hidden from the police. Gino, the leader of the Sandman, was at a downtown gang community center, attempting to straighten things out between the Chosen Ones, the Renegades, and his own gang. In his absence, Connie was in charge. Conversation was stilted and tense, and Connie interrupted anyone who spoke too long or too much, dispatching them to the corner to look out. At 3:30 Connie announced she had to go pick up her kid from school. The guys were told to keep watch. She pushed the bag toward me, telling me to use it if I needed it. It contained a .32-caliber gun. With that, Connie put on her sunglasses and left to collect her two-year-old daughter from the nursery.

In New York City there may be as many as four hundred gangs with a total membership between 8,000 and 40,000. Ten percent of those members are female, ranging in age from fourteen to thirty. Some are married and many have children. They are blamed as the inciters of gang feuds; they are described as "passive, property and promiscuous." They are accused of being more vicious than any male; they are praised for being among the few with enough power to curb male gang crime. For some they represent the coming of age of urban women's liberation, for others the denial of the best qualities of womanhood. The contradictions of their position have provoked speculation among the police, the media, and the public about their reasons for joining, their roles and way of life. Despite the volumes written on male gang members, however, little is actually known about the girls, the standard reason being that girls constitute such a small proportion of gang members and are responsible for an even smaller number of gang crimes. Writers have also found male gangs, apart from their criminological interest, to be revealing in far wider sociological and psychological ways.[1] Gangs have been discussed in terms of societal structure, class relations, rites of passage in adolescence, group cohesion, ecological pressures, learning mechanisms, even linguistic usage. Yet in most of these accounts too, girls are invisible or appear as a footnote, an enigma, an oddity.

Little enough is known in terms of hard numbers on the size of the gang problem generally; let alone on girls' involvement. In the sixties, for example, it was widely believed that gangs had finally disappeared. Absorbed into youth politics, some argued. Fighting in Vietnam, said others, or turned into self-destructive junkies. It seems likely that their disappearance was a media sleight of hand.[2] New York stopped reporting gang stories and the rest of the country followed suit. Gangs die out and are reincarnated regularly by the media whenever news is slow. As a phenomenon they have never been fully put to rest. When a crime involving a few teenagers from a poor area makes news, gangs "reappear" in New York City. When gangs return, they are not reinvented. Though they may be inactive for a few months or a few years, they are quietly living in the tradition and culture that has sustained them for over a hundred years in the United States.

Statistics on gang membership have only been available since the 1970s when police departments in major cities became sufficiently concerned about the problem to set up Gang Intelligence Units. In 1975, sociologist Walter Miller attempted to document the size of the gang problem in a government report.[3] He was criticized not only by academics but by members of the very police departments he interviewed for relying on gross estimates which in many cases were contaminated by changes in recording methods and poor record keeping. Often they were no more than informed guesses to unanswerable questions.

A more approachable question is the extent to which the roles girls play in the gang have changed over time, but even this is not without difficulties. In reviewing a hundred years of writing on female gang involvement, it is difficult to separate the true nature of girls' involvement from the particular interpretive stance of the writer (usually male), whose moral or political view most probably reflects the prevailing community standards. These must have affected the girls too and the nature of their involvement in the gang. Nevertheless, certain themes appear consistently throughout the writing and reveal important factors in the girls' participation, as constants and as historical changes in their roles.

Two factors can help in interpretting the roles of the girls. The first is the girls' class value orientation – their desire and ability to be upwardly mobile in terms of their life-style. Gang girls are almost unanimously working- or lower-class from the point of view of their parents' income and educational and employment status, but class value orientation is distinct from the reality of social class itself. Some of the girls described, while working-class, show a distinct desire to climb the social ladder. They value middle-class concerns such as the deferment of immediate gratification, long-term planning, and the desirability of self-improvement, and they also are able to deal effectively with middle-class institutions such as school and work. In the literature they are held up as "good girls." "Good girls" are feminine girls. It has been traditional to equate femininity with middle-class attributes (being well-groomed, charming, polite, passive, and modest), while masculinity is associated with working-class stereotypes (being direct, confrontational, nonverbal, physical).

Among the "good girls," some want to assume traditional complementary roles toward males. They look forward to a future as Good Wives, dependent financially and emotionally upon a man, living in a clean, decent apartment (perhaps not quite in the area of town to which they aspire) with children who are well dressed and who will grow up to better themselves in a respectable job as clerks or carpenters. Although this girl associates with a boy from the neighborhood gang, her aim is to save him from his rowdy friends who are clearly a bad element, bringing out the worst in him.

Some "good girls" assume relations with men that are not complementary but similar. These are the Independent Women. Ideally, they hope to go to college and become self-supporting with a decent job, as nurses, secretaries, or bank clerks. They may want children but do not want the financial dependence associated with total reliance on a man's income. If worse comes to worst, they will obtain welfare child allowance and raise the kids alone or with the help of their mother. They associate with the gang but only as an adolescent phase. They may go a little crazy as teenagers, but they are not lowlifes or bums. Nor do they plan to spend their lives in a grubby apartment, taking the children upstate on a bus every weekend to visit their father in prison.

The majority of gang girls, however, have a static class value orientation. They are not tortured by dreams of upward mobility and have a realistic view of their chances of success in society. They have not done well in school, and when they have money, they spend it (often when they don't have it as well). They watch television specials about the rich and famous but understand that, short of a win on the numbers, those life-styles are extravagant dreams. They certainly are not interested in the intermediate status of a lower-middle-class suburban life-style. Like the boys in the neighborhood, they enjoy excitement and trouble, which break the monotony of a life in which little attention is given to the future. They like sharp clothes, loud music, alcohol, and soft drugs. They admire toughness and verbal "smarts." They may not be going anywhere, but they make the most of where they are. Authority, in the shape of school, parents, and police, is the enemy but a welcome one since it generates confrontations and livens things up. Because these girls accept a lower-class value system, they are represented in the literature as "bad girls." Men may find dignity by being straightforward, unpretentious, and working class, but women do not.

Among the "bad girls," as within the "good girls," some take the traditional complementary role toward their men. Boyfriends take precedence over same-sex friendships, and boys are the ones who really matter. Because of this, these girls see other girls as possible rivals and are constantly on their guard. The major focus of their quest for excitement lies in romances with the boys in which they assume a passive role. This passivity can make them the victims of unscrupulous males who may lead them into prostitution or drug addiction. Even if such a dramatic fate is avoided, their undisguised interest in sexual relationships has led them to be branded as Sex Objects by many writers (in spite of the fact that boys who show a similar interest in sex avoid this kind of labeling). The only time this type of girl escapes her passivity is when she provokes fights within and between male gang members by her promiscuous sexual behavior and her treacherous revelation of one boy's secrets to another. But even in this, her behavior has a traditional female quality: scheming, divisive, and nonconfrontational.

Some "bad girls" choose to compete with males on their own terms and are therefore considered in the literature as Tomboys. They insist on accompanying their men to gang rumbles and on joining in. They pride themselves on being tough and take particular pride in fighting and beating male gang members. To prove their toughness, they emulate typically male crimes such as robbery, burglary, and auto theft, and some achieve the distinction of being arrested and, more rarely and therefore more prestigiously, of being sent to jail. Like the males, they have strong same-sex friendships within the gang and pride themselves on their solidarity.

However, Sex Objects and Tomboys have much in common. Both have romantic and sexual relationships with the boys in the gang, but Tomboys give equal attention to their female friends. Both will engage in fights with female rivals for their man, but Tomboys fight for other reasons as well, whereas Sex Objects feel that fighting is usually a man's job. Both will use their femininity in the service of the gang by acting as spies with other nearby gangs, by luring unsuspecting male victims into situations where they are robbed or assaulted by the boys, and by carrying concealed weapons for the boys since as females they cannot be searched on the street by male officers.[4]

These types of roles tend to suggest a no-win situation for gang girls. As Sex Objects, they are cheap women rejected by other girls, parents, social workers, and ironically often by the boys themselves. As Tomboys, they are resented by boys and ridiculed by family and friends who wait patiently for them to "grow out of it." Among lower-class women, the Independent Woman, as often as not, raises her children in an all-female household. In so doing, she becomes the target of government, academic, and media concern by those who accuse her of rearing a new cycle of delinquents or, if she works, of ousting the male from the labor force by taking low wages. Among the black population especially, as feminist writer Michele Wallace suggests, a covert war between the sexes may exist because of the male's perception of the Independent Woman as "castrating."[5] Clearly the most socially acceptable role is that of Good Wife. Yet even here the Woman is often characterized as the fun-spoiling petty bourgeoise who takes the high-spirited male away from his gang friends to a future of shopping expeditions and diaper changing. Perhaps this is an overdrawn picture, yet in a classic account of male gang life by William Whyte one can almost hear a groan from the author as two members of the Norton Street Gang fall in love with socially aspiring girls and leave their old street friends behind.[6].

With this typology in mind, we can now turn to some of the literature on the nature of girls' involvement with street gangs, tracing their roles from the last century to the present day.

The earliest account of gangs in New York City dates their inception from about 1825.[7] The first gang originated in the Five Points district of lower Manhattan at the crossroads of Cross, Anthony, Little Water, Orange, and Mulberry streets. Called the Forty Thieves, it was composed of Irishmen and originated from a drinking spot owned ironically by a woman – Rosanna Peers. Within a short time, other gangs had formed in the neighborhood, most also Irish: the Shirt Tails, the Plug Uglies, the Dead Rabbits, the Roach Guards, and others. The earliest accounts of gang wars indicate that the battles continued for two and three days at a stretch, during which the streets were barricaded with carts and paving stones and the police were helpless to intervene. Yet in these accounts there is no evidence of women being excluded from the fighting. In the famous three-day feud between the Bowery and the Five Points, we hear of some women performing their traditional auxiliary role faithfully: "On the outskirts of the struggling mob of thugs ranged the women, their arms filled with reserved ammunition, their keen eyes watching for a break in the enemy's defense, and always ready to lend a hand or a tooth in the fray."[8]

Gangs were diversified in the focus of their criminal activities even then. The primary distinction, similar to the later conflict and criminal gangs of the 1950s, was between those who were fighters and those whose motivation was primarily financial gain.

> While the early gangsters of the Five Points and the Bowery were frequently thieves, and on occasion murderers, *they were primarily brawlers and street fighters*, and most of their battling was done in the open. But the thugs who infested the Fourth Ward and swarmed each night into its dives and gin-mills for their recreation and plotting were *killers and robbers first of all. They seldom engaged in gutter rows with the gangs of other districts . . .*[9]

Women were represented in each of the types of gang activities, and some gained wide reputations. Their roles and personalities correspond well with descriptions of girls in gangs written 100 years later. Then, as later, females were blamed for instigating gang wars. Such girls were often described as Sex Objects. In 1908, Carroll Terry was a dancing girl of outstanding beauty in a dance hall in Coney Island. One day Louie the Lump (a Bowery gang leader) danced with her and finally exacted a promise that she would return with him to Manhattan after her night's work. She indicated to him her affection for rival gang leader Kid Twist. That same day Kid also appeared at the resort and Carroll, in true female style, told him of Louie's interest in her. Kid sought Louie out in a bar on Surf Avenue and forced him, under threat, to jump out of the window. Louie called Manhattan for reinforcements and, when they arrived, lured Kid Twist and his friend Cyclone Louis out of the bar and shot them down on the sidewalk, together with Carroll Terry. Sometimes motivated by vanity, sometimes acting under male direction, girls have been accused of contributing to male inter-gang hostilities by provoking fights and acting as spies and lures up through even the more recent work on female gangs of the 1970s.

When not depicted as Sex Objects, girls were described as

Tomboys. The Gophers had a ladies' section known as the Battle Row Ladies Social and Athletic Club or, more popularly, the Lady Gophers. In charge of them was Battle Annie whose prowess as a fighter was well known and who held classes to instruct her members in the art of combat. When the labor unions and employers began hiring gangsters, Annie became rich by supplying well-trained females to both sides. While Battle Annie presents an unusual figure of a Tomboy who never grew out of it, most young female fighters were saved by a good man. Wild Maggie Carson was one of the many girls who led a juvenile male gang – the Forty Little Thieves. She was a wild young fighter until; "The Rev. Mr. Pease taught her the joy of sewing buttons on shirts."[10] Subsequently, she married well and reformed.

All over the city, young men's social clubs had been in evidence for most of the nineteenth century, but they reached their zenith in the 1890s. They were largely controlled by the political associations formed by Tammany district leaders to strengthen their hold on the voters. The bosses provided money for outings and gifts for the poor and through the clubs made contact with gang thugs who would remove opponents and cast illegal votes. Some of these clubs had women members who were admitted with full membership privileges, and their names complemented those of the male clubs to which they were attached: the Lady Locusts, the Lady Barkers Association, the Lady Flashers, the Lady Liberties of the Fourth Ward, and the Lady Truck Drivers Association. The clubs met in barns, tenement basements, saloons, and back rooms. That the females were auxiliaries of male gangs was evident then as today. Furthermore, the dubious status of some "social clubs" continued into the early twentieth century with the accounts of Thrasher in 1927 and even Whyte in 1938.

The early years of this century, characterized by massive immigration, saw the establishment of thousands of local social clubs in urban areas such as New York and Chicago. The majority of these were pro-social in intent and provided the recently arrived immigrant with a social circle of others who spoke his native language and who could help him adapt to the New World. The settlement clubs were often run by established middle-class professionals in an area with a view to acculturating immigrants. They offered advice on practical matters and encouraged the use of English. A 1931 survey published by the Welfare Council of Settlements in the City of New York showed they had nearly as many female as male adolescent members (9,600 and 12,500 respectively). While the aim of such clubs may have been laudable, some at least were resented by the local youths, who saw them as an attempt to deny the validity of the group's own language and culture. Street gangs, by contrast, sprang from the youth themselves. But street gangs may not have been so prevalent in the United States without the role model of the social clubs with their use of names, emblems, rules, initiations, and dues. At any rate, it appears that girls were more willing to cooperate with these externally organized clubs and in New York joined the Elmer Pals, Comrades All, and Chums Social.

Frederick Thrasher one of the first American criminologists, made an extensive survey of Chicago gangs, which was published in 1927.[11] He saw gangs as a "natural" progression from a childhood search for excitement in a situation of social disorganization engendered by poverty, poor integration of immigrants, and failure of parental supervision. The gangs, however, were nourished and given a certain legitimacy by corrupt politicians and crime syndicates who exploited gang members in their own interests. Many of Thrasher's "gangs" were little more than social clubs that from time to time engaged in some suspect activities. He was able to locate only five or six all-female gangs, – four of which were social clubs and the remaining two organized around baseball in one instance and stealing in the other. What roles, then, did the girls fulfill?

During puberty and early adolescence, the boys were generally hostile to girls because in their view the girls were too young, did not like the boys, were never around, got nothing out of the gang, and wanted only to spend money and get them into trouble. Even as girlfriends, rather than members, they were felt to weaken group loyalty by demanding time and attention and to impair the gangs' functioning as a conflict group dedicated to fighting rival neighborhood groups. Boys in the gang were ridiculed and punished for overt interest in girls although, at the same time, a code of chivalry prohibited fighting with girls. Those gangs that did include girls were described as immoral rather than conflict gangs. Their chief activities included petting, necking, illicit sex, and mugging, and they had names like Tulips, the Lone Star Club, the Under-the-L gang, and the Night Riders. Thrasher believed such groups were the result of rooming-house environments which encouraged a precocious interest in sex among young people thirteen to fifteen years old. In spite of this heavy emphasis on sexuality, a few females played an equal part in gangs, either as sweetheart or gangster.

Thrasher concluded that one reason for the relative absence of girls from gangs stemmed from the closer supervision of girls even in disorganized urban areas as well as "the social patterns for the behavior of girls, powerfully backed by the great weight of tradition and custom," which were in opposition to the gang and its activities. Thus, for Thrasher, the essential nature of the girls was middle class, and, even under conditions of social disorganization, deviations from sex role were rare and temporary. The strictures of being female remained fundamental, constant and unchanging even when other social norms were in flux. There was no real place for females in the illegitimate opportunity structure. Once wayward girls had realized this, they reverted to the niche society had carved for them, and in the 1920s this was principally as Good Wives.

Whyte's 1943 account of Italian street life in Chicago documents the relationship between the upwardly mobile "college boys" settlement club, the Italian Community Club, and the lower-class "corner boys" group, the Norton Street Gang.[12] The community club was run by outside social workers who knew little of life in the Italian community and often did not even speak the language. Although they received a cross section of the very young boys and girls, with age many members fell away into their own informal groupings. Many of the senior girls' clubs remained inside the settlement and were composed of those girls who considered themselves more socially aspiring than their agemates. The same was true of the boys. The rest joined informal and less structured street groups. Nevertheless, the unity of the Norton Street Gang was severely threatened when some of the members became interested in a girls' settlement club, the Aphrodite Club. The girls met in the settlement house and greatly prized their friendship with the boys of the Italian Community Club. The Norton Street Gang began to form contacts with the girls with a twofold aim: to take the girls away from the settlement house and thus to prove their masculinity over the Italian community boys and to each other. The girls seem to have served only as a gauge of the boys' sexual prowess and prestige in the group. Ultimately, continued association with them led to the reform of one gang member (who abandoned gambling and began to attend the settlement house) and marriage for two members, resulting in their alienation from the gang. The force that "good girls" exert toward conformity is the logical corollary of the force that "bad girls" exert as instigators of gang feuds.

A 1949 description of New York juvenile gangs by William Bernard sounds quite contemporary.[13] Although official figures estimated the number of male gangs to be between sixty and 200, Bernard suggested the existence of at least 250 in Harlem alone, with membership running between a dozen and 200 per gang. Seven out of ten gangs at that time were limited to a single ethnicity: Negro, Italian, Irish, Jewish, and, by then, Puerto Rican. They had distinctive dress and many had connections with adult gangsters. Gang feuds were fought with daggers, bayonets, ice picks, and zip guns. Bernard reported growth in the number of girls in gangs at this time, principally in the role of Sex Objects. During the war years, groups of girls would pick up soldiers and lure them into side streets where their male accomplices, too young to be conscripted, would "roll" or rob them. In one incident a girl was dispatched to seduce a rival gang leader in a loft while her gang notified the police of her whereabouts and claimed she was being raped. Characteristically, the girls' function was to carry weapons (because they were immune to search by male officers), provide alibis, act as spies and lures, and provide sex for the male members. Any aggression had a typically "female" character: the favorite weapon was a lye and soda mixture that the girls hurled in the faces of their enemies. This concoction was used against members of their own gang who slept with opposing gang members, as well as in inter-gang disputes in which the females of one gang would fight the female auxiliaries of another. Virtually all the girls were affiliated with male gangs, although they took on their own names such as the Robinettes, the Chandeliers, and the Shangri-La Debs. Police probation reports described initiation rituals that required the prospective member to have intercourse with a member of the male affiliate gang. Older girls were reported to have procured younger girls for the boys with the express intention of rape. Girls in this account, as in many other, are seen in relatively few roles: as agents provocateurs, generating wars and feuds between otherwise peaceful male clubs; as fallen women; and as cat fighters. But the overwhelming impression, once again, is of gang girls as Sex Objects.

In the 1950s what was lacking in data on the gang problem was made up for in grand theorizing. Two classic criminological books were written on gangs, one by Albert Cohen, the other by Richard Cloward and Lloyd Ohlin. Both saw gang delinquency as a result of the strain between the widely held goals of success in a capitalist society and the realistic sense of failure among boys who had no chance of "making it" in acceptable career terms. Cohen stressed the negative, malicious quality of gang life as evidence of a reaction

to middle-class standards. Cloward and Ohlin pointed to alternative underworld success goals that supplanted the middle-class
ones: criminal gangs were oriented to adult economic criminal
careers; conflict gangs to proving manhood through gang rumbles;
retreatists were immersed in drugs, liquor, and music. Miller
disputed the notion of delinquents as failures in their own terms.
He stressed the separation of values and interests in different social
classes, arguing that lower-class males do not subscribe to middle-
class goals and that gangs represent an attempt to prove manhood
with respect to the focal concerns of the lower class generally.[14]

Most writers at this time made no attempt to explain female
gang delinquency. Cloward and Ohlin suggested parenthetically
that access to illegitimate career structures was denied to females
(also to blacks and other minority groups). Furthermore, girls were
unlikely to become involved in gang warfare. They were most likely
to be retreatists – the double failures who possessed neither
criminal skill nor "heart."

Cohen dealt more explicitly with girls in applying his theory.
While the behavior of delinquent male gangs could be accounted
for by their failure to succeed in a competitive society and their
consequent rejection of its values, the same could not be true for
females. Cohen argued that people universally want to excel not
only as people but as men or women. Even within a delinquent
subculture, this remains true. Since a girl's worth is defined not
with respect to society at large but in terms of her success in male-
female relationships, to fly in the face of the law would at best be
irrelevant to her status or, at worst, damage it, since criminality is
so widely recognized as a male domain. The girl then is most likely
to express the strain between long-term goals and the realistic
likelihood of achieving them through an appropriately female
channel – sexuality. Just as the "college boy" must relinquish
short-term enjoyment for later benefits, so must the "good girl"
learn to maintain her sexual attractiveness without becoming
sexually accessible. In this way, she increases her market value in
marriage with its concomitant promise of upward social mobility.
The "bad girl," who rejects this ethic, expresses her disdain by
allowing free sexual access to males. As Cohen says, "Sexual
accessibility, however, has this virtue: it pays the most immediate
and certain dividends by way of male attention, male pursuit, male
company and the wasteful public expenditure of the male's resources on the female – one of the most socially visible and
reassuring evidences of success at the job of being a woman."

From such a position, one might expect the girl to wear her promiscuity proudly as a badge of rebellion, just as Cohen's "rogue male" boasts of his criminality. This is manifestly not the case. There is no strata in contemporary society in which females have ever gained positive status from visible promiscuity. Cohen, formalized the predominant concern with female delinquency, which is that it "consists overwhelming of sexual delinquency or of involvement in situations which are likely to 'spill over' into overt sexuality." No mention is made of rapes, "gang bangs," or homosexual prostitution by the boys, let alone their involvement in normal, if precocious, sex. Girls' sexuality is singled out to the point that being "in trouble" for a girl carries the automatic connotation of pregnancy, not crime. Cohen picked up the mood of the times and reified it into a fact that would be considered axiomatic for the next two decades. Girls in gangs are Sex Objects, and to help them we must teach them how to trade their sexuality legitimately for marriage.

The 1950s was the era of the street worker. Academics had engendered a new sympathy for gang members and a liberal concern with dealing with them "on their own turf." Male gangs were seen as a distinct subculture. Street workers sought to understand that culture and to limit direct intervention to the prevention of injury. They were there primarily to keep a watchful eye and to offer practical help in problems of education, health, or work.

Many descriptions of gangs emerged, a few of which included references to girls. Those street workers who directed their attention to the female members apparently did not experience the liberal dilemmas of those who worked with boys. Their unanimous aim was to transform the girls from Sex Objects into Good Wives by introducing them to the finer points of makeup, hair styling, cooking, dress making, and etiquette. Unlike male street workers, who often found themselves identifying strongly with their clients, these workers seem to have found little in the female subculture with which to identify. Again this may be related to the essentially middle-class female stereotype which was so pervasive. While male workers may have envied the tough, aggressive life of male gang members, the same could not be true of women since no acceptable stereotype of working-class women existed. The "female" virtues of cleanliness, nurturance, and poise were seen to be equally desirable for all women at all class levels.

In 1950, the Welfare Council of New York City published a report on their attempt to work with four Harlem gangs: the Jay

Bees, the Gay Blades, the Royals, and the Knights.[15] Each gang was well organized with age-graded units and a girls' affiliate. The thirty-three Royal girls were between thirteen and nineteen years old, and most were either sisters or friends of the male group members. Once again, the girls are described as inciting and supporting the boys' law-breaking while playing little part in it themselves. However, six girls had appeared in court, three had spent time in reformatories, and six had been placed on probation. The majority are described as sexually promiscuous, and illegitimate births were "common." Some of the girls occasionally drank or used narcotics and a few truanted from school. They are described by the street worker as passive, exploited people with little self-respect and poor intelligence. One male told a street worker: "You take what you want from them. When they get off the beam and don't act right, slap them around so they'll know who's who." Once again, they are depicted as Sex Objects of the boys, and the street worker's aim seemed to be not so much to encourage their independence from boys as to inculcate "feminine" middle-class values about their sexuality and its worth.

The role of sex in Chicago gangs, described by researchers James Short and Fred Strodtbeck, substantiates this view.[16] Girls who spent time with gangs were viewed as cheap and available – easy targets whom the boys used to demonstrate their manhood. A street worker with the gangs remarked:

> . . . They just pull the girl off to the side and start rapping to her . . . Jake will lay a broad right on the bench but most of them will take the girl off somewhere to one of these junked cars and lay her there. . . . They'll discuss who's fucking and who's not, how much time it takes for this one and how much time it takes for that one.

The street worker sought to end this state of affairs by conducting classes in cosmetics and etiquette, organizing sewing parties, and setting up charity boxes to send to foreign countries. The girls were only accorded importance as a means of reaching the boys in the gang, as potential mothers of illegitimate babies, and as pawns who could be used as excuses for gang warfare.

A descriptive 1963 article by journalist Robert Rice on the Persian Queens (a pseudonym for a real female gang from Brownsville, Brooklyn) stressed the marginal and parasitic quality of the girls' gang and the rather dismal attempts of seven girls under the leadership of Ethel to organize themselves into a cohesive unit.[17]

The roots of the club lay several years back with the two principal fighting gangs in the neighborhood, the Mohawks and the Famous Dukes. Each had its own female auxiliary, known respectively as the Mohawk Debs and the Famous Duchesses. Ethel had been in the Debs. When the boys decided to decrease their street visibility (after a bout of police arrests), the girls were left without a suitably tough male group with whom to consort. Ethel decided to form her own independent female gang – the Persian Queens. However, the only allegiance the girls really wanted was with the Mohawks, who had passed on into being, at least officially, a regular social club. Rice concentrated most heavily on the girls' role as Sex Object for the boys. The girls were "delighted to drink with the Mohawks, sleep with the Mohawks and, if the occasion demanded, carry weapons and furnish alibis for the Mohawks." Yet there are also glimpses of the Tomboy girls in the fighting gang, the Famous Duchesses. One girl was singled out as the most fearless fighter: "when she fought, she fought to win with any weapon that came to hand though her favorites were a length of two by four and her fingernails which she kept long and sharp. She almost always wore pants rather than a skirt and she habitually kept her hair tightly bound in a black bandanna." Ultimately, Rice views all the girls as victims of their sex as well as their neighborhood:

> If a girl fights as well as a boy – and Youth Board workers know girls who do – boys don't like her, and in no walk of life is a girl whom boys don't like an object of admiration or envy to other girls. By the same token, the one kind of status that carousing can confer is manly status, and to the extent that gang girls carouse they merely lessen the possibility that they will achieve the womanly status of being considered desirable mates. In short, because gang girls aren't boys, they are in their own view barely people and this low self-esteem is naturally reflected in their personalities.

Needless to say, the local street workers attempted to salvage the girls' disintegrating egos by holding classes in cosmetics, comportment, and etiquette.

A 1964 book by Kitty Hanson about a Spanish Harlem female gang, the Dagger Debs, was based upon accounts drawn from New York City Youth Board's files and "in part, upon the personal experiences of the writer."[18] The novelistic flavor of the book does little to persuade the reader of the representativeness or authenticity of the material. However, in many respects it substantiates

Rice's account quite fully. The Dagger Debs numbered twelve members and more could be called upon if needed (although none ever appear in the book). Their structure included a president, prime minister, and war counselor, and the girls dressed in men's shirts, dungarees, and ankle boots with pointed toes and wrapped their hair in red bandannas. The ranking leader had achieved her position by fighting and defeating the former leader. They had a "clubhouse," an abandoned ground-floor apartment with sand instead of floorboards, which was used for meetings and "making out" with members of their brother gang, the Daggers. Many of the other female gangs Hanson mentions also had affiliations with male groups that were reflected in their names: Dragon Debs, Untouchable Debs, Emperor Ladies, and Elegant Queens. While passing reference is made to the girls' involvement in mugging and shoplifting, the major stress is on sex. Case history accounts suggest the girls' early initiation into sexual activities, an almost universal lack of genuine sexual enjoyment, and an ignorance of reproduction and birth control.

> They will oblige on rooftops or in cellars, on park benches or in the grass. They stand in halls and doorways or disappear briefly into dark corners. They behave like prostitutes, but most of them are not. They have such a low opinion of themselves, they don't even charge.

The street worker aimed to turn them into "ladies" by starting a charm clinic and teaching them how to eat in restaurants and shop in department stores. Her ultimate goal for each girl was that "One day she may respect herself so much that she says "No" and the boy who asked her knows she means it."

Violence was another central theme of the gang. Examples are given of the whole gang descending on a single female enemy and beating her badly, of two girl gang members attacking and shaving the head of a member who had sold out to another gang; and a rather improbable account describes a single member beating five members of a rival gang in the toilet of a dance hall for laughing at one of her gang members. A gang member discovered with another girl's boyfriend was subjected to a severe attack by the offended girl.

> Hanky was a fighter, but no match for the fury that jerked her off the park bench, gouged sharp nails the length of one cheek, punched her in the stomach and then pounded her into unconsciousness. Truelove leaped upon the prostrate girl, kicking and stomping and

kicking until her boots were bloody and the Debs had to drag her, cursing and hysterical, out of the playground.

Although the girls recognized the existence of "fair fights," Hanson is skeptical that fights among girls could ever be considered fair. Weapons might be excluded, but girls, unlike boys, fought dirty with nails and teeth, and only rarely did audiences succeed in staying out of it. Apart from issues of gang integrity and sexual jealousy, the other arena of violence was in supporting the Daggers in inter-gang war. As female auxiliaries, the Dagger Debs were definitely of inferior status to the males. They also received much of the blame for the gang feuding and individual fighting of the Daggers.

A 1979 study of data derived from interviews with black male youths detained at Juvenile Hall in the mid-1960s (40 percent of whom were in gangs) and with a further sample of male members of Los Angeles gangs suggested that almost one-fourth of the criminal acts reported by the males involved participation by girls.[19] Females were most likely to be involved in violent or "minor" incidents and less involved in acts of theft. If a girl had appeared just prior to the commission of a criminal act, 27 percent of the events would have been postponed and 42 percent would have been cancelled, according to the males. The authors assert that their data challenge the prevailing belief that it is girls who instigate male gang crime. They suggest that, in fact, the opposite appears to be true. Girls – perhaps "good girls" – are actively excluded from the bulk of economic crime planning and execution. But this belief seems only to confirm the recurring theme of girls' roles in gang activities. *Fights* have traditionally been blamed on "bad girls," and it is in the category of violence that girls are most heavily involved, according to their data. Also, as the authors caution, the data were derived exclusively from boys and may reflect more about masculine presentation of male-female gang roles than about the facts of day-to-day interaction.

During the 1950s and 1960s Miller investigated two girl gangs – the Molls and the Queens.[20] The Molls were an all-white, Catholic gang of eleven girls whose mean age during the study went from thirteen to sixteen. By age seventeen, five had been arrested, four had appeared in court, and two had been placed in reform institutions. The Molls favored playing hooky, stealing, drinking, vandalism, sex, and assault, in that order. Their rate of involvement in these acts was only one-tenth that of similar male gangs but was the same as one of the higher-status boys' gangs and considerably higher than that of the Queens. Their sexual activities were very discreet and were never boasted about in the same way as were criminal offenses. Although they attempted to gain favor with their male companion group (the Hoods) by emulating and abetting the boys' criminal activities, they did *not* freely dispense sexual favors to them.

The girls' overall leader as well as their secondary leader, who took over in case of emergency, were members of the more criminally active clique of six girls who set the general tone of the gang and whose official criminal records were more impressive. The two leaders never engaged in direct hostility or aggression but, like many of the male gang members, attempted to outdo each other in illegal accomplishments. "Best friends" cut across the cliques but were often short-lived, and their fast turnover ensured the overall structural integrity of the group. However, the girls made no effort to deny their dependence upon the Hoods. In fact, they seemed quite proud to acknowledge their reliance upon them, even though, as Miller ironically notes, the girls "will be called upon, at least as often as their male peers, to be breadwinners and heads of households."

The second female gang was the Queens, sister gang to the Kings (in more than one sense – seven of the Kings had siblings in the Queens). Black gangs were less homogeneous with respect to social class than white gangs, and, indeed, in terms of legitimate accomplishments both the Kings and Queens did remarkably well. Most of the Kings completed high school and 18 percent graduated college. They were among the least law-violating of the male gangs (at least up to the age of seventeen) and their characteristic activities (such as athletics, organizing public dances, and scrap paper drives) suggest more of a social club than a gang. The Queens, aged between sixteen and eighteen showed a wider range of class background, although most of the girls' fathers held lower-class jobs. Eighty percent of the Queens completed high school (compared to 20 percent of the Molls), but none went to college. About half of the twenty seven working members held "white-collar" jobs, such as secretary or key-punch operator, a third had low-skill occupations, and two subsequently worked as part-time prostitutes. Almost half the members had close kinship ties within the gang.

The Queens were not heavily involved in criminality in comparison with other gangs, with the exception of assault. Whereas the Molls displayed only two acts of aggression in the observation period, the Queens were involved in eighteen. The Queens were also less cohesive as a group than many of the other gangs, which Miller attributes to their race, sex, and social mobility. The gang was an association of four major cliques: two were "good," one was "bad," and one shared features of both types. Their leader was from a "good girl" clique. They were all highly dependent on the Kings. Many girls joined the gang specifically to gain romantic access to the boys. They followed and cheered their boys to athletic successes, tried to hold their meetings on the same night as the boys (to ensure none of the Kings would be free to engage in a "sneakie"), and at their all-girls meetings were particularly concerned with such feminine topics as dress, cooking, taste, demeanor, parties, and gossip. The Queens perceived themselves as socially mobile, and middle-class norms of conduct were clearly visible in their tastes and morals. In fact, as a group, they correspond descriptively more to a social club than a gang proper. Their value orientation strongly suggests a future as Good Wives.

With the advent of major civil-rights marches and increased political awareness in the 1960s, many social observers expected street gangs to become involved. After all, gang members were alienated, poor, often from minority groups, and had nothing to lose by immersing themselves in civil disobedience. They certainly had the time to become involved. Yet it appears that their involvement was numerically small, fleeting, and did not reflect a fully developed political awareness. Those gangs that were involved took part in two major ways, either by forming or joining community grassroots programs to improve the standard of living in ghetto areas or by aiding militant left-wing groups. The supergangs of Chicago, claiming thousands of members in citywide divisions – the Blackstone Rangers, the Vice Lords, and the Black Disciples – were awarded a substantial federal grant to implement various social programs, which ended in scandal at U.S. Senate subcommittee hearings, when it transpired that nepotism, fraud, and mismanagement had been rife. New York City police have suggested that similar apparently pro-social attempts to clean up areas by driving away drug dealers were merely a cover for the gangs to take over drug distribution themselves. The link between gangs and militant groups has not been fully established. Police Sergeant H. Craig Collins suggests that New York street youths were actively recruited and paid for terrorist work, but Miller suggests that their level of organization and political sophistication was too low to be of use to such groups.[21]

The 1960s also saw the beginnings of the woman's movement. Originating among women professionals and academics, many believed it was only a question of time before it filtered down to the lower class. Indeed, at least one female criminologist has suggested that increased rates of female crime in the 1970s should be attributed to the liberation of women. Others have challenged such a view with data suggesting that changes in the female crime rate did not match the correct time period to validate such an argument.[22] At this time of new social consciousness, a change in the role of girls in gangs might have been expected. But were they really touched by the woman's movement? Did they have the power or desire to alter their place in the gang?

It appears that no significant change occurred. A brief section of a 1975 survey of gang activities in major United States cities refers to girls.[23] Their fundamental roles had not changed and they still acted as weapon carriers and decoys. A few participated in individual or gang fights. The most common form of female gang involvement continued to be as auxiliaries or branches of male gangs. In New York, half of the gangs had female branches, but their total membership comprised only 6 percent of the gang population. Only six all-female independent gangs were reported in New York. In Chicago, only 400 out of 4,400 gang-related arrests (9 percent) were of girls. In Philadelphia, of the forty identified female gangs, not one was seen by the police as constituting a true gang or as posing a serious crime problem.

The brutal rape of a fourteen-year-old girl by gang members, described in William Gale's 1977 account of communal gang life in the Bronx, written with the help of two Gang Intelligence Unit officers, indicates very clearly the advantages for a girl of voluntarily entering a local gang.[24] The girl served as a prize in what was essentially a male gang rivalry. Her fate might have been averted had she been in a gang herself. While statistics suggest detected rape probably accounted for only 2 percent of gang crime at that time, the account eloquently indicates the role of females in male gang life – the trophy for demonstrated "manhood."

Other girls were less resistant to gang membership. Gale describes how girlfriends of members became brides through the outlaw wedding. The clubhouse would be decorated and members' contributions used to buy cake and wine. Cuts were made on the hands or arms of the bride and groom to allow their blood to be mingled. (The cuts sometimes required stitches at the local hospital after the wedding.) A can of beer was then ceremonially poured on their heads and the wedding was complete. The couple was then locked in a bedroom for twenty-four hours, armed with sandwiches, beer, and an empty can to be used as a toilet. Girls who joined the gang independent of a male were required to have intercourse with any male gang member who expressed an interest, and girls were expected to be exclusively heterosexual. Gale reports that one male member stated, "Once we had a dike in the gang. When we found out she was a queer, we gang-banged her and threw her out." Contraception was rarely practiced. The girls feared cancer from contraceptive pills, and the males refused to wear condoms on the grounds that it diminished their sexual pleasure. As a consequence, early pregnancy was very common and did not arouse much concern. Girl members who slept with outsiders were beaten first by the female leader and then had to pass naked through the legs of all female members, who were armed with improvised whips.

The marginal status of the girls was clearly illustrated when male leaders and members of twenty South Bronx gangs met at a Boys Club of America chapter to establish a formal peace treaty. Female members were not allowed in until the close of the discussion and only four girl leaders were admitted. Two were the presidents of all-girl autonomous gangs (the Alley Cats and the Savage Sisters). Their chairs were placed in the last row behind the warlords, and when the leaders joined hands in a circle to seal the treaty, they were entirely exluded. Two leaders of female auxiliary sections were allowed to accompany their male presidents.

The overwhelming passivity of the girls was frequently evident. They appeared to be constantly at the mercy of their bodies and their men. Both inspired a kind of nonemotional surrender, a sense of fatalism and the futility of resistance. Female friendships were tenuous and temporary, repeatedly interrupted and broken by jealousies over boys. The girls seemed natural victims, resigned and hopeless, self-obsessed and trivial, running through at best a pretense of emotion which lacked any foundation. Boys impregnated them, beat them, were sent to prison, or deserted them – all these consequences were accepted with equanimity and always with an eye to the next preoccupation, which more often than not was male.

Not all writers were so certain of the traditional role of the gang girl. Some stressed the strength of female-female bonds and indicated a definite movement toward more autonomy among the girl members. Among males, the 1970s was a time in which attention turned from ritualistic gang feuding to more predatory crime.

Violence was used increasingly as a way to gain control over schools or parks (as operating territory for drug peddling, extortion, and robbery). About 40 percent of the victims were non-gang members. The literature suggests no such shift among girls. At this time, their activities seem to be centered around the older concerns of "heart" or courage and "rep," the maintenance of a warlike reputation.

In 1974, John Quicker, a Californian sociologist, analyzed girls' involvement in Chicana gangs in East Los Angeles, based on interviews with thirteen female members.[25] The girls affirmed that their gangs usually began as affiliates of male gangs, often taking the feminized Spanish version of the male gang's name. None of these female gangs existed independently of a boy's unit, although some male gangs had no female affiliate. The majority of gangs were of mixed sex. Although the girls accompanied boys to inter- · gang fights (usually taking on the opponent's female unit), there were certain activities that were dealt with by the girls themselves, such as settling internal and external disputes of their own. Once in a gang, only girls in the most cohesive groups were required to restrict their romantic relationships to the affiliate male gang. In many cases, the girls were able to date other boys, providing no outright state of war existed between his group and her own.

To join the female gang, the girl first had to express interest and subsequently prove that she was not joining simply to gain protection against her own personal enemies. The major means of testing this was to "jump her in," whereby for ten seconds the initiate had to suffer and, if possible, defend herself against the joint assault of the whole female gang. A second method was the "fair fight" with an established girl member. Finally, a very few girls "walked in," that is, were accepted without initiation trials. Leaving the gang occurred either actively, when the girl had to fight a member or members (in the course of which she was likely to be injured), or passively, when a life event (marriage, getting a job, the demise of the gang) legitimately excused the girl from further involvement.

The girls denied any active leader in the gang, yet it was clear that some girls were more central in changing opinions than were others. Important decisions were generally taken by a vote. The gang came to command complete loyalty from its members and, as a result of the physical ordeals they shared together, came to act as a family to the girls. Members referred to each other as "home girls" or "sisters." Quicker suggests that the economic conditions facing poor nonwhites, the increase in freedom to these previously sheltered girls, and the ambiguity of their future lives were the major explanations of the increase in gang activity of girls in East Los Angeles.

Waln Brown, an ex-gang member himself, offered an account of female gang behavior in Philadelphia, in which he stressed: "To be a female gang member in Philadelphia's black gang subculture does not have the automatic connotation of being a sexual object subject to the whims of the male gang members. Rather, it means that the female is an intrinsic part of that gang's group identity who participates in gang activities and is involved in various gang functions rather than just ancilliary activities such as sexual fulfill-ment."[26] In mixed-sex gangs, girls, unlike boys, were not subject to initiation fights nor were they likely to be drafted. A girl was admitted as a "young girl" until she gained sufficient street ex-perience to graduate to an "old head" – a graduation which did not depend solely upon chronological age. She may have earned this title, as did the boys, by her performance in gang wars in which she would usually, but not exclusively, fight with female members. She may have earned status by defending the gang's name when it came under attack on the street or in school, or by vigorous assault on any other female gang that attempted to cross her group's "turf" or territory. Within the gang, fights sometimes resulted from disputes over boys or because an aspiring girl sought to gain status by beating a senior member and taking her "rep." Fights against male gang members were not uncommon. More traditionally, the females might be called upon to exploit their gender for the benefit of the gang by acting as spies in other groups or by luring males into situations where they could be attacked or caught in a com-promising position.

Brown also offers an illuminating and rare view of an all-female gang, the Holly Ho's, which operated independently of males. The membership fluctuated between twenty and thirty and ages ranged from early teens to early twenties. Their activities centered princi-pally on aggression, and consequently, would-be members were subjected to vigorous initiation tests. Each initiate had to fight the "runner" – a huge scar-faced girl. Victory was not expected, but the girl had to demonstrate some physical prowess. The gang was reputed to enjoy fighting and had been known to attack both males and females. They owned knives, handguns, rifles, and sawed-off shotguns. "Getting a body" (killing) was an important part of the gang's "rep." Brown asserts that the attractions of gang life – the action, the excitement, the camaraderie, and the opportunity to prove one's worth – were equally powerful for both males and females growing up in the black ghetto. The girl's function in the gang had clearly extended beyond being the passive property of male members.

At the end of the 1970s we are left with a picture of girls in transition. Whether this is a real change or simply the reflection of a changing attitude on the part of researchers is impossible to say. To deny that girls still value being sexually attractive or want to be wives one day would be ridiculous, but there seems to have been a general societal shift toward the acceptability of the Tomboy and the value of succeeding in male as well as female areas of life. The literature suggests a sociological lag on the part of females. In the 1970s, they are described as being influenced by the old male gang values of the 1950s. Little mention is made of girls as perpetrators of robbery, extortion, burglary, or drug selling. They remain marginal but not separate from the activities of the boys. Current awareness of the double standard of morality has directed researchers' attention away from a purely sexual view of girls' involvement in gangs, and we begin to glimpse the girls as whole human beings whose position is not solely predicated upon their relationship to boys.

As well as the noticeable changes in the girls' role in gang life, some themes also recur persistently in accounts collected from different parts of the country and at different times. In summing up the girls' position, these constants are important to bear in mind. It is equally important to disentangle the facts from the preoccupations of male writers, who have assumed the role of interpreters between the girls and the outside world.

The youth gang is a male phenomenon. Statistics clearly verify this even today, and every major theory has been predicated on the fact that it is males who participate in street gangs. Those girls who do join gangs seem to find themselves in subsidiary or auxiliary groupings, as are the very young groups called Pee Wees or Juniors. According to the literature, both groups are secondary to the male group. It is tempting to speculate that this marginal status results from the prevailing cultural bias of largely male writers who have seen the adolescent male gang as the prototype or nucleus around which these other units orbit almost parasitically. It is, after all, these young males who will become members of adult society and who, if not rehabilitated, threaten most immediately the future of "civilized" society.

Parallel with this is the preoccupation with the girls' sexuality and its abuse. Illegitimacy and continuing cycles of alienated youth represent the major concern of academics, street workers, and policy makers. Just as the gang males threaten to disrupt their futures in society by denying the appropriate goals of work and success, so the girls deny the validity of love, marriage, and passivity as prerequisites of sex and procreation. Is it no more, then, than an ideological sleight of hand that places so much stress upon the male gang member? It seems unlikely, for the fact that the ancilliary group depend for their very existence upon the male gang cannot be ignored. Neither juniors nor female gangs commonly develop without the impetus of the adolescent male gang. While their activities, goals, rites, and interests may be separate, they define themselves with reference to the male group. The girls accept their marginal role.

Although in recent years there has been evidence of changes in the girls' activities and autonomy, these have occurred as a result of shifts in the *nature* of their relationship to the male group. The relationship itself continues as a very real factor. Adolescent girls still place a high value on male approval. However, by the 1970s a clear pattern emerges. Girls care about the opinions of their own sex. Personal integrity depends not so much upon winning and holding a man against other females' competition but upon first gaining other girls' respect and conforming to their norms. This is shown in gang girls' tendency to initiate, discipline, and form "sisterly" relations with one another. This shift in emphasis may be the result of a new academic interest in girls' behavior in its own right or it may represent a real role change. Certainly, there is a move toward viewing the girls not as Sex Objects but as Tomboys.

Throughout the literature, sexual objectification is a second major theme. Girls join gangs to meet boys. Innocent girls are corrupted by sex and as "fallen women" slip into the underworld of gang life. Girls in gangs perform sexual roles (lures, spies), are "passive, property and promiscuous," are sexually and physically abused by men, want to excel as females by having sex with as many members as possible, get pregnant, and work as prostitutes. It would be absurd to suggest that adolescent males and females who spend time together do not become romantically and sexually involved with each other, but the disproportionate coverage given to female gang members' sexuality is wearisome. It is particularly annoying since writers on male gang members provide almost no information on the boys' sexual activity by which a comparison might be made.[27] This concern with the sexual nature of the girls' delinquencies is not confined to gang members. The discriminatory bias in juvenile court processing, whereby girls far more than boys are penalized for promiscuity has been noted by several commentators and is no more than a reflection of the previous double standard of sexuality visible at all levels of society.

Only recently has there been a decline in this prurient interest. It is, I believe, a meaningful one. For many years, a joint conspiracy assured the sexual nature of the bond between the girls and the gang boys. The girls themselves accepted the status-conferring nature of associating with a high-status male. It was, after all, not peculiar to them but a general feature of society as a whole. The boys not unnaturally found such a state of affairs to be in their own best interests. The striving for manhood in street life – the crime and the feuds – was sweetened by recognition of their success by the female spectators. Sex did not have to be searched out as long as the female affiliate was around. The cat fighting between girls vying for male affection maintained the males' egos and cost them nothing. Among the boys, however, the real business of life, the real proving ground, was crime and bravery, and for many years girls were excluded from these areas. The competition was between men; one of the prizes of success was sex. But with the advent of the 1970s, the male-female relationship began to alter visibly toward a relationship more of similarity than complementarity.

The Molls were one of the first clubs described in this country who sought to gain male favor not by trading their sexuality but by emulating male behavior and activities. This pattern gained strength over the following years up to the present day. Females changed from being responsible for gang violence (through their sexuality) to being actively involved in it, despite male attempts to exclude them. In California in the mid 1960s, males still resist the intrusion of women into criminal acts but cannot keep them out of violence. By the 1970s, Quicker indicates that Californian gang males, while expressing misgivings about female involvement in gang wars or "rumbles," do nothing to prevent their attendance. And in Philadelphia and New York, girls are actively involved along with the boys, although, as researcher Peggy Giordano notes, it is with other females that the girl gang member identifies and from whom she seeks recognition.[28] The trend, while growing, existed in a scattered way in the early literature also. Asbury notes the involvement of women in gang feuds at the turn of the centry, but the aggression is directed against males. Some writers suggest that the change from emulation of males to the romantic partner of males is a developmental one.[29]

What seems to be more recent is the participation of females in mixed-sex gang activities, in which the girls use traditionally "male" arenas of competition but direct their competition and consequent status against other members of their own sex. But have things substantially altered? Perhaps the achievement of such status even by these new means again functions only to win the attention of a high-status male. Brown and Giordano's work suggests not. In Philadelphia, girls are neither required nor expected to be involved with the boys, and graduation to "old head" carries no guarantee of sexual reward. Giordano's work indicates that degree of delinquency correlates only slightly with gaining a boyfriend's approval. Such trends, however, do not mean that the gang no longer engages in sexual activity – only that sex has assumed its rightful position as a part of the girls' life rather than the single hingepin on which self-respect and status depend.

Girls appear in the literature as both the cause and the cure for much male gang delinquency. Hanson, for example, notes how the Dagger Debs engineered conflicts and incited fights as a way of expressing their control over the boys. This theme appears often, sometimes with the girl serving as an unwitting pawn in the genesis of a gang war, sometimes actively provoking disputes among boys. At the same time, girls are universally thrust forward as the reason for the ultimate demise of the gang. Serious romantic involvement, much like heroin addiction, is seen to weaken intragang bonds among the males and usually signals the withdrawal of the boy from gang activities, or at least the more criminal ones.[30]

The apparent contradiction here is not an unfamiliar one, since it corresponds to the age-old distinction between "bad" and "good" girls and rests on the view of the female as being ultimately, although invisibly, responsible for the male's fate. "Good girls" get the male out of gang life; "bad girls" increase his involvement. It is tempting to equate the "good girl" with the "college boy" described by Whyte. The unifying characteristic of both is the deferment of immediate gratification (the girl who values her virginity and chooses to dispense it wisely in exchange for a suitable marriage). However, the distinction between "good" and "bad" girls exists even *within* delinquent gangs. The Kings described by Miller, for example, distinguish the "good" and "bad" girl members. This basic distinction is accepted by boys and girls alike even in youth subcultures. The basis for it seems to go further than sexuality.

"Fighters" and "drinkers" both fall into the "bad girl" category, although in different ways. A "bad girl" is one who cheapens herself by abusing her sexuality, but "bad" is also applied to girls who behave in breach of their complementary feminine role. Those very factors that Miller noted to be status-conferring among boys (capacity to drink in large quantity, to fight readily, and to be proficient in sexual performance) are the very behaviors that invoke the judgment of "bad" in girls. Nowhere is the stress on salvation of a "good" woman more evident than in the philosophy of the street workers of the 1950s. In reforming the girl members by inculcating self-respect and instilling in them a demand for more respectful behavior by males, it was clearly hoped that the boys would respond by forming romantic attachments to these new "nice" girls and ultimately withdraw from gang life.

From the earliest reports of the nineteenth century, gang females assumed one of two fighting roles. They appear fundamentally as Sex Objects (that is, girls who direct their attention to gaining men by assuming orthodox sexual roles), who will only fight other females over access to men and who, in these circumstances, use teeth, nails, and any means to gain victory. The fights over men are universally depicted as vicious, dirty, and typically "female." On the other hand, girls sometimes appear as Tomboys, denying their femininity by wearing trousers and bandannas or assuming names like Battle Annie. Parallel with the change in the relationship between the girls and the boys is a concomitant change in emphasis from the first to the second of these two types. Girls in contemporary gangs wear the same jeans, boots, and gang insignia or "colors" as the boys, which probably reflects at least as much about changes in female dressing habits as it does about the shift from lover to competitor. Nevertheless, both seem to spring from the same change in societal stance toward women.

Of course, today (as always) girls fight over boys, but the difference is one of the emphasis placed upon it. Traditionally, for a male to fight over a woman was legitimate, manly, laudable. The reverse (girls fighting over boys) was illegitimate, unfeminine, and either deplorable or humorous. The rightful place of the female was as passive prize. Deviations from this role generated the same fascination as deviations from girls' expected chastity and celibacy. Consequently, perhaps too much was made of it. Today, girls fight over boys but also fight in other arenas too – in gang feuds, against personal insults, and against police. Increasingly, they use "male" weapons such as guns and knives, the great levelers. The stress on cat fighting has diminished, and when a gun enters the picture, the sex of the person holding it seems less important.

Almost every account stresses that membership of girls' gangs compared with boys' shows a higher turnover, a shorter life span, a failure of effective leadership and organization, and pervasively a sense of purposelessness. In the light of the girls' dependence upon male gangs as reference points, none of these factors is surprising. The girl gang comes about after the establishment of the male group and ends with the demise of the boys' gang. The previously boy-centered attitude of girls meant that failure to find a boyfriend or – paradoxically – success in finding one often led the girl to abandon the gang for another hunting ground or for marriage. Pregnancy, not uncommon for many urban working-class girls whether in gangs or not, often meant leaving the group. In short, the social fact of being female for many years meant instability, for girls were all ultimately at the mercy of men and of their own sexuality. The internal structure of the girls' group, at least until the 1960s, was frequently dependent upon the status of the males with whom girls were involved, which during the stormy period of adolescence tended to alter frequently.

In the more recent literature, girls still depend on male gangs for their existence but no longer for their raison d'être or their internal structure. It is still the male gang that paves the way for the female affiliate and opens the door into many illegitimate opportunities and into areas that serve as proving grounds. But once begun, a more visible solidarity and "sisterhood" within the gang appears. A girl's status depends to a larger (or perhaps simply more evident and self-admitted) extent on her female peers. They show their evaluation of her through their own rites and meetings. To lose one's boyfriend no longer means exclusion from the gang. Worth extends beyond simple sexual attractiveness. The girls still, however, accept the male value system in defining the arenas of achievement. Girls increasingly want to succeed in male terms (as Tomboys). Perhaps in the future they may gain the confidence to succeed in terms they set up for themselves.

Chapter 2

Urban Living for Girls

Because girls appear in the literature as supporting players (prizes for male members' status, excuses for gang wars), they have an insubstantial quality about them. They are represented without context: Where do they live? What does their family think? Are they at school? How deviant does the community believe them to be? They are also represented without depth: Why do they choose to have the babies? Why do they hate so much? What other possibilities do they see in their lives? They are seen as being without community, without family, without a culture of their own. Yet these facts are essential in understanding the attraction of the gangs and in understanding the girls' decision to reject their conventional future.

Gangs have always sprung from conditions of poverty and alienation common to those at the lowest levels of urban life. Today 50 percent of gang members in New York are Puerto Rican and 35 percent are black.[1] They come from the poorest areas, principally in Brooklyn and the Bronx. In 1980, there were approximately two million teenagers under eighteen living in New York City: the majority were black or Hispanic. Families living below poverty level (defined as a maximum annual income of $8,532 for a family of three) accounted for 37 percent of all black families and 51 percent of all Hispanic families.

In her life a young black or Hispanic girl will attend a public school where she will encounter whites as a minority: they constitute only one-quarter of public-school students. Most of her teachers, however, will be white (80 percent in 1983). The students in her class will be poor like herself: 50 percent will be from poverty-level families. If she is unlucky, she will attend one of the 115 schools declared unfit by the United Federation of Teachers because of the number of attacks on staff. Even if she avoids such a place, she is likely to be a victim of assault, larceny, extortion, and routine narcotics dealing and consumption. Her academic achievement will probably not be commensurate with her age. Fifty-seven percent of pupils read below their grade level. In 1983, 73 percent of blacks and 80 percent of Hispanics left high school prior to graduation. Perhaps trouble will have already begun. She may be one of the 100,000 students who truant from school on any given day.

Her chances of a teenage pregnancy are not insubstantial. National figures indicate that between the ages of thirteen and nineteen, 225 out of every 1,000 white and Hispanic girls and 515 out of every 1,000 black girls will give birth. In New York, 30,000 teenagers become pregnant each year. In half of these cases, the girl has a termination. Nevertheless, in 1982, babies born to teenage mothers accounted for 17 percent of all black and Hispanic births in New York. If she marries, there is no guarantee that it will last: 55 percent of black and 37 percent of Hispanic children under eighteen live with their mothers only. She will then probably be poor because 75 percent of families who live below poverty level in New York are headed by women.

She will most probably live with her child on public assistance through the Aid to Families with Dependent Children (AFDC) program, food stamps, and government-supplied health care. It is estimated that 70 percent of New York teenagers giving birth will be on welfare within one year. Never-married mothers have the lowest rate of labor-force participation. The unemployment rate (those looking for work) among New York mothers is twice the national average. The median family income where a single mother does work is still far below the income of two-parent families where the mother remains at home because of the continuing disparity in pay for men and women doing comparable jobs.

These statistics can only hint at the day-to-day experiences of lower-class girls and women in New York. But by looking more closely at their lives, we may be able to place gang girls in a clearer perspective, to see them as emerging from a particular life-style with a very circumscribed set of future possibilities. What follows are modal patterns as observed by urban sociologists who have written about lives lived in inner-city poverty. From these back-grounds, girl gang members emerge.

In 1965, Daniel Patrick Moynihan's *The Negro Family: The Case for National Action*, a government publication which was to have substantial policy implications for the United States, reported that nearly a quarter of urban Negro marriages are dissolved; nearly a quarter of Negro births are illegitimate; nearly a quarter of Negro families are headed by females; and that the breakdown of the Negro family had led to a startling increase in welfare dependency among blacks. The "tangle of pathology" Moynihan went on to describe included the undesirable matriarchy of black families, which displaced the black male from the family and the labor market and resulted in the high use of drugs and the prevalence of crime among blacks.[2]

Critics attacked the tone of the report, which seemed to suggest that blacks had brought about their own downfall by failing to adhere to mainstream white family structure and morality. Black feminists were infuriated that the female's attempt to win jobs and raise children (forced upon her by whites' refusal to employ black males) was now the subject of criticism.[3] Fewer people, however, queried the statistics or factual base of the report. At the end of the 1970s, 40.5 percent of all black families were headed by a female and 65.5 percent of families lived below the poverty line. If anything, the situation had worsened, even though less concern with it had been shown in terms of welfare changes, long-range government plans, and academic interest. Urban ethnographers have documented the life-styles of black families living in poverty and have revealed much about the centrality of women.

In lower-class marriage generally, role segregation is high. The husband is expected to be a provider. Success in this sphere excuses him from further responsibility in the home. The wife is expected to maintain the home, raise the children, and make her husband feel comfortable. The structure of ghetto society does not provide an adequate niche for all men to be breadwinners for their families because of widespread unemployment among black males and poor pay for unskilled labor. These economic and racial factors mean that in many cases the male cannot alone provide the family income, even though the man's worth is directly related to his financial contribution to the home (whether in the form of wages or disability payments). When the man is not working, many women no longer feel that they are obliged to cook for him or perform other household duties until he pulls his weight. Job distribution in the ghetto involves relatively more women and fewer men than in mainstream society. Women are often able to find jobs beyond the ghetto in service work such as waitresses, domestics, and hotel maids. Ethnographer Ulf Hannerz notes that because of this, they are more likely to come into contact with white people and gain middle-class skills. Such women develop an "increasing attachment to mainstream values," learn standard English, and develop skills that increase their role as "external affairs" specialists, taking control of bill paying, parent-teachers meetings, and so on. Ghetto men are more trapped in their social niche.[4]

Stress is placed on girls to obtain a good education, while it is more acceptable for males to skip school or fail grades. Since it is the woman who is likely to support her family, this stress on education is understandable. Many "female" jobs are clerical, at best, and, at worst, demand a minimum level of math (store workers) and verbal skills (receptionists). Moynihan makes much of this disjunction of educational attainment – the difference in grade school years completed by black males and females shows that men lag 1.1 years behind. An alternative explanation is that women need more education to obtain employment than do men.[5]

While both black and white lower-class families tend to be matrifocal, there is less pretence of patriarchal authority in black households. However, one writer notes that "If women are the dominant sex among low-income Negroes, the women do not know it. On that score, one of them remarked, 'I've often heard of a woman wish she was a man, but I never heard of a man wish he was a woman.'" In the same vein, Michele Wallace has noted that the fact that black women work more often than do white women should not be construed as liberation so much as necessity. ". . . black women's 'liberation' consisted of being bound to the most unpleasant, unrewarding kind of work, work that did not enlarge her universe or increase her fulfillment. The black woman had not chosen her work. It was something she had to do, either because of the whip or to keep her family from starving – a necessity, a drudgery."[6]

Social workers for the AFDC program deal with the mother, not the father, which increases the man's feeling of inadequacy and displacement. Furthermore, in many states, a "man in the house" rule excludes families with an employable male from receiving public financial assistance. This may force the man out of the home or, more typically, make him officially conceal his presence. Thus, although the black woman economically may appear more independent of her husband, it does not *necessarily* follow that she feels liberated nor does her role invite envy. The lack of money in the household means that she is deeply suspicious of her husband's activities among his male peers; it is here that their income is likely to be spent in drinking, gambling, and highly uncertain loans to friends.

The lure of the streets carries with it also the possibility of extramarital affairs. Sex plays a major part in the ghetto man's self-concept. (In this context, Wallace claims that the black male preoccupation with sex not only results from his desire to live up to the "superstud" image projected onto him by whites but is also a way of punishing the black woman for "emasculating" him.) Lee Rainwater, who has extensively researched the black family, reports sexual infidelity as the leading cause of marital breakup. Unfounded jealousy may directly end marriages, as well as sometimes triggering actual infidelity. Hannerz notes that many couples reach an understanding whereby extramarital affairs, by the male at least and sometimes by both partners, are tacitly tolerated. Rainwater, in a 1968 survey, found that 85 percent of respondents supported clandestine marital infidelity. However, the majority believed that such activities broke up marriages, and the recurring theme of sexual jealousy in both Hannerz's and Liebow's ethnographic studies certainly supports this view.[8]

Although ghetto women tend to be the verbal and public upholders of morality, their actions do not always match their talk. Such women explain female infidelity by seeing women as the victims of men. Since all men have a "bit of a dog" in them, they are constantly on the lookout for sex, and "good" women may occasionally be taken in by them. There are other women who make no bones about their sexual activities, believing not only that "women want it as much as men" but that if their husbands engage in illicit sex, they have every justification for doing the same. Ghetto women in general tend to view the majority of men as "no good" because they do not work, do not keep jobs, are habitually unfaithful, drink, fight, and get in trouble with the law. Much of the socializing in the neighborhood occurs in same-sex groups, the men on the street and the women in each other's homes. Within these groups much discussion centers on male and female sex roles and behavioral propriety. Women tend to view themselves as heroines, martyrs, and upholders of local morality. Men are "no good," and thus it falls upon women to raise children, support the family, and preserve some standards against the dissolute behavior of males. Sons represent nothing but trouble, while daughters help in running the house and raising the other children and bring with them as well the promise of future grandchildren.

Wallace notes that "Moynihan bared the black man's awful secret for all to see – that he had never been able to make his woman get down on her knees." In the husband-wife relationship, the woman has been forced economically to provide and, in doing so, has challenged explicitly or implicitly the legitimacy of the male's position. She learned to hold her man away from other women, drink, and the streets. Yet the result has not been her assimilation by men but their rejection and criticism of her. Even in the radical politics of the 1960s she was given no place. It was as if the man was taking his revenge. "He claimed that she had betrayed him. And she believed it even as she denied it. She too was angry, but paralyzed by the feeling that she had no right to be."[9]

The childhood and adolescence of a black ghetto girl prepare her for a life in which men will not play a major part. Her early experiences may depend quite substantially on the birth order of the family. Psychologist David Schulz notes that first-born girls are considerably more involved in child rearing than subsequent children.[10] Even when the child is only five or six, the mother may "give" her the next baby to raise. That baby effectively becomes her child and may even call her "Mom," referring to her biological mother as "Grandma." One girl described by Schulz took sole responsibility for all her siblings during periods when both parents deserted the household. Generally, girls respond with a mixture of pride at being given such a responsibility and anger at their loss of freedom.

This pattern clearly substantiates the idea of childhood as a very abbreviated period of life for such girls. In the ten families studied in detail by Schulz, seven of the resulting children had serious emotional and behavioral preschool problems. Many of the eldest girls, as well as the mothers, were concerned that they might "go too far" in disciplining the younger children, suggesting a high degree of repressed anger. The result was often that the children were overindulged in terms of their behavior while rarely receiving the amount of affection they demanded. Middle-born girls are also expected to contribute to raising younger children and to do households tasks but are less often "given" a baby. Younger children manage to escape the duties of child rearing.

During grade-school years, the children receive considerably less attention at home. As they approach their teens, daughters once again cause concern almost exclusively in connection with their sexual behavior. They often have learned about sex from older sisters or friends and have begun sex play by age seven or eight. However, since sexuality is rarely discussed by parents, many girls are considerably older before they fully understand the link between sexual behavior and pregnancy. In high school, the girl faces the choice between a career and motherhood. The decision to "do it" with a boyfriend carries a high risk of pregnancy. Not to do it, however, means cutting herself off from a central aspect of teenage life, and same-sex peer groups are of great importance for both boys and girls. A pregnancy is also considered to mark maturity by black teenagers, who are often exposed to adults in various "high life" activities. In line with adult women, the girls recognize that any male will try to seduce them, and their ambivalence about going along with it is more pragmatic than moral, based on fear of pregnancy and of being taken advantage of. Although a girl may go with several boys, she will usually restrict full sexual intercourse to a small number.

Many girls become pregnant. In a 1960 sample of adult ghetto women, Rainwater found that 45 percent reported a premarital pregnancy, 27 percent of which were terminated. At the same time, 90 percent of women and 60 percent of men felt that premarital pregnancy was a significant event and did not approve of it. Eighty percent of women felt that it was worse for a girl than a boy to become freely involved with sex, even if she did not become pregnant.[11] While pregnancy is considered unfortunate, it is not entirely unexpected, and most families develop a means of coping with it. The girl agrees to have the baby as long as it will not interfere too much with her peer-group activities, and usually the mother is willing to take the child. Establishing the father seems to confer a kind of legitimacy upon the birth, and many boys are proud to acknowledge paternity as a sign of their masculinity and maturity. Marriage is only rarely considered. The girl returns to the peer group and frequently her relationship with the father ultimately breaks up. Getting married involves giving up a familiar home that places few restrictions upon her behavior, assuming responsibility for the child, and acquiring a husband who may not be able to provide a stable income. She will have other boyfriends and will later marry, but marriage is seen as a fragile institution related more to bonds of affection than to economic or instrumental ones. Nevertheless, to have been married does give the girl a certain maturity and respectability, which, even after a divorce, gives her a heightened moral position.

Often after one marriage, the women choose to remain technically single, although most continue to have boyfriends. After divorce many women live in three-generation households. Whether they work or receive AFDC, it is often to their advantage to share a house with their mother, who will help with child rearing. The child's mother has a permanent baby-sitter, allowing her to go out in the evenings, and the grandmother gains a share of family life and can hold court for other family members and their friends. The maternal household is generally run with little organization. It is open to the world, and friends come and go. The children learn to go to the store, cook, amuse themselves, and get each other ready for school. The streets present a perpetual threat to them in terms of drugs, crime, pregnancy, and truanting. But the mother can do little to counter the threat and so the home remains open to the comings and goings of both children and adults from the neighborhood.

Often the mother (and sometimes the grandmother) will have a boyfriend. Some men "pimp" off women, taking advantage of their hospitality, sexuality, and AFDC check. According to Hannerz, many street men fancifully view themselves in this role, but the majority of men effectively pay for the right to be a family member. The man may be the father of one of the children and therefore contribute support to the family or he may just appreciate the woman's (and her family's) company and make gifts toward the household. The alternative for many may be living alone in a rooming house. As Rainwater summarizes, "The female role models available to girls emphasize an exaggerated self-sufficiency (from the point of view of the middle class) and the danger of allowing oneself to be dependent on men for anything that is crucial. By the time she is mature, the woman learns that she is most secure when she herself manages the family affairs and when she dominates her men."[12]

In traditional Puerto Rican life, the family is of overwhelming importance.[13] It acts to orchestrate the majority of life events from marriage through birth to death. Although overt family control is stronger over females, both sexes develop a sense of family obligation. The family may include, along with blood relatives, a system of *compadrazgo* or godparents. For example, witnesses at a marriage may become the *compadres* of the named couple, or sponsors at a baptism, the *padrinos* of the child. They develop a strong sense of concern for each other in terms of economic help, support, and personal advice.

In the traditional Puerto Rican marriage – whether consensual or legal – husband and wife roles are again sharply segregated. The husband supports the family economically, while the wife is responsible for household duties and the rearing of children. The authority figure is the male, who makes all major decisions except in the areas of household management and child rearing. The male may involve himself marginally in household issues by purchasing family provisions and reserving the right to be "choosy" about the food that is presented to him.[14] In general, however, there is such a lack of communication between husband and wife that the wife may have little knowledge of her husband's job. She may be curtailed in her social life to the point that she may not leave the house without her husband's express approval, although the male can leave whenever he wishes and is free to "hang out" on the street, drink in bars, and often to have sexual relations with other women. This pattern may not begin until the birth of his first child, and, although the woman at first may react with bewilderment and hurt to these social restrictions, as time goes by and more children are born she comes to accept the situation, feeling that parties and dances are no longer her rightful place.

These external social situations come to represent activities that the "good" woman eschews – smoking, drinking, dancing, flirting. Nevertheless, she may continue to resent her husband's frequent absence from home. If another woman is involved, the correct response of the ideal wife is to ignore it or, if it becomes intolerable, to ask her husband to continue the affair more discreetly. Although occasionally aggressive confrontations occur, they are usually immediately regretted by the wife because "good" women do not behave that way: they maintain their dignity, respect their husbands, and put up at least a show of a good marriage.

This attitude toward male infidelity, at least as described in the literature, is in contrast to that of the black woman. Although the black woman may go so far as to say that all men are fundamentally promiscuous, she still holds her husband responsible for his infidelity and may even retaliate in kind. The Puerto Rican woman, however, is brought up to accept that men are by nature "hot-blooded" and consequently are prone to sudden flight, traumas, moods, and other women. The appropriate response is to turn a blind eye, to understand that it is less his fault than the fault of the women who tempt him and to stress her superiority over her rival through the bonds of marriage and motherhood. She assumes a motherly role to her husband, tolerating his excesses and not taking them as a threat to her marriage, which is based less on sexual passion than on respect. Thus, while the male role is predicated on the *machismo* image, the female role has been characterized as *marianismo* – the cult of the Virgin Mary.[15] The "good" woman nurtures, cares for her family, and, above all, suffers. The disjunction between her feelings of rage and her inability or unwillingness to express such emotions results in the phenomenon of neuroses called by Western doctors "The Puerto Rican Syndrome." An attack may last hours or days and is characterized by temporary semi-consciousness, convulsions, hyperventilation, moaning, profuse salivation, and aggression, including biting oneself or others. Afterward, the attack may be denied or attributed to bad spirits.

Yet, however subordinate her status, a wife commands respect from her family and her community. It is within marriage and the family that the woman's honor is recognized. Nor can it be concluded that women are powerless in marriage. Lopez-Garriga describes the non-confrontational strategies of self-assertion used by women to get their own way.[16] Sofa also notes:

> Nevertheless, women seldom confront their husbands with their dissatisfaction. Instead of protest, women attempt to manipulate men into doing what they want, and into believing that men are the real boss in the household while they are quietly running things. Much of the public deferring to male authority is based on this premise. This manipulative strategy is very similar to that employed by both men and women to all persons in higher authority . . . "Obedezco, pero no cumplo" (I obey but do not comply) is an old "jibaro" (Hillbilly) saying. In the attempt to avoid open conflict, manipulation employs a highly individualistic mode of gaining advantage over one's adversary.[17]

The effects of assimilation into American culture on Puerto Rican families have been studied by many researchers, principally among families living in New York City. Although the father remains the major breadwinner and the wife cares for the house and the children, husbands more often help around the house and the wife is free to leave the house to shop or visit friends and relatives. Leisure activities are demarcated by age and sex so that the husband may go out with the older children, while the wife remains at home with the young ones. In summer, the whole family may visit the beach or park, but it is rare that the couple goes out alone without the children. Family size tends to be smaller (two or three children) than in Puerto Rico, and husband and wife come to depend upon each other more and more for companionship and support. Individualism tends to take precedence over familism and extends to the wife, who increasingly takes part in decision making and becomes more assertive. However, studies of working-class homes suggest that the wife remains subordinate and obedient to her husband and the couple usually has separate social lives, the wife remaining at home with the family and relatives, the husband sharing outside activities with friends. Social class and acculturation both affect the individual's position in the Hispanic group.[18]

Traditional role stereotypes are slowly changing and nowhere have they been more explicitly and eloquently challenged than by the Young Lords Party, a grassroots political movement in New York in the 1960s. The following is from one female member's analysis of the current role stereotypes:

> The whole concept of machismo – that man is superior in all ways – has developed among our people because the Third World man is so oppressed by outside forces – by the system, by capitalism – that he's taught to believe that the only way he can get back at this is by being superior to women . . . In Puerto Rican society, the woman is taught to cater to the needs of her family, in particular to the demands of her father or husband. She's taught that she is inferior in her own ways. Like, sometimes she is taught not to enjoy sex – the man, of course, can go out and enjoy it – this is being very *macho* . . .
>
> I was living with a brother who was a real *macho*, a real street cat. He had been a dope fiend, you know. He was very respected on the street since he could fight, all the other men looked up to him – that's how brothers judge each other, like who's got more balls and who's more down . . . This brother's whole thing was he couldn't stand me to go out on the street in short skirts, not because he didn't like me in short skirts, but because other men would see my legs, and I was his property . . . He used to insist on my going to visit his mother all the time so that I would see what kind of woman he wanted me to be . . .
>
> Now, supposedly this brother liked liberated women, but I think this just meant sexually liberated women. A woman was still supposed to be a slave in all the other areas of the relationship. His whole idea of what was good in a woman was for her to be attractive, to be sexy (but not really sexy) and then to know how to cook and sew and eventually have a whole lot of children.[19]

Much research has been directed toward the traditional nuclear or extended family, in spite of the fact that figures indicate at least 40 percent of mainland Puerto Rican families are headed by women. What becomes of the male-dominated model when the male is unemployed or absent? Ethnographer Oscar Lewis suggests that in the absence of a resident husband, the woman is likely to have a network of relatives and friends with whom or near whom she may live. Although arguments and confrontations (often over money) may ensue, there are usually others who will take her in.[20] The welfare check helps to alleviate the extreme poverty she must face, but the short cash supply often means that food items are bought on a day-to-day or even an hour-to-hour basis. Many single mothers, overwhelmed by the complexity of living in a city where they have only a rudimentary grasp of the language, return to Puerto Rico. Many families are in a state of constant transition between the island and the mainland, where one spouse goes ahead of the other to find employment or accommodation or where circumstances (a broken marriage, an unexpected pregnancy) lead to a quick return home.

The single women described by Lewis are aggressive and independent (perhaps because of the inability of their husbands to provide economic support) and highly sexual. Yet in traditional Puerto Rican society the distinction between the "good" and the "bad" woman is still very strong. "Good" women (marianismo) are neither assertive, aggressive, nor sexual. Single women risk crossing the line by having transient relationships with men. Yet while voicing contempt for traditional sex roles and their dual standard of morality, the women Lewis studied still in their hearts dream of the old ideal of marital harmony.

> It had always hurt me to see my girlfriends leave their homes, dressed in white, wearing veils and crowns, because it had been my dream to have a real wedding and to be taken out of my house properly married and to have at least a photograph of myself in my bridal gown. I used to dream that I would marry a good man and that we would never separate. I thought I would like to marry an elderly man who would give me whatever I needed and who would respect me and my children and my family. My idea of a good man is one who would be pleased if I gave my mama a plate of food or brought her to my house when she got sick, a man who'd give me permission to put my family up in the house when they came from out of town, or let me rent a room for them somewhere and not interfere in what I gave them or they gave me . . .
>
> If the husband wants to go out and have some fun, she [the wife] should let him go because you can't keep men tied down. She should say, "Go ahead, but just tell me where you're going in case something happens so I can get in touch with you." She shouldn't fight with him if he comes home drunk. Supposing the man tries to pick a fight, you should try to calm him down, but if he really wants a

battle you have to give him one. If he comes home drunk or walks in talking nasty, you should say, "Take it easy. Go lie down," and give him a little plain black coffee. If he begins to drink everyday, you should say, "Now what? Are you fixing to be *un bum*?" or "What's wrong with you? Don't drink so much." But it's not so bad if he goes out on a Sunday for a little amusement.

Nevertheless, consensual marriages are accepted as a realistic situation and, from my experience in New York, the characteristic pattern of early pregnancy and (sometimes brief) consensual unions is common. Fathers, more than mothers, are upset by a daughter's pregnancy and sometimes even send the girl back to Puerto Rico for a few months (whether as a punitive or restorative measure is unclear), but by and large the situation is accepted and the baby welcomed into the extended family in the neighborhood. The women particularly stress the joy of motherhood above that of marriage and rally to help with baby clothes and advice. Grandmothers baby-sit. Sisters and sisters-in-law have young children too, and they also take the child on occasion. Welfare checks are eagerly awaited and shared between the family in a system that somehow succeeds in tiding everybody over until the next check. Perhaps most striking is the belief that eventually the ideal man will come along to rescue the girl. Often he is described in economic terms as a provider. At best, his income would be legal and he would be a hard worker. He would take care of her, protect her from poverty and homelessness, take her away from the neighborhood, and help her deal with the threatening demands of welfare people, landlords, and her children's teachers. True love continues to be seen to reach its highest expression in the old male-dominated marriage pattern.

Children are reared according to practices grounded in a belief in the physical and mental superiority of the male. From an early age, the young girl is taught modesty. While the boy may run around naked, the baby girl is always diapered, and nude female baby portraits are rare. By the age of two, she will find that a disheveled skirt evokes consternation from her parents. One woman kept her two daughters (age five and six) off the street because the father wanted "No other man looking at what he has."[21] Girls are taught from the beginning that their place is in the home and that only men and chaperoned women go out on the streets. In the traditional family, there are strong proscriptions on the demonstration of anger, especially the pent-up frustration of girls. As a child, the girl is encouraged to develop values that will suit her in her future role as housewife – for example, cleanliness. She is instructed in cooking from an early age. Within the family, there are especially strong bonds between mother and son, father and daughter. Often the attachment between mother and son is so great that it later interferes with the son's marriage because he feels no woman will ever live up to the marianismo of his mother and because the mother may continue to direct and control his domestic arrangements.

Children are considered incapable of responsible behavior until about age thirteen and their behavior is continually monitored, causing greater delay in the child's independence from the mother. The father is responsible for extreme disciplinary measures, but the mother copes with minor misbehaviors on a day-to-day level. Her discipline is tempered with compassion, and the close bond between mother and child is usually maintained. Her continual presence in the home makes her the immediate role model for her children at least in the early years. However, after the critical age is achieved, childlike behavior is severely sanctioned and the child is constantly enjoined to "grow up."

The traditional power boundary between parent and child has become less distinct on the mainland, where few parents subject their children to the extreme punishments they themselves may have undergone as children. That boundary may be further eroded by the child's fluency in English and the parents' need to use him or her as an interpreter with public officials. Nevertheless, the daughter is required to give at least a public show of respect for the parents.

From the time of menarche, a closer watch is kept over the girl than over the boy. Traditionally, a girl's social activities are dependent upon those of her parents. She may attend local dances and social events with them, but her "street" interactions are usually on the front steps of the house under their watchful eye. Her sixteenth birthday party is a big event, signaling that she is of an age to marry, and about that time, she will start to "go steady" with a boy. The boy will probably already know her family, but, whether he does or not, he will go to the father to ask permission to become his daughter's boyfriend. Once again, this is a token of respect for the family rather than a meaningful request. In strict families, the young couple will be chaperoned whenever they are together and the boy is expected to support the father's efforts to protect the girl's virginity. Great pressures are placed on the girl, who is probably at a school where her classmates have far more liberty, and many Puerto Rican girls in New York become pregnant or elope to escape parental restrictions.

Most girls' ideal marriage includes a church wedding and reception. According to Massara, the wedding night is shrouded in mystery for many women even today, their mothers' only advice having been that they should do their duty. Most of the girls I spoke with, however, had experienced sexual intercourse from a relatively early age (twelve to fifteen years old). Consensual marriages are, in fact, very common and are recognized as bona fide marriages especially after the birth of children. Many consensual unions are "legalized" by a formal ceremony at some point and photographs as well as the license are proudly displayed. Some women display wedding photos even after divorce, for they remain a constant source of joy, pride, and legitimacy.

Motherhood marks another important transition period for the girl. As noted earlier, it is often the time when her relationship with her husband will subtly alter from companion to mother figure. The husband may begin to stay away from the home and even to become involved with other women. She, by contrast, must now find her greatest satisfaction in being a mother and relinquish the pleasures of dancing, smoking, and taking too much care over her appearance. In recompense, the social value of her evident fertility and motherhood may be high. In motherhood, the Puerto Rican woman attains the zenith of her female role. She learns to suffer, as her mother did, for the children. Their happiness makes it all worthwhile. The enforced isolation from social contact, the virtual prison of the apartment, the company only of other women, the alternating pride and humiliation she experiences at her husband's hands, the tolerance of his infidelity are all part of womanhood. To register anger or frustration is in breach of her role, to regret her children a sin, to hate her husband a betrayal. To do other than accept the life mapped out for her puts her in fear of crossing that line that sets "good" women apart from "bad." But times are changing, and young mainland Puerto Rican women, as we shall see, are chafing against the controls.

The girls in this book are, of course, individuals and broad sociological descriptions cannot capture the particular biography or outlook of any one of them. But their futures are constrained by the cultures in which they live, and such futures do not evoke enthusiasm among them. Each of these girls has become involved in gang life with all of its attendant problems: the risks of arrest and imprisonment (to say nothing of injury or death); the stigma of being labeled a "bad girl," with its implications of promiscuity as well as criminality; and a life alienated from regular work, school, and sometimes family. Having understood a little of the lives they have chosen to reject, we can now turn to the life the gang has provided for them.

Chapter 3

Connie and the Sandman Ladies

The Sandman is a Manhattan biker gang. It is arguable whether or not biker is an appropriate description, since while I was in contact with them there was only one functioning motorcycle (a BSA 650), although there was much discussion of the purchase and renovation of other bikes. However, biker seems appropriate in the light of the age of the leading member (thirty years old), the sense of brotherhood the gang felt with other biker gangs (such as the Wheels of Soul), and the conversational preoccupations and attitudes of the members. Discussions of drug experiences and trips to the country "runs" and the predominance of Satanic and Nazi badges and emblems were very reminiscent of descriptions of the Hell's Angels. But the members in general had little sympathy for this group. They rejected their size, criminality, and fascistic political views, arguing that the Sandman, by contrast, was a social club and an unofficial family. Local biker clubs were seen as very different from the national, almost institutionalized, structure they attributed to the Hell's Angels.

Although they described themselves as a club, the Sandman was designated as a gang by the New York City Police's Manhattan Gang Intelligence Unit #1. In the final report by this unit in 1979 it is identified only as a Hispanic gang with an alleged membership of thirty five and a verified membership of ten. No information on its activities is available. Many members did not live locally but commuted in to Manhattan from the Bronx or Brooklyn to hang out. The membership was not particularly stable because of this and also because some of the members, especially girls, periodically drifted back to the Times Square area where they were involved in drugs or prostitution.

The major source of income for the gang when I was in contact with them was drug dealing. Prior to establishing their own area of

49

operation, they had worked downtown, keeping the streets of another drug-selling group "safe." They were also involved in an ongoing dispute with the Chosen Ones (a group from uptown Manhattan), which seemed to be related to drug sales and to other gangs' belief that the Sandman had provided the police with information that led to the imprisonment of their members. After the incident reported by the *New York Post*, in which a chase occurred along the subway tracks, the dispute continued. Two of the Sandman were shot at (one escaped injury, the other had four bullet wounds) and Connie's teenage daughter was the object of a shooting, although she escaped unharmed. Connie continued to care for her four children, support her husband, and lead the Sandman Ladies throughout.

A Day with Connie

Connie lives in the Upper West Side of Manhattan on the thirteenth floor of a project apartment building. You can spot her windows easily from the ground. A Puerto Rican flag hangs from one and heads bob in and out of the other to check what's happening on the street. Inside, the lobby is painted a pale lavatorial green and echoes with the laughter and shrieks of children in the nursery on the ground floor. It smells of a musty scent that covers the odor of chemical used to control cockroaches. The two elevators operate spasmodically. A ten-minute wait is not unusual.

No one answers Connie's door at first because the knocking is drowned out by the thundering bass of the rap disco blasting out of radio speakers. The door's spyhole cover opens, swings shut, and OK is standing there. He waves me through, smiling with exaggerated politeness. In the corner of the living room, the color television is on with the sound turned down, and quiz-show hosts grin and chatter idiotically. JR is stretched out luxuriously on the sofa beneath a giant Sandman insignia depicting a hooded face on an iron cross, which hangs on the wall. He wears a yellow T-shirt that proudly states "I love Brooklyn," in graffiti writing and a leather vest. A bottle of Colt 45 beer rests on the floor next to him. Mico is in the kitchen, helping Connie bag up marijuana for the day.

Connie, perched on a stool, looks up and smiles. She wears no makeup and her hair, scrupulously clean, falls around her face. She is small – five feet two – but the tall stool gives her a certain stature. Up high by the window, she can see down onto the street. She is wearing a check blouse, jeans, and two belts, one with a demonic

Connie, leader of the Sandman Ladies, in the project building where their clubhouse was located

goat's head and the other apparently a chain from a BSA motor-cycle. At the side of one belt is a small leather case that holds a knife. Connie always carries a flick knife and always in a visible place – as long as it is not a switchblade (which shoots the blade forward from the handle) and it is not concealed, the police will leave her alone. I pull up a chair and the three of us talk over the blare of the radio, yelling to make ourselves heard or leaning together conspiratorially to catch some complicated story.

In the mornings, Connie and Suzie, her daughter, get up early at 7:30. Suzie is fourteen, taller than her mother, and very capable. The girlfriend of Connie's six-year-old son Raps comes by to pick him up and often she dresses and feeds him as well. He is out of the house by 8:30. JJ, Connie's youngest son, has to be dressed and given breakfast along with baby Dahlia. She and Suzie take him to school, put Dahlia in the nursery downstairs, and sometimes manage to eat breakfast together in a donut shop. By 9:30 the kids are usually dispatched for the day.

This particular Friday, Suzie has stayed home to help out and hang around. Gino, Connie's husband and leader of the Sandman, is not going to work today and is sleeping through the early morning hubbub. Connie is happy to have all her family around her. As we talk, she bags up with a dexterity she has developed over years – snipping up the grass and packing it into tiny yellow envelopes. She seals each with Scotch tape and then, with a small piece of cardboard, scrapes another bagful from the white plastic bowl. We talk about jealousy. Connie leans over and pulls a notebook out of the kitchen drawer. Each page has neat paragraph entries, the visible results of years of sitting, thinking, bagging, and talking. She writes down each new insight about life and relationships.

This morning she announces that she has to get on with her "automated routines," so she gets up, washes the dishes, puts a pile of dirty T-shirts into the washing machine, and lights a cigarette. OK is now listening to the radio through headphones, but the volume is so loud that we can all hear it. JR has turned up the television and sits absorbed by a soap opera. Connie runs out of cigarettes and OK is sent to the store to buy a pack of Kools. Connie tells me about when she had Suzie at fifteen. After her fourth child at twenty-eight, Connie "closed down the factory." "I felt like a damn incubator. There has got to be some balance in life, but who should decide who's to live and who's to die?" she ponders as she slaps Scotch tape onto the tiny bags.

At one o'clock, Wolfy from the Satan's Wheels in the South Bronx arrives. He has a black handkerchief around his head, held in place by a piece of string, and wears a T-shirt and a cut-off denim jacket without gang insignia or "patches." Patches seen on the subway cause trouble. The guys get up to greet him as he comes into their clubhouse. They exchange news from different clubs, and Connie and I sit by, half-listening from the kitchen. From the bedroom comes a warm roar and Gino appears with arms outstretched to Wolfy. "Hey, hey, what's up?" They embrace and Gino's presence as leader is felt.

Connie divides the plastic bags and hands them to some of the guys who pull on their leather jackets and denim patches with SANDMAN MC NYC on the back and go out for the day to the street. Gino, wearing a black leather biker's cap with his leather jacket, jeans, and motor-cycle boots, comes over and kisses Connie. Then he leaves to go down with the guys.

At 1:30, Shorty arrives. She is small and curly-haired, perhaps only nineteen. She is gang member Sinbad's girlfriend and wears her denim jacket over a blue sweatshirt. To be Sinbad's girlfriend is not a direct entry into the Sandman Ladies, however. She must prove her capability, just like anyone elso who wants to join, and she has not yet earned her patches. Connie will decide when she deserves the title Sandman Lady. Connie says that she doesn't care about a girl's fighting history; what she looks for in a possible member are brains. Shorty is still learning. Later, when she answers the door and leaves it ajar as she tells Connie who it is, Connie tells her never, never to leave the door open. How does she know that someone they don't want to see isn't out there about to walk right in? Shorty nods. She sits in the living room quietly watching and listening to everything.

Connie's favorite song plays on the radio. She jumps up and whistles for Suzie to come in from the bedroom. Together they take over the living room floor, doing the hustle. Suzie acts the male's part perfectly, with minimum body movement and an expression of total boredom. At the end of the song, Suzie walks back to the bedroom and Connie, out of breath, laughs to herself. At 1:45, Connie's mother phones from Queens. Connie talks with her mother frequently on the phone but does not see her often. Her mother disapproves of the club, and Connie feels caught between duty and love.

Everything is quiet now. Family members have gone their ways for the day, and only Shorty sits quietly in the next room, clutching a hankie. Connie tells me more of her life story. When she was nineteen – eleven years ago – her father died. She shows me one of the letters he wrote to her while he was in the hospital for drug treatment. The handwriting is scrupulously neat. He complains that the doctors think he is crazy and tells Connie that if anything should happen to him, she should investigate it. He writes with great pride about Connie's new career in nursing and about his beautiful granddaughter (Suzie). Among his letters, Connie finds some official papers. One is a charge sheet from the police or a court, signed by a doctor, testifying that her father was found unfit to plead because of "imbecility." The other is a telegram from the hospital telling her that he is dead and asking her to make funeral arrangements. Connie never saw the death certificate and never knew what her father died from. Now she remembers his injunction and feels guilty. She never did check the circumstances of his death. She looks at the clock; it's time to go pick up the kids.

Halfway to the elevator Connie runs back to the apartment to get her sunglasses. Last week she got beaten up. Her nose was broken, she had stitches, and both her eyes puffed out. The swelling has gone down, but two plum-colored circles remain around her eyes. Until they go, the sunglasses are compulsory public wear. She has also changed into a pair of dark red boots – lovingly cared for with daily doses of cold cream – that are pulled over her jeans. Over her blouse, she wears a fur-lined leather jacket, a couple of sizes too big, and on top of that her patches. Sewn on the denim jacket are the full colors of the club: SANDMAN NYC LADIES. With Shorty, we go into the weak afternoon sunshine.

Outside on a bench, Gino is recounting to the gang how the police beat him up when he had tuberculosis: "They beat the TB right out of me!" Sitting on the stone bench and the wall are seven club members all with their colors on. Wolfy and Lalla, a girl of twenty who deals around the area, are there too. Lalla wears a baseball cap back to front and a red jacket. She looks young and jumpy in comparison to Connie, severe and feminine, who sits on the stone chess table listening quietly while her husband speaks. Gino's story gets increasingly boisterous, and there is much laughter as they slap one another's hands in appreciation of the tale. The group appears insulated and self-contained. Their uniform jacket patches and their red bandannas divide them from the rest of the world. Nevertheless, neighbors, janitors, social workers, mothers of children who share Dahlia's nursery greet them as they pass, and Gino and the group wave back or shout "Hi. What's up?"

Dahlia stumbles out of the front lobby, watched by her teacher. She heads straight for Connie who picks her up, kisses her, and switches her shoes, which Dahlia has put on the wrong feet. Gino kisses Dahlia hello, and he and Connie decide who will go to pick up JJ from school. Gino goes, since he is usually at work these days and misses the daily ritual.

Every so often, someone approaches one of the group – the guy who is "holding" that day. The drug deal is transacted quietly. The girls sit separately. We talk about the neighborhood, about fights, about men. Now and again one of the guys asks for a cigarette or tells Connie something in Spanish connected with today's business. At the end of the day, all the money goes to Connie, who does the bookkeeping. Connie gives Suzie a couple of dollars from the roll of bills in her pocket to take Dahlia to the store to buy some candy. Today Dahlia gets some marshmallows, but Connie doesn't generally approve. She doesn't want her to get a taste for too much sugar.

Gino returns, and now the whole family is together. Raps, six-years-old, tells about a fight he had at school: "Yeah, I really dogged him. I fucked up his shit." Gino teases him about his ten-year-old girlfriend, offering some fatherly advice: "You tell that bitch that she can't carry your gaddam books to school no more." Everyone laughs except Raps, who looks down, embarrassed. He

Connie's youngest daughter Dahlia wearing her colors as a Sandman Tot

likes the attention but doesn't really know what is so funny. The teenage girls from the project are coming home from junior high school. As they pass, they greet Connie with a kiss, exchange a few words, kiss her cheek again, and go inside. They all know her and Suzie. Members of the club who have been at work or school arrive one at a time until there are fifteen of us. We each throw in a couple of dollars, and JC goes off to the liquor store. He returns with small plastic cups, a bottle of Coke, and some Bacardi rum. The girls' drinks are poured into the cups and are very strong. Sinbad notices me sipping at mine and instructs me to "Drink like a *woman*." The guys pass the liquor bottle around, drinking theirs neat. Before each one drinks, he pours a little of the rum on the ground in memory of those who are dead or in jail. The bottle ends up on the stone chess table in front of the girls and, the guys gravitate toward it. Gino and Wolfy speak half to each other and half to the kids who climb on and off the benches, threatening to upset the liquor. Raps drops his lollipop on the ground, and Gino picks it up, wipes it off, and pours Bacardi over it to sterilize it. Raps puts it back in his mouth and grimaces.

The conversation turns to Gino's time in Vietnam, where, he tells us, he was a combat photographer. He tells how many of the injuries he saw were perpetrated by the Americans on themselves when incendiary bombs were dropped short of target or when machines backfired. He was injured in the leg, but when the U.S. Army withdrew, his medical papers were lost. Now he has no way to prove that he is entitled to veteran's compensation, unless he were to take his case to court and that would cost him thousands. "If I had that kind of money, I wouldn't need their damn compensation, right?" Gino interrupts the story to wave and yell at a guy across the street who is something of a local celebrity because he had a role in *The Wiz*. Gino also sees two guys in surplus army jackets crossing the street – plainclothes cops. Gino watches as they enter a flower shop, which is a local drug-dealing center. Later, a local guy comes over to tell Gino that he followed them but they split up and went different ways.

It's 4:50 and it's getting colder. Gino announces we are going to a party tonight at the house of the president of Satan's Wheels in the Bronx. Upon hearing of the party, Connie, who has been standing back with Shorty, occasionally chatting to her, decides it is a good time to give Shorty her first patches. They disappear upstairs to sew them on her jacket and to check that Suzie can baby-sit. As we sit drinking, the daylight fades quickly. People coming home from work pass the apartment building in a steady stream. Some stare curiously at the group. Others, more familiar, simply hurry past. The light in the lobby spills out onto the concrete in front and the yellow street lights come on.

Connie and Shorty return. Shorty spins around triumphantly to show off her new patches: LADY NYC. Later she will earn her final patch: SANDMAN. The guys yell and whistle and, led by Gino, pour bottles of beer over her head in traditional gang congratulations. She squeals. It's very cold by now and her hair is soaking wet, but she smiles and flicks back her curls with the back of her hand. Sinbad hugs her proudly.

Connie disappears and returns with a sandwich wrapped in silver foil from a local Spanish store. We pass it around and share it with the kids who have come downstairs. By now there are about twenty of us. From time to time, one of the guys comes over and looks through my notebook, curious to see what I have written down today. They borrow my pen to make illustrations, additions, or subtractions. Connie and I stand together. She points out females who pass by, some friends and some potential enemies. I am shivering from the cold, but Connie teases me that my knees are knocking at the thought of going to the South Bronx. There is talk that the Satan's Wheels will send a van to pick up everyone. That would be better than going by subway. On the subway, twenty people dressed in gang colors attract attention, which often leads to problems with the police. But the Sandman must wear their colors as a sign of pride in their club if they are going to another club's turf. Maybe they'll carry them over their arms on the train and put them on when they get out. Some of the guys who have come from work look tired. Gino tells them to watch out for being burned. If they fall asleep at the party he will set fire to their pants, a disciplinary custom that reminds members always to be on their guard when they are away from their own area.

Gino announces that we will go by subway but no one is to wear colors on the train. Five of us take the kids and their various toys and carts up to the apartment. Suzie has two girlfriends over for the evening and is playing disco music. Connie leaves a small bag of grass for them. Suzie tries for a pint of Bacardi too, but Connie refuses. Dahlia cries for her mother but quiets down when Suzie picks her up. We go downstairs after I have been given a plain denim jacket so I won't look completely out of place.

OK and Shorty carry down motorcycle helmets, which they offer to Gino. Gino asks what the hell they are for. OK protests that Gino told him to bring them. Gino says he didn't. OK mumbles some curse and turns away. Gino loses his temper and begins yelling at him. Everyone freezes and watches to see what will happen. OK does not say a word. Gino berates him for not listening, for not following orders, for being insolent. Wolfy, even though it is not his gang, joins in: "He's your leader. You'd better damn well respect him." OK, head down, walks away. Gino does not let up: "And don't you be sulking like that neither." OK seems to look happier afterward. Gino's threat to leave him chained to the iron fence at the edge of the project buildings is forgotten.

We walk in twos and threes to the subway station five or six blocks away. Gino stops to urinate behind a wall. I walk on with the Hulk, talking about his future, his school, his clothes. Connie calls out, "Hey, where's Annie?" She is looking out for me all the time. At the subway, Wolfy and I walk down the steps while the rest of the group gathers at the entrance. I put my token in the stile, but Wolfy walks through the swing doors without paying. The subway clerk calls him back, but he walks on. When Gino and the others appear, the clerk has already picked up the phone to call the transit police. Gino intervenes and pays everyone's fare, including Wolfy's. On the platform, he bawls Wolfy out, telling him it's crazy to get the cops down for the measly fare. Gino shows a roll of money in his pocket to reinforce the point. This is, after all, their turf. They have to use the subway all the time, so why make trouble? Wolfy is a guest and, as such, he should respect their turf.

Gino tells us to split up because we look too conspicuous in a group. Connie, Shorty, and I walk down the platform. Near us two black girls are casually rolling a joint. Connie watches them – there is something about their manner that she doesn't like. When we get on the train, one of them leans on the center post of the car, ignoring the available seats. Connie walks over and leans on the opposite post four feet away, staring at her through her dark glasses. They stare each other down, but the other girl breaks first. She looks away, then at her feet, then gets off the train. We change trains at 182nd Street. A train pulls in, but it's not the one we want to take. Inside a car, a man in his thirties, dressed in a suit, smiles at us. It isn't clear to me whether he is leering or laughing at us. As the train pulls away, Shorty smashes her fist at the window where his face is. He jumps back and the train disappears. Shorty clutches her hand. In a few minutes, it begins to swell and turn red, but she does not mention it.

We board our train. Two Puerto Rican girls are standing by the door, whispering and laughing. Connie watches them, wondering whether to "bug them out." She approaches them, but I cannot hear what is said. One girl reaches into her bag and pulls out some gum, offering Connie a stick. She takes one and offers it to me. I decline. Connie pops it in her mouth and leans over to kiss the girl on the cheek. Connie is smiling. The girls look pleased, embarrassed, and confused. The guys walk up and down the train in ones and twos, checking that everybody is on and knows where to get off. Although they are carrying their colors over their arms, they look conspicuous in their chains, boots, and bandannas. Some have sheath knives in their waistbands. Passengers watch their comings and goings uneasily.

We get off the train and climb the unlit stairs to the street. The guys take the girls' arms to guide us up. Several young girls are standing by the subway entrance. They seem excited at our arrival and particularly interested in Connie and Shorty with their patches. As we cross the street, Sinbad authoritatively holds up his hand to halt the oncoming traffic. We straggle along a side street, and Gino peers down an alleyway to a handball court where some kids are playing by floodlight. The game breaks up, and after a few seconds one of them appears in patches: FLAMES NYC. It is Felix, a friend of Gino. He greets all of us and cordially offers a small plastic cup of vodka and grapefruit juice, which we pass around. He has recently redesigned his club patches – from a swastika into a more complex design with a skull set in red and orange flames – and turns around so we can admire them. I reach out to touch them, wondering how he got such a complicated design so professionally done. Connie pulls my hand back and tells me that it is forbidden to touch someone's patches. And there are rituals surrounding them: they can never be taken off carelessly, but must be folded and laid down safely, they must always be worn with boots, never with sneakers.

Felix decides to escort us through his turf to the party, which is several blocks away. He is on good terms with Satan's Wheels. We walk on down dark streets with huge empty tenements on either side. Doorways are covered heavily with graffiti and smell of urine. Connie, Shorty, and I walk at the rear, and Sinbad turns every few yards to make sure we are keeping up. Connie advises me to sit quietly at the party and be careful that nothing I do be misunderstood. I am white and, as such, am considered to be available property. Don't say too much and stick close to her, Connie says. We gaze around at the buildings. We are both completely out of our territory, although Connie points a few blocks downtown to where she lived briefly years ago. She tells me this isn't a real nice area. Broken bottles crunch under our feet. Finally we halt outside a grocery store, waiting while Gino and Felix finish their discussion.

We walk into an old tenement building. The huge hallway is painted crimson and lit by long fluorescent tubes. Initials and names are emblazoned on the walls. We walk up one flight of stairs and ring a doorbell. After a few minutes, we are let in and walk down a hallway. Three or four girls are sitting in a bedroom through some French doors. Gino greets the guys in the club who are in the kitchen drinking, and Connie goes into the bedroom. In perfect Spanish and very politely she introduces herself as head of the Sandman Ladies and thanks the girls for their hospitality. They are much younger than she is and struggle to summon an equally dignified reply. They are dressed casually, but when they reappear several minutes later, they have put on sweatshirts that say PROPERTY OF SATAN'S WHEELS NYC, with the name of their particular man underneath. Connie tells me that *her* girls don't belong to any man.

We all assemble in the living room. Connie points out that the room is "typically Spanish" – velour-patterned sofa and many mementos on the tables and shelves; dolls, candles, crucifixes. The Satan's Wheels move the sound system into the room. Bottles of beer and Bacardi are passed around, interspersed with joints. When the music comes on, it is heavy rock – Stones, Led Zeppelin, Pink Floyd – and is deafening. Conversation is possible only by leaning right up against the other person's ear. The main lights go out, and the room is lit only by three ultra-violet lights, which illuminate eyes, teeth, and the white in jacket patches. One by one people begin to dance. Connie sits next to me on the sofa with her back straight.

It is the Hulk's sixteenth birthday. Suddenly the lights are switched on and he is drenched by several bottles of beer. He waves his arms, apparently enjoying the experience. The floor is awash with liquid, but one of the Satan's Wheels later mops up. Everyone is also scrupulously careful to flick their cigarette ashes into ashtrays, rather than on the floor. Amid the apparent chaos, there is a definite order. The Hulk moves around the room, embracing every member of the club, and by the end, we are all nearly as wet as he is. Gino spends most of the evening in the kitchen, discussing club business with the Flames and Satan's Wheels. Connie and I sit together drinking. Everybody is loosening up. Chino gets his beard set alight as a reminder that he is getting a little too loose. He climbs onto the fire escape and peers down, announcing that he is contemplating suicide. Then he laughs.

Connie and I, as we drink more, consider the implications of everything in the world being a product of our imagination. If we wished it all away now, only *we* would remain, suspended sixty feet in the air, discussing this very thought. A guy next to me searches vainly for some matches. I hand him some and Connie warns me about body contact. If you touch someone accidentally, they may take it the wrong way. I move away from him, suddenly aware that I have been half-leaning on him. Connie motions me to lean forward and tells me that if we keep talking together, maybe the guys will assume that I'm with her. That way, I'll be safe. Gino returns to sit by us. He and some other guys are throwing a bottle back and forth with eyes closed, a kind of test of everybody's reaction speed. I notice Connie's hands loose in her lap but ready in case it is thrown her way. The music changes to disco – a whole album side of it – and Connie gets up to dance alone.

It is after midnight and I decide to leave. Connie forces twenty dollars into my hand for a cab. Gino assigns two guys to walk me to the taxi office. Everybody yells goodnight, and I make my way back home.

Connie's Biography

Connie's mother left Puerto Rico for New York after the Second World War, when she was only nineteen. Along with thousands of others she came to the United States looking for a better economic future. She met a dashing young man who, from his photographs, bears a marked resemblance to Clark Gable – mustached, with the brim of an expensive hat tilted over one eye and a trench coat tied at the waist. In 1949, Connie was conceived. Her mother returned to Puerto Rico to have the baby in her mother's house. There were already nine children in the small shack, six from Connie's grand-mother's first marriage and three from her second. Her grand-mother was a warm person and very religious, attending church every morning. There was little money and Connie's mother sewed gloves at home for bad wages to make sure that Connie had pretty clothes. From time to time she took the child into town to have professional photographs taken. They were expensive and precious; Connie still has them. In the pictures, she has short, straight hair cut in bangs and an expression of great seriousness. While she was in Puerto Rico, Connie rolled off a table and fell onto the rough concrete floor. Since then, she has been deaf in one ear.

When Connie was two and a half, her mother brought her back to New York to live with an aunt. Her mother still saw Connie's father from time to time, but he had become a drug addict. Connie remembers him as a quiet, kind man. By the time Connie was four, her mother had become ill with a lung disorder and was unable to care for the child. Connie was returned to Puerto Rico to live with a paternal aunt who already had a young daughter. Her sense of rejection still remained, as, years later, she told me.

I also threw that up in my mother's face. I told her, "Look, I used to go from house to house. At least I never did that to Suzie. I always kept her with me. I didn't get rid of her."

Did it affect you?

Yeah. Because I was dealing with a lot of situations for too young a child. Like the first time I was separated from my mother it wasn't something that she wanted. It was a physical thing. She was sick, so she had to go to a hospital for months and I was in Puerto Rico. While living in Puerto Rico, I had to stay with my father's sister. And my cousin every night would do the same thing. Put her leg over me and piss. Every damn night I'd have to wake up with piss in the bed.

How old were you?

About four. Same age as JJ. I came to consciousness of this world very young.

I don't remember much from being four.

I do, I do. I remember being so lonely, so lonely. Like an outsider. Like I didn't really belong because my father was like a black sheep of their family. Here they are stuck with this kid – even though they were supposed to be my godparents. I don't know. I always felt like an outsider. From there I would go to my grandmother's house – my mother's mother. And I remember singing to her a Spanish song, "Who is it that loves me?" I always used to sing that. I would always remember feeling so lonely. By myself, by myself, by myself. Yeah, I had all these people to look after me, to make sure I was well clothed and fed, but I was like alone. Even though I knew my grandmother loved me. And of all her grandchildren, I'm the one and the one that died too that she can say are really hers. I don't even write to her, man. I don't know what to write to her. She speaks no English. If I do talk to her – like once when I wrote to her, I wrote to her because I was feeling very lonely. Because my father had died and my cousin had also died and I felt so bad. I just wrote to her. Then I said, "What am I doing? All I'm doing is depressing her more."

Connie was back in New York for her fifth birthday party. She lived with her mother on 76th Street. Shortly after she arrived, she was diagnosed as having worms and was hospitalized for two weeks. Separation from her mother was now becoming the norm. She was increasingly withdrawn. She began school but hated being away from home, especially as her mother had met the man who was to become her stepfather.

Then she met my stepfather because a child can't be everything to a woman. A woman always has to turn to a man. But I used to hate that man because at that time I started school too. I didn't go to kindergarten, I went to first grade. Every morning she would take me and every morning I would scream and holler and rant for her to take me home. So the teacher would say, "Look, I don't want to upset the other kids. Take her home." She would take me to the five and dime and buy me stuff. "Now are you going to go and keep your mouth shut?" "Yeah, yeah, yeah." Then I'd do the same thing all over again. It's hard getting away from Moms. And then she met that man, and to me, I felt I was totally shut out and I hated him. And at that time my father used to come around and they would let me see him – weekends and stuff like that. He was a very intelligent man. He also had beautiful handwriting, he could draw. He wrote a poem about Mr. Trouble: "No matter where you go, he'll always find you."

She was torn between a love for her real father and a continuing need for love from her mother. At six she was already playing hooky from school with friends. Since her mother spoke no English, it was easy to get away with. She faked accounts of her days at school and scribbled odd pages of English that she passed off as homework. She had a lazy eye and had to wear glasses, which she hated since she was becoming increasingly conscious of boys. Although she was quiet, she was getting tougher inside.

I told you that when I was six years old I had my own conscious mind and I had to dodge a lot of people in order to survive. I wasn't raised in the streets. I was raised in a different way. From 9 to 3 the streets are much different than after school. Those will be the street kids, the ones that are always outside. I had a street life but within confinement. I do have a middle-class background too.

You grew up fast.

I knew a lot for my age. A lot of people didn't want their kids hanging out with me. Then again, lots of mothers trusted me with their kids.

Sent to summer camp at six, Connie was determined to prove her toughness against all comers. She took a knife with her and, in an attempt to demonstrate her fearlessness, threw it into various imaginary targets in the ground. She misthrew once and the knife penetrated her foot. Rather than lose face, she pulled it out herself and spent the next three weeks limping.

At seven, she moved to 135th Street, with her mother and stepfather and began at a new school. They lived in the basement of a building, and Connie's uncle came to stay, bringing with him a stream of pretty young girls. Connie continued to play hooky. From 9 to 3, she was on the streets with her friends, playing rough and dangerous. She remembers how one day a little boy fell from a roof on which they were hiding. They also used to jump rides on the backs of buses as they pulled away from bus stops. The day that she fell off into the traffic, she could not go running back home to her mother who thought she was in school.

Life in the basement apartment was far from luxurious. And Connie's relationship with her stepfather was not improving. He would force her to eat all the black rice on her plate, which she hated. It became a battle of wills, which Connie won by surreptitiously throwing her food behind the stove. But there were bright days too. She remembers how her real father came to meet her one day, bringing her a brand-new pair of tap-dancing shoes.

When Connie was nine, her stepfather's position in the family was firmly established by the birth of Connie's brother. The family moved back downtown to 74th Street. Connie was sent back to Puerto Rico, first to her grandmother's, then to her aunt's.

It's very difficult raising a family with a child from another marriage. Everybody has different reasons for getting married. The second sibling, it doesn't necessarily have to be [through] marriage. The first children always get the rotten egg. Being the oldest is a bitch. But then again, it's a bitch to grow up period. That's why I'm glad I'm grown up and not a child. I don't think I can cope with being a child again.

When I went to Puerto Rico when I was about ten, they were always trying to find a place to place me where I could just really fit in. I was staying at this aunt's house – she was very strict, man. She had packed up my clothes to come to New York about three days before. Over in Puerto Rico they change their clothes like three, four times a day. And here I walk to the store every day with the same clothes. They had a record they used to sing to me: "Here she comes and she's walking with the same old clothes and look, she's getting skinny." And I *was* skinny to top it off. So I mean that's why I say I would never want to go and live in Puerto Rico. That's why I say I'm glad I'm not a child anymore because you had to go through so many changes. A lot of people say they want to go back, but I say, "No, I don't. I like it just the way I am now."

You were six when your mother got the new guy, then at ten you went to your aunt?

But before that I had been in Puerto Rico living again, going here and going there.

Was your mother upset that she couldn't keep you with her?

I guess she was, but I just didn't get along with her old man because I wouldn't respect him because, no matter what, he wasn't my father and I would tell him, "You're not my father."

At ten, Connie returned to live with the family in New York, now on 34th Street. Later that year, they moved to 105th Street, then to 78th Street. Every move meant a new school for Connie. She became adept at dealing with the changes. She succeeded by withdrawing socially or by asserting herself through fights. Connie had pride and a strong character and she felt much older than her contemporaries, who had been together in their cliques since kindergarten. When she was ten, her sister was born. Connie was the only child to remember her real father – a fact that her stepfather found hard to tolerate.

One time I remember I was sitting down taking a pee 'cos we used to live in like a rooming house and I was looking at his [father's] pictures and my stepfather came up to me and he just tore up the pictures. I was always the third wheel. No matter where I went. And since I didn't get along with him, I would defy him. Like one time, this was on a visit I think, I had gotten dressed up on a Sunday and he wanted me to shine his shoes and I said, "No, shine them yourself. I'm not going to get dirty." And he said, "No, I want you to shine my shoes," and I wouldn't do it, so he beat me up and I still wouldn't do his shoes.

At eleven, her relationship with him became so problematic that she was sent to live in Queens with an aunt and uncle. Connie still saw her father two or three times a year, although he was in and out of jail frequently because of his problem with drugs. In Queens, Connie acquired three female cousins who resented her presence. They would hide and destroy her possessions. She could not adapt to the middle-class life-style for which her aunt and uncle were training her. It was a miserable two years.

My aunt and uncle were trying to teach me the value of money, so they would give me a quarter every week. But I would have to take that quarter and put it in a little jar. I give my kids money, so there'll be no reason for them to steal from me. 'Cos I used to steal from them. Because I used to go to school. Everybody had their candy and stuff like that, so I used to go into the supermarket after school looking for my aunt, and I would even be so bold – even ask the workers, "Have you seen a lady that looks like this, like this?" They'd say, "No, look around." So I'd pass by the candy and I'd take some candy and put it in my schoolbag, then say, "Well, I guess she ain't around, maybe I'll see her later," and I would walk out.

Then my uncle's mother, I used to take money from her and I figured "Well, she's old anyway – what the hell? She'll probably say, 'What the hell did I spend it on' And she won't realize." And then one time, I got caught. I had the money in my belt because everyone had been treating me for a few days so I wanted to treat them too. My aunt found the money. See, I used to wear a belt with a pleated skirt and as soon as I walked out of the house, I would fold it all the way up and make it real short and put the belt around it. And even if I had to wear the same skirt over and over again at least it was the way I liked it. They used to buy me some real messed-up baby, baby clothes, you know. I guess that's why they [schoolmates] made so much fun of me. And then she found the money, and I got whipped for it and she asked me, "Where did you get it?" and I said the first thing that came to mind [which was that it] was Brenda's money – this girl that used to live down the block. She used to steal from her housekeeper and – but then Brenda didn't want to come over and claim the money because she was saying, "Oh, my mother found out I was stealing and she gave me money and I don't have to steal now. Like I can't do it." I kicked her ass for not doing it. So then I went up to my aunt and I said, "Look, man, I tell you the truth, man, I found it." "Where you found it?" "Well, I was crossing the street and I was with some friends and I found it, OK?" So she came up to me – I never told her where I got the money from – she came crying to me and she kept crying and saying, "Look, I don't –." What kind of hell I put her through! I only think of my side, but thinking now, she must have gone through hell too. She cried and she said, "Look I don't know if a man gave it to you and you let him do –." you know? But I would not tell her. I couldn't tell her because I would think that's just as bad.

How old were you then?

About eleven. And then, the lady died after I was older, you know. And then one day, I mean in my dreams, this lady used to chase me all over. I mean I would open up a closet and there she was. She would start coming after me and I'd be running and I'd wake up in a cold sweat. I'd be scared as hell and then one day I realized "What the hell, man? I was only a kid. She can forgive me." After that my dreams just stopped. I finally realized "Hey, I'm sure she doesn't hold it over me." But I mean I had such bad guilt feelings because she had died.

At thirteen, Connie moved back in with her mother and stepfather, who were now living on 96th Street. She attended eighth grade there and in spite of all the changes in schools took pride in the fact that she had never been held back. She was bright and was able to skip school without failing any important tests. When she was at school, she developed hopeless crushes on boys and lived in a kind of fantasy world fueled by the romance magazines she used to read. These fantasies were often sexual. She was becoming more and more attractive as she got older, and by the ninth grade, she was very popular at school, although she had by no means settled down. Fights were still frequent, but other kids were somewhat in awe of her independence. By the time she graduated from junior high school at fourteen, her stepfather and mother were constantly arguing. He was increasingly drunk and began seeing other women. Connie went to high school on 19th Street, although her mother, when she split from her stepfather, moved to 90th Street.

Connie hung out downtown after school and uptown with friends from her neighborhood. There were lots of parties, and she never had any shortage of admirers. At fifteen, she discovered she was pregnant.

The thing that got me was when I was pregnant at fifteen, everybody was trying to find out who the father was because I don't talk. She [my mother] started crying at the doctor's office 'cos he said, "Your baby is going to have a baby." She suspected it 'cos I hadn't gotten my period for a while, then I – morning sickness. One time I ran out of the house and I did it under the stairs. And the super was a lady and she started saying, "Who the hell had to be vomiting?" Then when my mother found I was pregnant, she said, "Oh, it was you, was it?" I couldn't hold anything in.
Did she want you to have an abortion?
She didn't know what to do. She was like totally lost. And then she used to hang out with this lady who was working in an agency and the lady told her, "Take her to Catholic charities. Have the baby given up for adoption." So we went through the procedures

and you go into the place and right away they paint such a picture where "Yeah, I'll give my baby up. They're going to have a father and mother and a good home and everything." And my mother said, "What are the chances of the baby being adopted?" And my mother freaked and said, "No, I can't go on a train and see a poster [of adopted children] and not know which is my grandchild." So she said, "I'll raise her." She was going to give her her last name and everything.

Connie quit school and lived with her mother on 100th Street. At sixteen, she began working as a sales clerk, moving from job to job. She and her mother shared the job of raising Suzie.

At nineteen, Connie enrolled in Jobs Corps to get her High School Equivalency Diploma and to train for nursing. It meant living in New Jersey Monday through Friday and returning on weekends to be with Suzie at her mother's place. One positive aspect was that it gave Connie the time to do some of the growing up that she had missed.

During the time I was supposed to be a baby, I was at home taking care of my own kid, not baby-sitting. That was a responsibility that I always had to think about. Now when I was over there, she was staying with my mother so I knew she was in well-kept hands. I didn't have to worry about her, so I could really let go.

While Connie was in New Jersey, a chaplain from Bellevue Hospital contacted her to tell her that her father was in the hospital and anxious to get in touch with her.

He was a drug addict so he was really a lost soul roaming in life. As far as I know I was his only daughter – as far as I know. He always wanted to change my name to Dahlia – that's why I named Dahlia after him – for him.

. . . When I was in Job Corps, he used to write me letters. They went looking for me till they finally located me 'cos they told me he was dying. I went to the hospital, and this man was in merry spirits. He sang a song to me. He was so happy to see me. Then after that, he started disintegrating till he died. The thing that kept his life going was to see me before he died, and after he saw me, he just died. And he saw Suzie too. He was in a mental institution. I think I still have some papers – where he had gone to Bellevue for a hospital appointment and he got beaten up and his skull was broken. They had to take his brain out and they put it back with a metal plate on his head.

Throughout Job Corps, Connie visited her father and they wrote to each other regularly. Connie took a clerical job on Wall Street, and it was there that her mother phoned to read the telegram saying that he had died. Connie got on the subway to go home and cried.

At twenty, Connie quit her job to take a college preparatory course through Manpower. She was accepted at Brooklyn College and began introductory courses in sociology, history, and politics. She gained forty credits in the next two years as well as taking part-time jobs at hospitals, stores, and the New York Housing Department to support herself. She was still living with her mother, although by now she and Suzie had their own room. She was working hard at school and learned a lot from other students about literature and Puerto Rican culture. She also learned to play chess.

At twenty-two, Connie and Suzie moved into their own apartment near her mother's. It was a nice place with a doorman and a balcony. Connie was happy to have this new freedom. It had been crowded at her mother's with the two other children, and Connie and her mother often disagreed about raising Suzie. Connie was always very firm with Suzie and was determined to establish which one of them was the boss. She never hit her, but often it became a battle of wills because Suzie, like her mother, had a very strong character. Men came and went in Connie's life, but there were no serious relationships.

When Connie was twenty-three, she met Gino. It completely changed her life. They met at a party and went home together. From that night on, they have rarely slept apart. Initially, Connie's mother disapproved of Gino, and when Connie quit college seven months later, it did little to improve her mother's evaluation of him. But Connie had never been so happy. Emotionally, socially, sexually, she was completely absorbed with him. She felt released from the "machine-like" existence of work, school, and child rearing. For a while, she taught reading and writing in a local school. Gino had a veteran's grant to obtain his High School Equivalency Diploma and worked as a gym teacher. Three months after quitting college, Connie found that she was pregnant. They were both delighted at the thought of having a child. Their son Raps was born in August when Connie was twenty-four. Suzie, although at first disconcerted to find out that she could no longer share a bedroom with her mother, came to love Gino. And she enjoyed the new baby as much as Connie and Gino.

Connie and Gino's relationship was, and still is, stormy. They fight and are both intensely possessive, but so far, in spite of everything, they have stayed together. Their day-to-day life when I saw them was very close. Neither of them went to work, and they spent all their time together.

When I was living with him, I wasn't alone. We would watch TV together. Then the kids would come. We would all be together. He'd pick one kid up, I'd pick up the other. He would wake up around 12 anyway or 1. Then we would get on the bicycle every day and go to his [drug detoxification] program. Come back. In the morning I'd go take the kids, have my coffee break round there, come home, clean, bag up. Then I would be with him all day. We still argued. We argued, I guess, from the beginning. I'm always telling him to leave. Like right in the beginning, when he said, "You think maybe I should leave?" I said, "Maybe you should." Then he tried to convince himself "Why do you want me to leave? I'm not that bad." This and that.

When Raps was nine months old, Connie became pregnant again. By this time, she and Gino were married and quite happy to have another child. Their son JJ was born prematurely with an underdeveloped liver and had jaundice for the first few weeks of life. It was hard looking after two babies. Gino provided materially for the family, but Connie was responsible for feeding, cleaning, and raising the children. She often felt exhausted. She considered having a tubal ligation, but at twenty-six, she still felt too young for something so permanent and Gino didn't want her to do it.

At twenty-seven, she had her fourth pregnancy. Connie was still not in the best of health. She was anemic and had developed a heart murmur. The question of an abortion arose. Although Gino was keen for them to have another daughter, he was also worried about the physical and mental toll it would take on Connie. He gave her money for an abortion. She took the money but could not go through with it. Instead she bought maternity clothes.

In 1977, the family moved to a three-bedroomed apartment in a housing project and on Mother's Day that year a girl was born. She was named Dahlia – the name Connie's father had always wanted for his only daughter. The two boys loved having a baby sister, and Suzie was sufficiently old to be a real help in taking care of her. But by the age of twenty-eight, Connie had spent three years of her life being pregnant. Pregnancy made her feel ugly and deformed, and she and Gino had neither the space nor the income for another child. Connie got sterilized.

A club called the Sandman used to hang out in front of the apartment building where Gino and Connie lived. They often watched them from the window. The guys had patches and bikes, but their wives and girlfriends were usually out there with them and sometimes even their kids. It was like a family club, and so when Gino wanted to join, Connie approved. After an incident in which Gino was beaten up by the police and hospitalized, the president of the Sandman left and Gino took over.

It seemed at that time that most of them [the Sandman] had gotten girls pregnant so it seemed they were turning into a family. So as for me, I thought maybe it won't be so bad. But then Gino got arrested and the President didn't care that much. He cared more for the patches than what he [Gino] was going through. Then Gino came out and the guy said, "I want to talk to you" – the President. Then Gino took over, got to him, and the guys just went over to Gino.

How long was Gino away for?
About three weeks.
How did you get by?
Well, we had money from dealing herb.
What happened to the other guy, the old president?
He's still around. He looks like he's retired. If it hadn't been for Gino, I don't think he would be working. Now he works. His wife and his child – he's a working guy. Otherwise, I don't know.
He respects Gino?
Now they're starting to talk to each other, but it took a while.

Gino encouraged Connie to start a girls' club, even though at first she was skeptical.

He just wanted to give me recognition. Then, being that he was a Sandman, he wanted me there 'cos he wanted to make everything a family thing. So he said, "You're going to have a girls' club." I didn't want it. You know what I'm talking about? Sometimes I just don't want to be bothered. I just want to be alone. And I felt we were going to have lots of problems. 'Cos I know where I am and I know where he is and I know where people are and I just knew we were all going to be clashing all over. But I said, "Alright, I'll give it a go ahead." But I wanted to give it up. He begged me to keep it. I said, "Alright." When they wanted to go to Boston [for an inter-gang conference], there weren't no girls allowed. But they had to take me because I had my own girls' club. He's always giving me that identity and he always wants me to know I'm his lady.

In November 1979, the girls got their own patches, SANDMAN LADIES NYC. Connie was their leader. Gino and the Sandman became involved with the Inner City Roundtable of Youth (ICRY), an association composed of and designed to help New York gangs resolve feuds, find or create jobs, and form a political base for inner-city youth. The organization lived up to the equality they so often talked about by recognizing Connie and the Sandman Ladies as a legitimate club.

Connie in the Family

You have to be playing games with your old man. Sometimes you might have to be the sister, sometimes you have to be the lover. I don't want him to be with me because he married me and I'm his wife and he comes home every night to his wife. No, I want him to come home to his WIFE. "Wow, my wife." Sometimes I feel my love for him is too strong. I've always been so lonely that for him I don't mind giving up. Not lonely, lonely because I've wanted to be. I've been in my own shell. That's why I say my dream was to be a hermit . . . It must be that love is always being jealous. Love does hurt. Love is *always* saying "I'm sorry." I hate him for loving him and I love him for hating him.

Connie's statement indicates the confusions in her relationship with Gino: the need to play games to ensure his interest, the jealousy and insecurity of possible loss, the safety of total with-drawal from him, and the day-to-day swings of love and hate. After so many years, the passion and confusion have not dissipated. It is a theme to which Connie frequently returns in her conversation. The dilemmas she tries to solve are between wife and lover, commitment and withdrawal, jealousy and loneliness. For this reason, Connie can never sit back and relax. She tries to be different each day. Threats are seen in the time Gino spends away at work, in other women, and in the possessiveness he in turn feels about her. When these threats become real, Connie reacts with anger, sometimes violence.

I told you I choked a girl because I had the feeling that something was going on. That's the one I said I can't stand. And I wanted to choke her to death. I went and I broke a pizza shop window because I thought the owner had been my friend and I thought he cared for that chick's life. Because I knew she ran in there and she probably said, "Connie wants to kill me," and I know she must have been shaking because she got away from my grasp and ran. But I took my time running because I said, "I'll know how far she ran when I get to the corner by the people." So I took my time running over and I ran to the corner and I didn't see like nothing, so I looked and I saw a pizza shop and I went and waited outside. She came out, "Oh, Connie, please, please, please." You know, "What did I do? What did I do?" To me, Gino is going like this, showing her how to go on the bike and I had never even done that. So to me, I thought he was showing her special attention. I'm the *only* one, but now I'm beginning to get upset because I'm very, very jealous. And it's not jealous of the fact that he'll be taken away but jealous of the feeling that he would laugh and smile with somebody else and when it comes to me, he argues – he says, "Why isn't this done? Why this?" And I'm not there on that part. He can communicate and talk to somebody – that's jealous of a feeling.

OK, when he went out to work first of all, we had been together since the day we met – twenty-four hours a day. So when he asked me, "I want to work, what do you think I should do?," first of all, I knew he was asking me because he wanted to work. Otherwise he wouldn't have asked me, he would have said no. I was very angry because I knew he wasn't going to be around me anymore and that was my life. I said, "Gino, give it a run." He says, "You going to be angry?" I says, "I don't know, I can't guarantee you anything, but give it a run because I know you want it." So now I was alone so I wanted to work. I wanted to keep busy during the day. He didn't want *me* to work because of the male egotism. Oh. I said, "Look, Gino, I could have an affair just the same way around my neighborhood as I could at work." "No, people would tell me." But would they really? And I said, "Do you think it's going to be with somebody you know? All I got to do is go to the park, find me somebody, just do it and then I'll go right on my way." Because to me it's just a self-gratification of a certain feeling that you're looking for. Yes, you have a man – then again, there's something else that you're looking for. I finally realized I like being lonely. Feeling lonely in the sense that I've lost my lover, which I did. Because Gino was my lover. And I lost my lover. And he's not willing to play any more games. Like I tell him, "Why don't we carry on an affair while you're working?" He thinks it's stupid. So I say, "Well then."

For Connie, sex lies at the heart of life. She makes a distinction between sex and the sexual act. Sex exists in a relationship between any two people – even friendship depends on an attraction at a fundamental physical level.

I didn't say it was a sexual thing – you and I share a private world and it's not a sexual thing. It could [be] if two people consented – a private world can be sought to the extreme, not to the extreme, to the finality. That's as final as you can know a person. A lot of people go through their lives just knowing people like that – a sexual act and that's it. So one world I was talking about was a nonsexual world. But see he [Gino] doesn't understand that, that's why he is afraid of me. He won't let me go to work because he feels that he'll lose control over me. Sex is everything in life. If you're attracted by somebody sexually, it doesn't mean it's ever going to get there. It's just that you say, "I like the appearance." And that will tend to influence you. Like remember before they used to say, "Oh. Ted Kennedy. He's so cute" – the women – "I'll vote for him 'cos he's cute"? That's it. Everything is sex, sex, sex.
Is that good or bad?
Like you're sexual from the minute you're born. And then JR, he told me about women try to sissify a man. Shit like that. And I said, "Look, man, a man is always under the care – from the minute he is born – he's being influenced by a woman." It gets down to the main ingredient of life is just sex. And that's the most important thing in a relationship. Male-female or whatever-the-hell relationship.

Connie is therefore attentive to any indication that Gino "shares a private world" with anyone. Her jealousy stems from an emotional rather than an economic basis. She does not fear the responsibility of bringing up four children alone.

I said, "Don't think because I have kids I'm going to put up. I'm not." Like some women will put up, I won't. I'll leave him. I don't have to put up with him. I'll find somebody else that will give me more. Because I've had opportunities where men have told me, "I'll take you and the family."

Connie's jealousy is proportionate to the commitment she has made to Gino. Throughout her childhood, Connie learned to contain all her feelings except anger. When she committed herself to Gino, it was a gamble against the odds and it was important to her that it should be a success. The sheer amount of time and energy she had to give him came out of her abandonment of her own life and her alienation from her family. When Connie senses, however remotely, that Gino is becoming separate from her, she retaliates sharply both behaviorally and emotionally. She treats him as no more than one of the club, and sexually she becomes withdrawn and unresponsive.

I'm possessive and I want every feeling. I want that man to give me every feeling in fucking life. Every, every feeling. That's how bad he turned me on. Where I wanted every feeling off him whether it be – if he wanted me to be a prostitute, I was going to be a prostitute and I wanted to play every part. That was it. I had him home and I was satisfied. Now he's not mine anymore. So I can't have the same feeling and I can't deal with him the same way. Because to me, he is just another person. The only thing is I just sleep with him, that's the only difference. It comes down to sex. And I've had to learn how to deal – well, he's not mine anymore, he belongs to the world. In order to deal with it like that, I have to treat him like any other individual. The only thing is when I see him in bed, we fuck and that's about it. But during the day, he's just like one of the other guys. Otherwise, if I had that feeling for him, then no matter who talks to him – I might even be jealous over you.

But I'm learning how to deal with it. He doesn't want me to and I say, "Gino, you sure you can handle that, man?" Because he wants me to love him 100 percent and I can't. See, he wants to control me. OK, when we first met, he controlled me mentally. Because I let him then. But now I'm not even willing to play act anymore. I don't want to act anymore. And I'm not afraid of him physically. He can kill me if he wants, motherfucker, because I don't give a fuck. So now I'm coming out. Then I'm finding, "Well, it's not too bad." I socialize over here and I be talking over there – talking with all these nice-looking guys ordinarily I couldn't talk to. Being that it's never going to be involved, you feel more at ease on the friendship. So I said, "Well, fuck it. I'll enjoy it too. I'll make the best of the best situation. Alright, so I'm stuck at home, but no, I'm not licked. I'm meeting all these other people coming and going."

When withdrawing from Gino, Connie occasionally flirts with other members of the gang to gain his attention.

So what I do is I flaunt it. I flaunt it. I say, "Yeah, here I am, fellas, but you can't take me. Just try and I'm going to stomp your head. 'Cos the only one I'm going to let in here is Gino and that's about it." So I flaunt it, fuck it. Let them suffer. Let them put up with just being around me. It's better not to be trusted than to be trusted. Because when you're not trusted, they're always checking up on you. You see more of them when you're not trusted than when you're trusted.

Connie's feelings for Gino are still as much sexual as emotional. In order to keep him with her, he must remain sexually attracted to her. Sometimes she worries that her body is no longer attractive.

I thought I was marked anyway because I have all these stretch marks from when I first had Suzie at fifteen. So I said, "My body is ugly." To me, I don't know, I always had this dream of being the perfect sex symbol of the world. I would see myself as being able to play all these games and getting anyone I wanted – or anything I wanted. That's why I say, when Gino says he loves me, I say, "What do you love about me? I got a fucked-up body." Maybe it's because I only love his body – I don't know.

While she sees sex as a kind of testing ground of love, she is worried by the fact that many men see it only as a demonstration of machismo. She is equally worried by women who take advantage of this weakness.

There's a lot of women who are fresh. They'll just come up to him walking along and say, "I'll open my legs." They say, "Well a man is a man, so if a woman gives it to him, he's supposed to take it." Not to me. I feel he's an animal if he can't say no.

Although ultimately she blames men for cheating on their women, she has a natural hostility to girls who lead them on. As she sees it, they know this male weakness as well as she does, and if they try to take advantage of Gino's masculinity, they are indirectly challenging her. At that point it is no longer a private matter between her and Gino; it becomes an issue of public face, pride, and dignity. She has no regard for women like Laura, an ex-Sandman Lady, who do not challenge their rivals openly.

Is Laura still with the same guy?
From what I hear, he's got another woman and she's willing to put up with that. I don't even bother talking to her because she's so simple-minded. She's telling me that the girl is saying, when he's kissing her, that he loves Laura. And I said, "Laura, you mean to tell me that you sit and listen to that shit? Man, I would have whacked that bitch in her face so fast. You got something to do with my old man? Fine. Keep it to yourself. I don't want to know about it." So I'm letting her know – you got to scare her, you got to whack her. She knows I don't play around.

During the days, Connie remains at home cleaning, cooking, taking care of the kids, and just being there for any member of the club that needs a place to go or somebody to talk to. When the club is at war with another gang, that role is particularly crucial. She is not only leader of the girls but, in Gino's absense, takes responsibility for the males too. Often the days are humdrum. Sitting, smoking, thinking too much make her edgy and discontented. When she gets like this, she blames Gino, or blames being female, or simply blames life.

Gino gets the blame when there are tensions between them and the tedium of the day gets unbearable.

I tell him, "You're not going to eat? Like, damn, I've been here over this stove slaving, all these frigging niggers around. Like I could have been in my own world, but I took time out to think about you because that's my function, right? Dinner would be ready when you come home." I say it with irony. I say, "Have you got to go play with your image or have you got time to eat?" It's hard communicating our feelings – it's not that they're not there. We're challenging each other, I guess. Because he'll know when I'm up to that point where I say, "Fuck it," and I know when he's at that point. I try not to aggravate him, so what I do is I worry him a lot. I'll leave him even if it takes killing myself to do it. If I have to escape and that's the only way because he's watching, because he doesn't want me to get away, I'll do it. I'll kill myself. I will do it. I told you. I live my life on the line. I almost was thrown out the window so –

Gino?

Yeah. That's how we argue. I said, "You're gonna throw me? Well, let me jump then." So then he had to hold me back.

Gino worries that staying home all the time will stultify Connie, but at the same time he does not want her to work. He thinks she should go out more, to visit or to shop, but Connie is firm: it is all or nothing.

Gino tells me, "If you stay home you're going to wither." Like when I started growing up, developing, my aunt and uncle said, "You're getting too old to be running around. You got to stay in the house, you can sit on the porch if you want." So I went and sat in the basement. I'd rather have nothing than not have what I want. Oh, he argues, we argue, we argue. But what I'm saying is we argue all the time but we can never come to a conclusion because I don't know. A man always feels he's got to dominate a woman. I'll stay home. I'll clean and I'll cook. So when he asks me, "Are you going to go to work with me?," I say, "No, I got to clean." I refuse to go to work with him and sit there like an idiot, waiting around for him. I won't put up.

They argue about Connie's role, although she really accepts the fact that she is needed at home. She never lets him forget that she, as well as he, made sacrifices for the marriage.

That's what it's all about – that fascination. Then you're thrilled that you're the one he picked. And you know he has to rub that in your face. 'Cos men will do that. "Oh look, I had so-and-so and so-and-so, but I chose you instead." And I tell him, "Look, let me tell you something, motherfucker. I gave up my career for you." He tells me, "What the hell are you talking about?" I said, "Goddamit, I was going to college. I could have been a career woman and kept it like that, but no, I decided I wanted to give my career to you. So don't be telling me you gave up shit for me – I gave up shit too. Don't be thinking you're the only one."

At other times, Connie sees her frustrations as arising out of being female. After all, Gino is a good husband who always provides for the family. The problem is in the female role itself, which she sees as relatively incontrovertible, at least for the foreseeable future. Sometimes as she speaks about her day, she becomes aware of the constant references to domesticity and children. When she catches herself, she feels trapped by her femininity.

It's a very busy routine trying to get everyone out of the house for the day. That is my function as a woman. To make sure everybody leaves the house clean, fed, to go out into the world . . . I am a housewife, therefore I take out the steak in the morning that is going to be done for dinner. That is automatic. Automation procedures that have to be done every day . . . Sometimes I feel like an "it," a machine. I'm not supposed to think, I'm a woman. I'm not supposed to think. They're supposed to function. Pussy, pussy. No matter what you do, whether you're writing a book, you're still going to reflect that.

In society in general, it is the division between the sexes that strikes Connie as the most important. Religion and race are less relevant. The oppressed groups in society may change in terms of their color or beliefs, but, for her, women have always been at the bottom of the pile. On the other hand, since sexual attraction is a critical factor in her life, her security depends, as she sees it, on remaining attractive to Gino. This contradiction prevents her from being a whole-hearted feminist.

Well, now the blacks and the Puerto Ricans don't have nothing to worry about – it's the Cubans now. You know, I saw a movie that said, "If there were no niggers, we'd invent them." Do you know what? The Cubans are taking over the oppressed group now. They're the oppressed group. Before that it was Dominicans or Haitians. There's always some group that somebody's going to pick on. But that's the way it always is. Whenever you go into a new neighborhood, since you're the newcomer, you're always going to get all that hard stuff and everything until you finally fall into a category – whatever group. You either fit in or fit out. I think it's always the way of life, 'cos, like I just said, you move into a neighborhood and automatically everybody is watching you. You got to have somebody to pick on. I think what it is, like I also noticed, each individual has to have one person they hate in life, like they got to have people they love. You got to have someone you hate because these are all feelings that keep everybody going. So when it comes to society, society is a group of people. Some are wife snatchers, some are husband snatchers, that all makes society. No matter where you go, what economical background, you still find the gossips, this and that. That's society. The world is full of a lot of different needs – and you don't even need to find them in your own culture or your own race or creed or whatever distinctions they make between people. Male and female. I just see it as male and female. I don't see it as anything else but just that.

At other times Connie sees the constraints of life as her real problem. If she has kids, they have to be taken care of. To take care of them, she needs money. To keep her body going, she has to "eat, shit and sleep." At times she wants release from just being alive. She wants solitude and silence. At times like this, she blames no one.

What do you think about marriage?
I don't know. It's just a legal thing to me. I've learned to deal with feeling. It happens to most wives. Because if your husband didn't want you to write this book, you wouldn't be writing it. For him to go to the extremes of letting you go out and meet people and not be possessive, you have to put up from him something in order to get that. But I feel I'm trading a lot with him [Gino] and I ain't getting nothing in return. I'm still right here doing automated things, washing clothes, doing this, doing that.
Is that your main objection to marriage?
To life, to life. It's always got to be something makes you do your automated routine. Eat, shit and sleep. Basic survival. Now, how it's done is different. People do it in different ways. Sometimes you got to do it the way other people do it because there is no other way.

Connie never expresses any desire to reverse the roles, so Gino would have to be at home instead. All in all, she is content with being female, although life, for both sexes, often seems an uphill struggle.
While Connie is a mother to her own children, her mothering extends beyond her immediate family to her children's friends, the gang itself, and males in general. Often her feelings toward Gino are strongly protective. He is more open and impulsive than Connie and sometimes she sees dangers that he doesn't. By virtue of being male, Connie believes, he cannot always see what women are trying to do to him.

All men are itty-bitty babies. They're always after pussy and that's where a woman comes in 'cos she'll play any kind of game. If it ain't straightforward – any kind of game to get there. She wants it, just like the guy will try. Women are always conniving.

But on the other levels too, Connie feels protective toward Gino.

Well, sometimes I wonder about my relationship with him. When I met him, he had so many problems and I was still in school taking sociology and I said, "Hey, he's fine-looking. I'll take some time to help him out." . . . We're going to travel and I got to get myself together and realize that I got to share this man with the world. But I got to be by him to show him who is acting and who's not. Who's trying to use you and who's not.

Connie's apartment is a kind of home base for various local kids. Because Connie knows the dangers of growing up on the street, she encourages them to come to her place where at least she can keep an eye on them. So much of Connie's early life was disturbed by constant moves from one home to another that her main goal as a mother is to provide stability.

What do you want for your kids?
Mostly what I'm doing now. Giving them a family background where they do have a father image figure. Because he is there. Just being a warm family. All being together without having to be in their own world. All communicating together in a circle.

At the same time, simply being a good mother hardly seems enough to want out of life for Connie.

There's got to be more than just being a good wife and mother. What's my contribution? There is no job I really want to do. My first idea when Gino started to work was to run out and get a job. Then he said I couldn't work and blah, blah, blah. Everything males say to females. Sometimes I feel it's too bad I'm not really needed here. What's my purpose? People can do without me. That's when I start wondering, what am I doing here? My kids can do without me. My mother could always take care of them. So then it makes me feel like – fuck, fuck, fuck.
Don't you want to live just for yourself?
But there's no time for me to be me. I don't know what I want and I don't know what I want to do. I think – and by thinking I've already done it, seen it. Just by reading. Like I'm more of a watcher than a doer.

Connie is not a clinging mother by any means. She sees her role as getting her kids ready to make it alone without her.

Some mothers will influence their children so much that they can't go out into the world. And those are the ones that will be more dedicated to their parents. Now my children are going to be totally independent. I'm going to kick their ass out of here.

I know what you mean.

It's like my mother. Maybe sometimes I'll bother her, but like I'm not always over there knocking on her door all the time – "Help me, Mom, help me." It's like Gino's mother, she's thrown all of her kids out. She sells smoke in the park and everything. She is like a young teenager. Hey, I respect her for what she's doing – she's living her life. Her children – she already knows what to expect from them. If she don't kick them out, they'll always be on her ass.

In Connie's case, this is particularly important because she always feels death to be imminent. This is not an entirely un-realistic fear, given the life she leads.

Hey, I'm not going to insist education is very important. It's important that she [Suzie] spend time with me here. 'Cos the way I look at my life, I might be here one minute and gone the next. And I always try to make my children survive without me. I wrote a letter to Suzie and Gino. A suicidal note. I think that's probably when I came up pregnant with Raps. Then life goes on. It don't make me want to stay. And now I'm up to the point where I'm just flaunting my life. And even accidental things are happening to me. The children have to be survivors, fighters because I won't always be around. So I do have to teach them how dangerous life is out there. How very aware you have to be of life.

The daily frustrations of rearing children provoke contradictory emotions in Connie. For example, Connie and Suzie are very close, almost like sisters. They dance together and play together but Connie will pull back very sharply to discipline Suzie if she thinks the closeness is leading to any "disrespect" from her daughter. When she talks of incidents of conflict between Suzie and herself, her tone sounds frighteningly harsh. But with Connie, love and hate are part of the same bond of trust. Whatever she may say or threaten, Suzie and Gino simply take the brunt of being the two people who are close enough to her to cause her real pain.

Even my daughter. We dance, we goof, we got a good relation-ship. Sometimes she grabs me, comes by like playing. I say, "Don't ever do that." And I told you about the time I jumped her with my brass knuckles? 'Cos she said, "That *lady* . . ." When she said "lady" every fiber of my body stood up on my head. I said, "Don't you ever refer to me as 'that lady' 'cos I'm your mother." I stop it right where it is. Because I told them [gang members], "If you get on my nerves, you've got to leave. I demand this and I demand that and I'll let you know where it's at from the very beginning. If you don't like it, then get out." And I gave Suzie the choice – you can go to your grandmother's house, but no, she likes the excitement over here. No, she's got more recognition over here. Over there, she don't really like it that much. That's why I told my daughter, "You're a selfish bitch." I don't trust nobody. Nobody I trust. I told her, "Bitch, you stabbed me in the back. Don't you ever stab me again." And I tell people, "Don't ever be on my shit." I told her too. I said, "Look, I don't need you here. Don't think that what you do for me, you're doing me a favor because nobody does me favors. I don't need no favors from nobody." I hate it when somebody does me a favor. That's why I always try to have, because I don't want nobody saying, "Hey, you owe me one."

At the same time, Connie trusts Suzie totally to defend the good name of the Sandman on the street. She respects her daughter's courage and loyalty and seems somehow surprised that Suzie turned out to be such a good fighter.

With my daughter, I want her to be worldly. I'm going to push her as much as I can. I tell her, "You are today what I made you." A lot of people tell me, "You expect too much from your daughter." I say, "Yes, I expect a lot so at least I can get a halfway decent move." Because if I don't expect a lot, then I won't even get a try. If you're around me, I expect you to act accordingly. Respectful, everything. One day there was this girl came from down there saying the Sandman weren't shit. That's her [Suzie's] age group, she got to take care of it. So she went over to the girl and went "whop!" The girl said, "No, Suzie. I didn't say . . ." "What? What?" She didn't let the girl go. She said it, she said it. She's not going to get her way out of it. My daughter really dogged her up – dogged means really messed her up. She don't care. She loves to fight.

Although in many ways Suzie is treated as an adult, Connie also worries about her as her daughter. Connie is proud of Suzie's good looks but recognizes that they mean Suzie must always be ready to defend herself against men. Connie sets a forceful example.

This morning I'm walking with Suzie and I'm just minding my own business, just talking, and this man just comes up and I hear out of the clear blue sky, so clearly him saying, "Come up to my apartment" and I don't know what the rest was but it sounded like "Let's party." So I look at him and I say how in the hell is he going to have the nerve to come up to me and think I'm a whore, that I'm just going to give up just like that or be that fresh. So I just went and I took out my knife, and then I went ["flick"] and I jumped at him and he jumped back. I said, "Come on, motherfucker, say it again. Come on, Come on." I can't really remember, but I do remember calling him – why doesn't he come over here if he thinks he's so bad? He said, "No, you think you're so bad, you're the woman with the knife. You come over here." And I said, "No, you're the one that ran, why don't you come back?" Then he said something about "You should stick that up your asshole." I said, "You're man enough, why don't you come over here and let me stick it up your asshole." And he just kept on walking. Because he knew if he would have come over, I would have stabbed him because the feeling that was vibrating from my body was showing him, "I'm going to stab you, motherfucker." I challenged him because I felt that men have long gone too much without respect for women. That every woman they see, they see as a pussy. And that cannot be so. Some guys really have a bad image of themselves where they look at a chick and they think she'll cream all over. Just like my daughter too. Beautiful girl. Her body – you've got to look at it but they [gang members] still have to stay around and remember that you don't touch.

Every member of the family has their own set of club colors. By birth they are in the Sandman. So far, this has proved a source of pride, and the children feel it gives them a particular status among their friends. Soon Suzie will be old enough to decide whether or not she wants to remain in the club. For the time being at least, Connie has managed to reconcile her family life with the gang. She stays with her children but also has contacts beyond her cramped apartment. The gang offers her compensation for the frustrations of three young children. Yet, ambivalent as she feels about motherhood, this is very much the role that she plays in the gang also.

Connie in the Gang

For Connie, the club is like an extended family. Members are treated as such when they are in her apartment; they are expected to fix their own sandwiches, buy their own liquor, tidy up the room, wash the dishes, behave responsibly. Connie's role is indisputably that of leader. There is always a little distance between her and members of both sexes, as is also true of Gino. She holds back, often watching quietly and saying little. When she does speak, she expects attention; she does not repeat herself. She sees herself as a mother figure as well as a leader.

These are my people in the club. OK, this club is family. Other clubs I can't speak for because everybody has their own different ideas. I seen other clubs where it's more like an army thing. So-and-so's head. And it's just guys being together, that's the way I see it. Doing drugs, brawling. Whatever it is. You know when I was telling you about groups of people who have friends and so on? The only difference is that your close friends don't wear patches and stuff. Like we've been dealing for a long time – smoke. And we always have people around. But now the only thing is the people around us close wear patches. People will always be there. Girls and guys too. But now to hang out with us you have to be more down. Down – to be fully down – remember the word "hip"? That's fully down. So it's more like a family thing, where I'm putting patches on friends or kids that I adopt into the Sandman. We make it more into a family group. I represent mother, father. And it's the same routine you always get. "Ma, can I do this?" "I don't know, let me ask Pop." "I don't know, go ask Mom." Dealing with the same routine as when you were younger but you weren't able to relate to. For one reason or another you can relate it with us and understand a bit more about life.

Some of the members used to hang out on 42nd Street with some of the clubs there. Hassles with the police occur there every day. Heroin is everywhere. Protection, friendship, shelter cost money, and prostitution is the easiest means by which to get it. Kids of twelve and thirteen work as hookers. Some of the girls in the Sandman Ladies worked there in peep shows or as prostitutes. Connie and Gino believe that clubs, whatever anyone says about them, are preferable to that kind of life.

These young girls run away from home, they end up there, and they have to what? They wind up being prostitutes, fifteen-, fourteen-, twelve-year-old girls, runaways. They can't go back home, so I'm

*Seven of the Sandman Ladies on Halloween night. Suzie, the oldest daughter, is
in the center. On the far right is OK, one of the Sandman boys*

showing them a way they could stay off the streets. They're not
living wild. It's not going to be something that's going to be fast
action all the time. It's more relaxed 'cos you just want to enjoy life.
You don't want to be out there fighting and arguing. So we're
trying to live as easily as possible. This is all it's taking to keep us
going. We're not working that hard. We're not killing ourselves.
And we're not harming anybody. We're just chilling out – relaxing.
We all feel the same way. Because if we have any bad vibes or
whatever, right away we stop it. Because I can feel it. And then it's
stopped.

What do you do?

An outsider or from the inside?

Insider.

Let's say they all walked in today, I looked at all their faces. I
didn't see no beef against anybody. Like they could have had a
fight in the nighttime, they couldn't settle it? I would tell them,
"Look, what's up?," and then try to referee it, sit them down, talk it
over, whatever. We want everyone to feel comfortable with everybody else. I don't want bad vibes because that brother is the one
who's going to be there when you're going to be there – both of you
together. Can't afford to have no bad vibes at all, no misunder-
standings. No member is supposed to hit another member.

If a member needs money, she or he will be given it. Money is not plentiful, but there is enough to get by. The smoke the gang sells locally to the community is one source of income as well as Gino's job at ICRY, where he works in the office. They spend little on clothing, and their entertainment is homemade: hanging out, talking, dancing, partying at another clubhouse. Many things they can buy cheap from friends in the neighborhood with no questions asked. If money arrives unexpectedly, it is pooled for a common use, like buying a walkie-talkie or a trip to Coney Island.

Entry into the Sandman Ladies occurs through Connie. She makes the initial decision on the girl's character and decides whether or not to let her hang out for a trial period.

It's hard to find girls to come into a club that – to set up totally on their own. And then they all have different ideas. We're not here instigating any trouble, but we don't want any trouble either.

Who did you get?

Well, first of all they have to be able to follow orders. They have to be able to know they're under my ruling and Gino's ruling.

Do they have to be able to take care of themselves?

Well, I don't care about fighting because anybody can fight. But I would rather have more intelligent 'cos anybody can fight. When it comes to it, you fight.

I guess if you're angry enough.

Sure because – hey, I proved it. I'm not a fighter. I'd rather talk my way out. If there's no choice, then you fight. We all like each other. That's why you have that period of hanging out with us, to see how you blend in with us, because if you have bad feelings with one club member then you can't. If it can't be settled, then it's going to be a personal grudge. Because we have to be . . . Like if I'm walking down the street with you, you have to be able to count that I'm going to throw my life for you. Just like I expect you to do it for me. I'm not going to go down the street and pick a fight and expect you to die for it – no. But if it comes to . . . if a situation comes where we have to fight, to be able to say, "I'm going to stay here and fight because I know you're going to stay here and fight with me too." And you're not going to run and I'm stuck there with nobody by myself. Because guts do count too.

What if a club girl ran?

Well, then she's chickened out – she has to leave. But then again, I don't think it would get to that point because most of the girls in my club do have guts . . .

Do you have meetings on special days?

No, whenever there's a meeting to be held, we just hold it. There's no need to call one.

How often do you see them?

Oh, they have to come every day. Yes, because clubbing is just like a house. You saw the fat kid. He goes to school, so I don't expect him to come hang out from 9:00 to 3:00. During the day I would say, "Hey, go to school!" Now after school, when he's finished doing his chores around and stuff like that, he says, "Mom, I'm going down. I'll be back whenever." That's the time he has to spend with us. Your social time belongs to us. The girls have to be here every day. Everybody has to be here every day. At the same time during the day, you have to come check in, see what's happening. And hang out.

What's hanging out?

Hanging out is being together. Spending time together. When you go to your friend's house you're really hanging out. Just there. Whatever you do when you're there doesn't matter, but you're there. You could be talking, eating food, having tea. But you're hanging out . . .

Do the girls have jobs?

It depends. Most of them work. Or if they're young, they might have their parents or if I'm here, I'll give them anything. They help out. Like Angela, this girl who's fifteen, she'll come here, help me out, whatever. Takes care of the kids for me. Whenever she needs anything, I will give it to her.

When they go to work, they dress all normal?

Yes. They feel they're being themselves in the club. This is being what they want to be.

Once a girl is in the club, she is expected to commit herself totally to it, and her loyalty to other friends and sometimes even family must be overridden. She must make this commitment herself; the club will not take responsibility for helping her leave home.

Well I told her, "Once you're here.– this is your family here. Your friends from before can come and visit you whatever, but you're not involved in their lives anymore." And here's this young girl, sixteen-years-old. She's telling me her brother was beating her up. I say, "What reason?" He thought she was getting high. I said, "Well, look. Since these people live in Long Island, obviously they

got a lot of money, and from what I hear that's a Mafia's daughter."
I said, "Look, they're doing this for a reason." It's like if Suzie does
something against me, I might go to the extreme in punishing her
or whatever. You can't get involved with family. No, but I mean . . .
if you go over there, it's like you're kidnapping. If you were to tell
her, "Meet me here in New York," you could always tell her
parents, "Look, I took her off the street. At least she is not doing
anything against her will." You go up to Long Island? That's
kidnapping. Then she's underage, so you're contributing to the
delinquency of a minor.

Once accepted, the girl gains her patches: first the bottom line,
which reads LADY NYC, then the top line – SANDMAN. As they
receive each patch, the girls sew it onto their sleeveless denim
jackets – their colors. In the summer, they wear their colors over T-
shirts; in winter, over sweatshirts or jackets. To earn their MC
(motorcycle club) patch, the guys must own a motorcycle, an
undertaking which can take months or even years, given their
limited income. Triumphs or Harley-Davidsons are preferred over
Japanese makes. The girls have no such requirement. To gain full
patches, a girl must only have demonstrated loyalty and guts on an
enduring basis.
    As leader of the girls, Connie has to show decisiveness and
control without overawing them. She prides herself on not making
any of the members feel threatened by her presence, a quality she
can allow herself, while Gino cannot.

When a girl is around me, she will feel my equal. She won't feel
I'm trying to compete with her in any way. If she's one of these
people where they show their toughness – I don't play that. I don't
play at all. I don't play games. I'm not giving them competition. If
she thinks she's pretty – well yes, you are pretty. I won't give her
competition in any way. I'm not competitive. Well, I'm competitive, but I'm not going to . . . I know you feel comfortable around
me because I'm not feeling like I'm tougher than you or I'm more
of a woman than you. You don't feel threatened by me being here.
You feel my equal.
Does Gino do that with the guys?
No, with the guys it's different. With the guys, it's toughness.
He has to prove it?
Well, now he has people to do it for him. People that know him,
know he's not playing. My thing is I don't give anybody competi-

Connie with three of her children. From left to right Raps, Dahlia and JJ

tion. When a woman thinks when she's coming in here, that she's real bad, I let her. The only competition with me is mentally. If I can't deal with you mentally, forget it.

By not competing, Connie aims to act as a reference point, a kind of image to which the girls can aspire yet set apart from them.

Well, everybody has their own image of what a perfect woman would be like. I see women who I say, "When I reach that age, I would like to be like that." I guess I'm in that kind of role too. Some of the girls would say, "When I'm her age, I'm going to be like her." It's my own thing – my husband and my kids. But still do your own thing and still take care of your kids, still be able to hang out. Because a lot of women have kids and then some men would never let you hang out at all.

Connie also gives advice on dealing with men, families, jobs, and court cases. Sometimes she does no more than just listen.

Your feelings are true feelings, that's what I try and teach my girls. Bring your feelings out into the open. Tell me. It's not going to go beyond me. Because I'm just a listening wall. There might be times when I'm telling you problems. I tell you anybody that comes around me starts thinking different. They're showing you something that might remind you of some kind of security when you were younger. That's why some people might call me Moms and can relate to me on that level. It's not really what I look like, it's the feelings that come out of me that they see which are there. So I give the girls good advice they can listen to for the rest of their life. "Connie said this." That's all I care about, that they went through my circle and have gone by. And they have changed. I've done something for their imagination. I have to be with the club, but me as an individual, I want you to remember me. Whatever I've taught you, remember for the rest of your life. Because I don't teach them in the way where I say I'm better than you are. You can always teach me. And I feel that if you want to take my advice – fine. If you don't – fine. I'm saying if you want it, you want it. If you don't, you don't. But always remember what I told you. Don't let nobody control your mind – not even me. Not even me.

Do they understand?

Some people think I'm crazy. They don't know where I'm coming from. Sometimes I find myself like that. I see myself like an outsider sometimes. It's hard for me to communicate with people. It feels as if when somebody talks to me, I sound like a book to them, so they go, "Oh my God, when I'm around Connie I'm going to have to be very alert and get all my knowledge together just to talk to her." That's the way I get when people come around me.

Do you think they feel that?

Yes. Because if I walk into a place and everybody is screaming right away when I walk in, everybody calms down.

Sometimes Connie uses subtle leverage to change a girl's behavior. Wire, for example, has a serious drug problem.

Wire has problems and if she nods, it don't bother me because at least I know she's off the streets. To me, they're my kids and I know she probably goes and gets high behind my back. But at least she's trying and she sees that I still love her because I tell her, "Look, Wire, we're going to be going to important places and I'm going to need you to represent me because you're someone who could talk to a lot of groups." I don't want some dumb ass you can't talk to. I want someone to talk to they know. And I tell her, "But if you're going to be like that, you can't go." So one day I'll probably leave her home. That's going to hurt her because she's going to want to be with Moms.

As leader of the Sandman Ladies, Connie has precedence over the males too. The power relationship is simplified by her position as "Moms," which automatically negates any sexual relationship between her and them.

Well, I would be the woman that they look up to. There's no competition and sex there. Because most women that you meet, there's this sex thing – where it *could* happen. But not in my case, it's not supposed to. So sex is right out. As a woman, I would be the woman they could look up to like the mother. You can't have sex with your mother either.

Do you like that?

Yeah. Because I feel more comfortable around them. And I don't have to feel afraid of the macho rap. That's why I'm Mom. They don't have sex with Moms. They respect me. Honey, everybody respects me – male, female, or whatever. I *demand* respect. You see me that day we were talking and everything, somebody don't just come up to me and they say, "Hey, excuse me." And then I tell them, "It had better be something important if you're going to interrupt me when I'm talking." 'Cos if I'm talking about a heavy subject, it's going to be hard to get back into that feeling. It had better be something important.

If a guy came on to you, would it mean he didn't respect you?

It's just that, you see, I'm the only woman in their lives that they'll listen to, without labeling her for her pussy. I'm just Moms and that's it. The most they can do is kiss me, maybe give me a little hug. But that's it – that's what you do with Mom. That's it. I don't think sex would even come into the picture at all or their friends. Because I'm Moms and that ultimate need – it's always been that you don't do it.

Connie, as leader of the Ladies and wife of Gino, can talk to the male members in a way that no one except Gino would ever get away with.

Like when I was in the hospital, everybody was so totally lost. What can I say? You have to teach them what's more important. When we're at war, like remember the other day? I had to stop Willy because we were all talking, trying to find out . . . The chief is not here so we heard that the people [another gang] were coming down and we're trying to find something to do. We're trying to find out and this guy started to tell me that he was in the army and he

could have been this . . . And I say, "Yo, Willy." See, I'll stop him.
"Willy we're not here to talk about your personal life right now.
We've got something. We don't have time to sidetrack. Got to keep
on the subject of what to do." And I go downstairs, and the guys –
the way I see it – they wanted really protection because they could
have been attacked, so I went over there and I started putting
people in different spots. And I never been in the army or anything
like that, but it's more or less thinking.

Connie also exercises her leadership in dealing with outside
figures, such as the police.

Didn't I tell you the cops came up here the other day? I looked
up and I hear it you know. Then I hear more. I look out the
window, I see five or six cars there, housing [police] everything. I
look down – the guys are playing checkers. They didn't say nothing
to them, they walked into the building. We live here, we got a right
to hang out. So then, they came up here, but my kids are sitting
there watching the TV and I was reading this book. And I hear the
knocking, I had the book in my hand and I opened the door. I said,
"Yes?" He said, "Did anyone here call the cops?" He said there's
been a big war going on and they [the other gang] had knives and
guns. I said, "No." He said, "Who's the owner of the apartment?" I
said, "I am." "What's your name?" I gave him my name. I said,
"You want to come in to look?" They said, "No." I said, "But I
insist that you come in so that you can see for yourself." So they
came in and my kids are just sitting there watching TV – all calm.
But they're supposed to know how to act also. So like they look and
they're still like watching – and I had a rifle over here and I had
smoke in the house but I'm so calm about it. They all left, but they
dug it.
Who told them?
I don't know. Sometimes we have enemies or something. Sometimes they just want to come and check up on us.
If some guy has it in for you, all he has to do is call the cops?
Yeah. That's what I'm saying. We've had it done a lot of times.
Like you know most of the cops there already know what we're all
about and they – we did help get that guy who was putting out the
gun. And check this out – we had to go before a grand jury. Like
they have all kinds of people. I went there and we all went outlaw
and the're looking at us like, "Gee we thought *they're* bad and
they're saying somebody else is worse." The guy copped out, so we

didn't have to testify. And the cop tells me, "Let me see the thing [knife] that you used to get the gun back." And I said, "No, because it's illegal." So he says, "As far as I'm concerned, I didn't see it." So I had it on me, so I went and I took it out. So he can't say nothing.

In some situations of conflict, Connie will directly challenge Gino's authority in a way that no other club member can.

Like one time, this chick came through the door and we're all here. So one of the guys gets up. I hate the door to be opened and closed. You're in or out – what the fuck? You know. So then this other guy gets up. And finally Gino gets up. I says, "What the fuck is going on?" I go over there and there's this bitch. She swears she's *it*, you know. It's Friday night so she's going dancing and she's like . . . I said, "Man, send her fucking ass to 9J." And Gino says, "But Connie," you know. I says, "No, man, fuck that shit. I don't need her fucking three dollars. If she don't buy, somebody else will." I can't stand for that humiliation. I felt she was humiliating the lot of us. So he's trying to convince me and tell me the chick is just trying to check out what she bought. I say, "If she ain't heard that the Sandman smoke is on, then fuck her. We don't need her because we don't have to put up with shit like that." We got the best herb around here. So I can be choosy. And I *will* tell people, "Don't ever come to my fucking house again." I don't need none of that. I'm not greedy. You don't buy? I'm not in no hurry. I'm going to be here tomorrow. I don't need nobody's money that bad, where I have to be humiliated.

In the main, however, Gino is responsible for most of the decisions which involve males and females. In matters relating only to the girls, Connie's word is final. Connie is responsible for disciplining the girls. In most cases, she achieves this without any physical aggression. If a girl blatantly misbehaves, she may get slapped, as two girls did when they insisted, against order, on going to 42nd Street and then had to be brought back by a group of the Sandman. But discipline is far more severe among the males in gangs.

Yeah, we had that. The guy got thrown out. He got beaten up and they were rough. 'Cos like in another club they say – what we did that time – if a guy in a club gets drunk or something? When he

gets home they throw gasoline all over him and light it on fire.
Every club has different rules. So this guy was lucky he got away
with a beating.

Wire, on heroin and nodding out a lot of the time, has caused
repeated problems. She was an attractive girl, and several of the
guys liked her. She went back and forth between Mico and JR,
unable to decide which one she wanted to stay with. Naturally, this
caused a certain amount of tension between the guys. One day a
member of the Savage Nomads was visiting. Wire and he met in the
elevator going up to the thirteenth floor. They smiled and began to
talk. Later he came to ask Connie and Gino if it would be OK if he
made out with her. Gino said no, partly because of JR and Mico
and partly because Wire was apt to talk too much because of the
dope. Given the currently good relationship between the two clubs,
he did not want to risk anything on account of Wire. Connie and
Gino talked to Wire too, explaining the situation and asking her to
cooperate for the time being. She said OK. A few minutes later,
however, she was back, flirting and laughing with the guy. Connie
warned her to leave it, but again she returned to the guy, behaving
very flirtatiously. Finally, Gino exploded. He ordered her out of the
club. In this club, he told her, you had freedom, but you insisted on
behaving like a club momma (a whore who runs from one guy to
the next). If that's how you want to be treated, he told her, that's
how we'll treat you – as property. And I'm giving you right now as
a present to the Nomads. You are theirs now, they can do what they
want with you. Reluctantly, she packed her things and left. A few
days later, she phoned Connie:

"Ma, I want to come home." "I want to tell you again. It's
harder coming back the second time. I watch you more. You were
fucking up a lot before, you were always nodding. Always told to
shut up and you didn't listen. If you blend, you blend. If you don't,
you don't. Here you can't be in my way. You've been to a different
place. So just pretend you never left. Don't be talking about it, I
don't want to hear nothing you got to say." She started blending. I
said, "Go ahead. Socialize. Let's see what you do." She said she
was afraid – Pops told her to leave. I said, "Yeah, but you could
have always said I don't want to leave or whatever, if that's what
you really wanted. But you just took it as an act of defiance and just
walked away. And now you come home crying. You thought you
knew better and I told you. But you never listen to Momma." Wire

came by that day. Gino said, "Look, you left once, you'll leave again." The thing with her is everybody has their own individual thing. She needs somebody to be telling her what to do and what not to do. She's not her own person. And I don't have time to really spend too much on one person. I hate to repeat myself.

After staying a few days, Wire left again during the night. She took three pairs of Suzie's jeans and left the door open behind her. The apartment had recently been firebombed by another gang and for her to leave the door unlocked was an open invitation for another attack. Connie was furious, then hurt, silent. Wire will not be coming back. Even when she was in the club, Connie had to watch her because often she was too disoriented to know what she was saying.

Do you discipline the girls?
When they get out of line.
Get out of line how?
I just say, "Chilly on what you're doing." And they'd better know what I'm saying. And they got to do it inconspicuous. Like when I'm on the elevator and there's somebody there – a citizen or a Sandman – I don't care what you've got to say. So like one other day, Wire was in the elevator. So she started talking something about the club. So I say, "Chilly." So she changed – started talking something unimportant like about herself or something. I said, "Chilly period." She just kept quiet. That's 'cos she knows what I'm talking about. Now this other chick Mia said something I didn't like. When she walked in, I'm looking at her like this, so she smiles and I don't smile back. She knows something is up. So I tell her, "Do you want me to tell you in public or do you want me to tell you in private?" So she looks at me, she says, "Mom, what did I do?" I said, "I just asked you a question, now answer me." And by the way I was coming out she knew. She said, "Private, Mom, private." When I tell them to stop arguing, they'd better stop arguing.

Connie believes that discipline is essential to the club for two reasons. The first is tactical because in a state of emergency – an attack by another club or a raid by the police – someone must be responsible for thinking fast and making a decision. Orders have to be followed if everyone is to come through safely. Second, Connie believes that discipline is one thing that practically every member has lacked at home. She tells them how far they can go. She sets limits on their behavior. Either they accept them or they leave.

Fights occur from time to time – very occasionally within the club but mostly with other gangs. Connie tries to stay out of fights now, but if she is drawn into one, her philosophy, she says, is to fight to kill. She feels too old to be bothered with petty skirmishes.

Do girls fight different to guys?
Well it depends on the individual. Most girls, they pull hair, scratch, but a lot of girls fight just like a guy.
How do you fight?
I said, "From now on I'm not going to be giving out any black and blue, I'm going to fight to kill."
When did you decide that?
I guess lately.
Why did you feel that?
So that I won't be bothered anymore.
You haven't been involved in fights with girls?
I don't have to. It comes to a showdown, I'll just tell you where it is right then and there. I don't argue. I'm not allowed to argue. Those people just start snapping when they start talking. I had to fight with a chick and I had my .25 automatic and I had my switchblade. This is the chick that any time they wanted a chick beaten up, they would get her – I told you about that incident. I had high heels on, chasing her.
The talcum powder story?
Yes. Yes. I mean I was put on the spot. The thing is whenever the spotlight is on me I'll always try to do my best. Because I don't want to come down. So you take the biggest one and you make your best of what you're going to do. Like the way I say is once you get up, you're going to be arrested anyway. If you leave her dead, leave her dead. Just grab one, and the way I'm going now I'm going for eyes. I feel if I'm going to jail anyway, I'm going to make the best job of it.
You got nails?
No, I don't. But I got fingers and they can still poke. It all depends on the strength and what you're using behind it.
Girls have a reputation for pulling hair.
Well that's usually girls fighting, pulling hair and scratching. That's why I say – one time I was fighting with a girl she grabbed my hair. I don't like pain. If I'm getting pain, I'm going to make sure you're going to stop. She grabbed my hair and I got so pissed and I went and I grabbed her hair and I started banging her head

and I said, "Bitch, you let go of my hair and I'll let go of yours."
She let go. She ruined my hair style because once I combed it, I
don't want nobody touching it. That's the girls' way of fighting,
just like when they run. Not my daughter though. My daughter
goes whop. That chick is always fighting, man.

What do they fight about?

My daughter loves to fight. Always fighting. Everything can turn
into a fight. Anything. We get girls fighting for anything. We get
girls say, "We heard someone is gossiping" – that girl will get her
ass kicked.

Same reasons as the guys?

Nobody is supposed to say anything bad about the club. If they
say, "The Sandman ain't shit," you're supposed to kill that person.
Jump down their throat.

Do girls fight out of jealousy?

Not in the club. Yeah, we have had a couple of girls that like the
same guy, but they would just compete for the guy, they wouldn't
fight over him.

What about the guys – they fight over girls?

No, they usually have girls coming to them on their own.

Are guys more likely to use weapons?

Depends. Sometimes you can just mess a person up with just
your dukes.

Doesn't sound like fighting is that big a deal with the girls.

They do fight. It's just the way I feel. The one that's fourteen,
you can't give her a dirty look – she'll just jump on your face.
Because I walk down the street sometimes and, say we're passing
each other and I'm dressed outlaw and you look at me funny, I
might just turn round and give you a look. Or you might look at me
up and down – depends on the mood I'm in – I might turn around
and just pose for you or I might just turn around and curse you out.
This is what I'm saying, sometimes you do have to fight. Speak up.
You do have to have spunk.

Although Connie believes that everybody has to fight, often the
club's life-style makes it a more frequent event for these girls than
for others. One fight Connie described occurred as a result of the
club's job, which, at that time, was working on 72nd Street where
drug dealing took place.

They had a job at 72nd Street. They were like bodyguards on the
block – any customers that were giving problems, stuff like that.

Since Gino like was the last one to come in, Gino had to take care of everybody. Like he was doing all the fighting, cleaning up the block. Yes, well, when we were working on 72nd Street, this guy gave me some coke so I didn't do it – I'd sell it. So this girl says, "Right, I'm going to buy it from you."

Did you know her?

Yeah. She was one of the workers down there. So she took the bag with her and she comes back and she gave me the bag and says, "I can't buy it, I can't wake up my mother," and she had put like talcum powder in it. And I went and I sold it to somebody else. And then I found out she had been working in a community situation. She had got the job and then she had come back and Gino had told the folks, "Look, she's going to work, she's going to pay me my money." Community situation right? So I had to get her back. So I stopped her and I said, "Where's my money?" She gave me part of it. I said, "No, I don't want part of it. I want all of it." Because Walter [an ex-Sandman] told me that if she didn't come up with it, he was going to give it to her. But then it turns out he was saying, no, he wasn't going to give her any money. I had to go and get my switchblade. So I ripped her chain off. She said, "Give me my chain." We were holding it like this. I said, "What do you want? Are we gonna be here all day pulling this chain?" She wouldn't let go and I wouldn't let go, so finally I relaxed and then I went "grab." And I pulled and it snapped. And I said, "I'll give you the other half when you give me the rest of the money." She didn't like it. She said, "Oh-oh my chain, my chain." I walked out, then I ran to the phone. I was dressed up. I called Gino and I says, "You better hurry up and get down here." The girl's name is Patricia. Black chick. I said, "Gino I just stole Patricia's chain. She's right here following me around."

So I'm standing in the park and she took me by surprise, she punched me right on the neck. So I went to get out my switchblade and I said, "You're not going to hit me again." So she said, "No, you're the one that's going to go to jail." But I don't talk. I just stay quiet. So she was telling me, "You're the one that's going to go to jail." Trying to get me to go over. So I'm still going like this [jabbing the air with the knife] and everyone is watching. Every time she came near me I'd go like this. 'Cos I wasn't going to let her get near me. And then the boys came by in their car and they took her and they were holding her so I went. And this cop came by. So he said, "Go ahead, go, go." So I crossed the street and I stood there 'cos I wasn't going to walk because Gino was at that time the

Boss's bodyguard and I couldn't show him up. Everybody was scared of Gino. So I'm standing there and nobody wanted to hold my gun 'cos everybody was on her side 'cos that's like not my neighborhood. It's more her neighborhood than mine.

So I finally got somebody to hold the gun for me and then I went back to the park and she was saying, "I'm going to kill that bitch. She thinks she's tough. I'm going to kill her." And I said, "Oh no." And then the boys had thought that I wanted to fight her, so they let her go. I said, "Oh my God." Damn, she was big and everything. I said, "No – once you decide you're going to do something, that's it." So I was standing on the corner. Everybody said, "She just pulled out her switchblade." So she ran after me, I was still going like this . . . not letting her get near me. She went and she starts picking things up from the garbage. She starts throwing them and I was bobbing. I start chasing her. This guy gave her a bottle and she said *I* was fighting dirty. I didn't even touch her. She threw that bottle at me. She knew then that I was really going to go after her.

Did you feel scared?

No. I just wanted things my way. I didn't really think about being scared, I just thought, "I can't let her go over me."

On another occasion a gun was taken after a fight in the lobby of the apartment building. Although the fight was none of the gang's doing, they had to recover the gun because the police would certainly suspect them of having taken it.

I don't know if you heard about the time this guy had a gun out in the lobby and he started shooting it. Finally, when they took it away from him, this other guy picked it up and started running. So I'm looking and I see the guy that picked it up. So me and Perry [Sandman member] started running but Perry's leg is bad so he hobbles, so I just ran after him by myself. When I get to Broadway, I look around – like nothing. So I say, "He went to the train stop." So I said to – finally Perry got there – so I said, "Go downstairs and check." He says he didn't see him. So I'm still standing there. All of a sudden I spot him across the street from Broadway. I'm not thinking about fear, I'm not thinking about my family, I'm not thinking anything. I'm thinking I got to get that gun because the Sandman are involved and if we don't get it, they're [the police] going to think we're the ones that got it. I had a switchblade at the time and that's illegal. Till I finally got this [a flick knife] but at that time it was a switchblade.

So I ran towards Broadway with all the cars coming and then I says, "If I go behind him on the sidewalk, he's going to hear me and he's going to run faster. I can't run that fast." So I ran real fast in the street and I came up in front of him and I took out my knife and I said, "Yo, nigger, give me that gun or I'll stab you." And my hand was not shaking and I was serious. So he said, "I don't have the gun." So I grabbed his hand. This guy was bigger than me. First time . . . I grabbed his hand, I say, "Yo, nigger, give me the gun." I said, "Give me the gun." And then I said, "We're going to walk over there." He said, "No, but people know me." I said, "I don't give a fuck. You should have thought about that when you took the gun. Now walk." And I made him walk back through the block and everything. I had on high-heeled boots because it was Gino's birthday and I went and I changed into my other boots, I really was able to run. And that's why I always say I really like my people to keep in shape. You always see me, whether it's dancing or whatever. I want everybody to do some kind of exercise 'cos you never know when you got to run. And, baby, you got to know how to run. 'Cos you can run to get out of a situation just like you can run to get into a situation. You got to be using your mind.

How did you feel afterward?

I felt good, I said, "Man, I did that with that guy? No bitch better tell me nothing. 'Cos I don't want to be bothered with no chick. If I was able to go up to a guy, I *know* I'll fight any chick." After a while I started thinking, "Damn, did I really do that?" So my mother can't understand her daughter running through the streets. A thirty-year-old woman, who should be home cooking, ironing. Which I can deal with that too.

Simply wearing colors on the street can often provoke fights but as Connie gets older she is less often drawn into these situations.

Does wearing colors cause problems?

Sure. But then again they [people] look at you no matter what. Because if you're in a black neighborhood and you pass by – they'll look at you. So really wearing those clothes, people look at you no matter what. What you wear, what you are.

Do people say stuff to you in the street?

Sure. But then again, they say it to me if I'm Spanish, just for being Spanish.

What do you say?

I don't know. Depends on the mood I'm in.

How does Gino deal with it?

The same thing. He's more calm. Like I got to the point the other day where I said, "The secret is not letting people see your true feelings." No matter what they are. I don't want to be bothered with fighting, so if you want to make me come out, you'd better make me come out for a good reason. Because life is too short. I have my health to worry about.

The guys in the gang are more sensitive to slights from passersby.

We were busted the other night. All the guys. They [the police] took them all in. One guy got beaten up, and he said that the whole club beat him up. The guy didn't press charges because he asked for it. We were all downstairs – we were just minding our own business. Drinking, talking. Here comes this guy coming up and calling some of our guys faggots. Then he walked up and said, "I'll take any of you on!" So like, "Oh yeah?" So one of the guys jumped up. He was fairly drunk, but we don't care.

Women who are disrespectful are treated with as much contempt as men.

You see, one time I go to the store. In the middle of the night, they have all different kind of classes go in there. OK. But there's this white chick over here – the white people are always putting down the Spanish people and the black. But we expect the white people to be better than us. To me, I feel "manners." Here comes this chick and she just pushes me out the way. "Hey, what's up with you?" And then somebody said, "Oh, don't mind her, she's crazy." I said, "What do I care? I'm crazy too. Just because she's crazy, I'm supposed to allow her to step over me? Hey, why couldn't she say excuse me?" So right then and there, you know, I waited for her outside. I was going to fight right there for just pushing me.

Did she apologize?

Oh yeah. She wasn't as crazy as everybody was making out.

Fights with other females that occur when they are disrespectful often involve accusations of promiscuity.

So during this week, I see the chick right. I'm minding my own business and she comes out, "I hear you want to talk to me," this and that. So I thought she was very disrespectful right there. That got me angry. I am her elder and at one time I used to be her teacher. I was walking with Betty [a friend in the building]. I had a bag in my hand and I said, "Here, Betty." And I'm standing and I'm watching her so she told me that. Lucy – now this is another chick I isolate from my life or as much as I try to, here comes her name again – "There goes Lucy with the rubber pussy" like I told her. See, 'cos lots of girls do use their pussy to get what they want. But they don't understand that you don't have to use your pussy to get there. You can get what you want and with respect and dignity without having to use your pussy. Because, goddamit, you're a lady.

Connie has also come to blows with girls in the club who have come on to Gino sexually. Two girls have left the club because of this. Even among the other female members, a girl who spends too much time with their man or who seems more interested in sex with the guys than friendship with the women will soon be the object of a great deal of hostility. When such tensions develop, Connie can discipline the girl or ask her to leave or she can grant permission for a fist fight between the girl and her accuser. The same procedure goes for the boys. In the main, Connie tries to deal with the dispute herself through words, since fights within the club are bad for morale and destroy solidarity. The girls accept the general rule that if you are attached to one of the guys, you direct your attention – socially as well as emotionally and sexually – to him alone. Sometimes couples join the club together, but the acceptance of one of them does not necessarily mean the acceptance of the other.

Girls are independent of the guys. Just because a guy has patches – his old lady, doesn't necessarily mean that I'm going to put patches on her. I have to watch them together. If I see the relationship is cool together and how they are . . . maybe I would want to deal with her and put her in my club. Some people you just can't deal with, like the way they are, their attitude. If they show off or something or they think they're it.

If a girl enters the club alone, she is not under any obligation to become sexually involved with all or any of the guys. The Sandman have no club mommas.

A club momma is a girl who would like support the club, get

Connie dancing with daughter Suzie in the clubhouse. On the walls are the club insignia and memorabilia

money for the club, and she's passed around all the guys. Now everybody gets their own girl.

Do some gangs still have club mommas?

Yeah. Some are very sexually open. I can't deal with that. The Chingalings – you heard of the Chingalings, yeah? – they asked my husband if he wanted to take two of the girls home for the night or something like that. Just take them home and send them back.

What did he say?

He said no way. He knows how I'm going to feel about that. 'Cos I tell my girls, "You're not no man's object. No, you're not an object. They say, "You going to be mine tonight?" No. *You* pick out the guy *you* want and then you work on the guy. You're a Sandman Lady – do it like a lady though. Always act like a lady."

However, Connie will utilize the attractiveness of her girls to encourage guys to join the club. Sex, as Connie says, is at the heart of everything.

You also have to know how to use your girls. She's [Wire] attractive, so wherever we go, sex is everything . . . Well anybody just to try to get into her pants will probably even join the club. Because people will put up when you like somebody, even if it's just talking to them, just having them in your vision. Because attraction is not just all the way sex.

Wire, for example, had been hustling for guys before Connie met her. Connie took her out of that and tried to encourage her to be her own person. Among the girls, she was free from being exploited sexually.

Let me tell you. Any girl that comes around this block and gets to be put under my care – the guys can't handle her anymore. So I mean they brain her because it was their thing and I end up taking it. They had her hustling down there for their habits and stuff and I went and I just took.

Was she glad to be out of it?

Yes. It's a different routine, it's more like a family thing – you got the kids and you got Mom. She's a very beautiful person to be with.

While Connie chafes against her role of mother (not only to her family but to the club in general), she maintains and guards it. While she voices frustration at being female, she accepts the necessity of remaining physically attractive if she is to keep Gino away from the constant overtures of other women. While she longs for a sense of unity with other women, she mistrusts them, for she believes sex is at the heart of everything. And behind all of her roles – lover, mother, gang leader – she experiences a pervasive sense of isolation.

After threats were made against her family's life and two gang members were shot, Connie, Gino, and the children disappeared for six months. When I met her again a year later, they had relocated and continued to keep their whereabouts a secret from people in their old area. Their new apartment was in a vast project, bleak, isolated, and a far cry from the lively area they had enjoyed in Manhattan. They had sold the motorcycle and bought a car. They continued to associate with a local social club of bikers, but Connie became more involved with the local school after her two sons were said to have learning and behavioral problems. She joined the PTA but always remained her old self. When I met her, she had just come from a classroom meeting where she had inscribed "Fuck the World" on the blackboard to the apparent confusion of the other mothers.

Chapter 4

Weeza and the Sex Girls

Wenna

The Sex Boys and Girls correspond most closely to the classic New York street gang. Prior to 1972, they were part of the Ghetto Brothers, a large black and Hispanic gang with divisions in Brooklyn, Queens, the Bronx, and Manhattan. Ralphie, the first leader of the Sex Boys, took fifty or sixty members in the East New York area of Brooklyn, deleted the "ES" from "Essex Street," the name of the street where they hung out, and thus named the new gang.

The Sex Boys are surrounded on all sides by other street gangs, although their most sustained rivalry has been with the nearest gang, the Montauk Chestbreakers (derisively known as the "Cheeseburgers"). In the early seventies, they were involved in standard gang feuds, often using guns and cars to effect forays into neighboring turf. In recent years, their criminal efforts have been directed to acquisitive crime, principally robbery, burglary, and drug dealing. Official police reports, available for the group from 1976 to 1978, show that their membership numbered about one hundred, with perhaps ten central or core members. There was a steady increase in the number of arrests of gang members.

In early 1981, when I was in contact with them, the gang had almost disintegrated. A dozen members were in and out of each other's homes on a regular basis, but they no longer had a clubhouse and most were voicing desires to "cool out." About half of them had children; some were receiving treatment for drug addiction or for mental-health problems. None that I met had succeeded in obtaining a regular job, in spite of efforts to do so. The last available precinct records of their criminal arrests end in July 1980. Seventy-one percent were for assault, robbery, and auto theft. Only 5 percent were drug-related, although this was another irregular source of income.

The Sex Girls were formed at the same time the Sex Boys came

106

into existence; their number then was alleged to be around fifty. Their leadership structure is much less clear than that of the males but has at various times included Booby, Weeza, and Blondie. Only six or seven of the girls remain now, and many of these became sisters-in-law through marriage, since brothers and sisters were often in the gang together. At the time of my contact only Booby remained without children. Since then, she has had a baby.

In this chapter, we will focus on Weeza. She is the sister of Afro, one of the original Sex Boys, and she joined because of his association with the group. She has been romantically involved with Lefty, Chico, and Popeye. She continues to be close friends with Booby. She was twenty-six when I was with her, and had two children.

A Day with Weeza

Rain is falling steadily as I emerge from the subway in East New York. The grayness in the sky matches the streets and the houses. Every other house in the area is vacant or burned-out and every other lot is empty but for rubble and rusting cars, in which the kids play in the summer. Some streets are better: houses are adjoining and windows and doors are occasionally painted a bright red or blue. Behind the wire fences and gates huge 1960s cars sit with Doberman pinschers or Great Danes sniffing around them and barking angrily as you walk by. Decals on the car windows testify to religious convictions: "Jesus – Say It Louder." The two corner stores at the end of Weeza's street are open for business, although it is not immediately obvious. They are covered in metal sheeting instead of windows, and the doors are entirely cased in metal grill. Inside one, it is dark but for the refrigerated cold-drinks cabinet. I buy a six-pack of Budweiser and some Hostess Twinkies for breakfast; they are not cheap. In the back of the store are two telephone booths which do a good business.

Weeza's front door is painted sky blue and is never locked. The hallway is pitch black even on the brightest day, and the old mosaic floor is strewn with bricks and pieces of wood. Her parents live on the ground floor and as I walk by, I can hear her mother shouting angrily in Spanish. The stairs are rotten and halfway up them is a hole in the wall, converted into a window, that looks out on a courtyard created by the demolition of the adjoining building. The window's glass has been smashed and rain falls onto the stairway. Outside, above a pile of bricks, hang washing lines that lead to

Part of the Sex Boys' turf. The neighborhood which they controlled was among the most derelict in Brooklyn

Weeza's apartment. Two forgotten sweaters are soaking wet on it.

I bang on the door and Weeza shouts "Who?" I call back my name and go in. The kitchen is empty but meticulously neat. The Formica-topped table is cleared; the stove does not hold its usual assortment of pots and pans ready for action. The glass-front cabinet at the side of the room sits empty as usual and is adorned with her son's decals of allegiance to various baseball teams and cartoon characters. In the bedroom adjacent to the kitchen there are two double beds with a curtain between them, which is now drawn back. Although the apartment has two bedrooms, it got so cold after the heating failed this winter that Weeza and Popeye brought their bed into the children's room for warmth. The land-lord disappeared three months ago, so there is no money to fix the boiler. Their old bedroom is now piled high with cardboard boxes packed with toys, clothes, and household items ready for the move to New Jersey, which they plan to make when they have enough money.

Weeza and Popeye are lying on the bed watching a portable TV on a small trolley by the wall. On the other bed is Weeza's ten-year-old brother, Carlos. Popeye, in jeans and a sweatshirt, is curled on his side like a cat. Weeza, who's wearing some dusty pink pajamas, lounges against his stomach. They are smoking marijuana through a tiny Coca-Cola bottle with a plastic tube – a souvenir from 42nd Street. On Wednesday the welfare check came, and Weeza has been out spending. Her children Sita and Paul, each got roller skates. Sita also got a new pair of shoes and, to even things up, Paul was given a foot-high model of the Alien. In a final gesture, she and Popeye had gone out the previous night to a Beefsteak Charlie's restaurant and then to a movie. The evening had cost twenty-eight dollars and delayed their move to New Jersey yet again, but Weeza felt that they had been saving long enough and deserved a treat.

Popeye grins, letting Weeza do most of the talking. The apartment is warm, for Weeza is cooking baked potatoes in the oven. The heat seems to suit the cockroaches, who are particularly evident this morning, crawling boldly over the walls. Weeza has long ago given up the unequal struggle against them and simply ignores them, except when they crawl on her. I kid her about being a slob – in her pajamas at 10:30. No, no, she explains, she and Popeye got up at six o'clock this morning and she just went back to bed. Sita and Paul had been left overnight at her sister's house a few blocks away so she and Popeye had gotten up at 6:00 and walked to her sister's by 7:00 to get them up, feed them breakfast, dress them in clean clothes, and do their hair. Then Popeye had walked Paul to his school and Weeza had taken Sita to hers. Weeza had then bought a chicken for the evening meal and come home. She had climbed into her pajamas, and she and Popeye had sat for a while across the kitchen table, reviewing the movie and smoking a joint. Weeza had gotten hungry, put some potatoes into the oven, and they had retired to the bedroom to wait for them.

Popeye gets up, pulls on a ski jacket, and leaves. He is going to phone Weeza's brother-in-law about his welfare case. A few months back, the welfare office had found out that Weeza's brother-in-law owned a thirteen-year-old car. Because he had "undisclosed assets," it was decided by a tribunal that he was no longer eligible for welfare support. Weeza hands me a letter from the welfare authorities and asks me to read it. She has trouble reading and writing. It is an official document in bureaucratese which basically says that the tribunal found against him and that if he wishes to appeal, he should apply for legal aid. In the meantime, his welfare checks have been stopped. Popeye has already read the letter and has gone to offer some advice by phone.

While we discuss this, Weeza fries pork chops, shreds some lettuce in a Tupperware bowl, and takes a small packet of powdered salad seasoning from the refrigerator. She sprinkles it over the lettuce, then puts Italian dressing on top. When it is all done, she sits down across the table from me and starts to eat. Popeye comes back and takes his meal from the stove, where it is resting atop the frying pan. Weeza pulls in the TV, and we watch "The Price Is Right." We join in the quiz game, hazarding guesses as to the price of dishwashers and candy. Weeza is the most accurate of us all. Whenever somebody wins, she gazes enviously at the set. I ask her what she would do if she won the money, and without hesitation she says "Move."

Outside, the rain continues falling. The windows are steamed up from the heat of the cooking. Weeza lights a bunch of incense sticks and puts them behind the stove to clear away the smell of frying. She stacks the dishes in the sink. Today there is no hot water and she cannot wash up until later. Popeye announces that he is going out on the street to see what is doing. He is always restless and frequently comes and goes during the days. On the street he can usually find some way of making money. Often it comes from the copper piping, lead, baths, and fixtures that he takes from abandoned buildings. Today Popeye gives Weeza a kiss on the cheek and, wearing his new ski jacket, goes off to see who is around.

Weeza decides she is still hungry. She is sitting at the table smoking a joint. Carlos has been joined by his younger brother Juan, and they sit on the floor playing with the roller skates. She says she would really like some chocolate chip cookies, the kind you bake yourself in the oven. The trouble is, she would have to walk to the big supermarket on Sutter to buy them. "Family Feud" begins and Weeza wishes she had her color TV back again. A few months ago Popeye was arrested and she had to put up the color TV for bail money. Now that the case is over, she should be getting the set back soon. The little black-and-white set was for the kids, so they could watch cartoons after school, but now the whole family has to share it. When the kids have it on, Weeza pushes it into the sitting

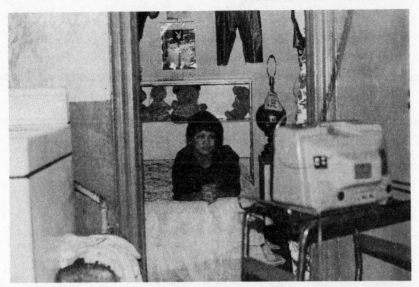

Weeza watching television in the bedroom which she shared with Popeye and her two children

room so that they are not under her feet in the kitchen. During the day Weeza is generally alone, and lately she has been getting bored. She says she spends too much time thinking and it isn't good. She finds herself reviewing her life again and again. She wants another kid and, in the meantime, a dog. She shows me an ad in the *TV Guide* for a place on Long Island where you can get stray dogs and cats free. She doesn't want a mutt, she says, but maybe a German shepherd or even a poodle. Her brothers, though bored by now, are listening to the conversation, and occasionally she speaks to them in Spanish.

Weeza puts on some socks that are still wet from the rain she walked through early this morning (everything else is dirty). She wants to get her hair cut, she says, as she pulls on a woolen cap and jumps up to show me the Curly Kit that she bought yesterday. It cost six dollars and is a kind of cold permanent that changes her short frizzy hair into a mass of curls. But all the curls came out in the rain this morning. The only makeup she wears is blusher on her cheeks. This morning she washes her face with Noxzema cream, then combs out her hair. She pulls on a pair of jeans but decides to keep on her pink pajama top, which she tucks into her waistband. Last she dons a bright red shiny bomber jacket and sends her brothers downstairs to her mother's as we go out into the rain in search of chocolate chip cookies.

We walk down the avenue, dodging the puddles, Weeza points out places of interest en route. Her sister lives over there. Paul's school is just down this street. The whole neighborhood used to be beautiful when she first came here years ago. All the houses were occupied, and this avenue was filled with stores. That was before it got "all messed up." Now, in the rain, it looks particularly desolate. The street is empty, the pavement broken. Occasionally, a bare light bulb shines from a broken-down house. Most noticeable are the vacant lots strewn with debris – beer cans, bricks, smashed wine bottles, rusting cars. A long time ago Weeza applied for an apartment in the housing project we are walking past, but she didn't get in. The project complex is huge, eight or nine towers with patches of grass between them. They are not very beautiful, but at least they are fully occupied and gas and electricity are provided. If Weeza had gotten in, she is sure she would not be "hanging out" anymore. Even though it is only a few blocks from Essex Street, psychologically it is miles away.

On the way back, Weeza tells me about Paul's problems in school. He had been constantly getting into fights with the black kids, and Weeza had decided he should change schools, but she wanted Sita to go with him. The move turned out to be fairly simple, and, after the first month, Paul had settled in and was working better. Sita, however, was miserable without her old friends and pleaded with Weeza to let her go back to her first school. Weeza saw the principal and asked if he would take her back. He said that Sita was his special girlfriend and she could come back to him whenever she wanted. So she did return and now things are running fairly smoothly. Sita reads and writes in both English and Spanish with great proficiency for a nine-year-old, but she tends to be lazy about things she finds more difficult, like math. Last week Weeza had a meeting with her teacher and then gave Sita a severe scolding about her behavior in school. Since Weeza began cutting school at five and so never really learned to read or write, she is determined that her children will not wind up the same way. She supervises their homework every night, even though she doesn't always understand it, especially the math. Popeye, who stayed at school a bit longer, usually checks their finished work. There is no point in being bright if you can't read and write, Weeza points out, although at the same time she is obviously proud of both her children.

Weeza and the author returning from the corner store on her block. The abandoned building was once a local high school

Back upstairs, Weeza sits at the kitchen table, carefully cutting the sausage-shaped roll of cookie dough into slices and then quartering each one and placing it on a baking tray. She puts the tray in the oven and switches on the TV to catch the end of "Ryan's Hope." Every day she watches all the soap operas, as do all her friends. At the beginning of each one she gives me a rundown of the story to date, with particular reference to the moral fiber of the various characters. She gets up to take the cookies out of the oven and we begin to eat. As we finish one tray, she puts in the next. When I can't force down any more, Weeza is still going – a fact that she attributes to the grass she is smoking.

At one o'clock Weeza takes the chicken out of the freezer and puts it in the washing-up bowl, where she leaves it with cold water running over it to defrost. We settle down to "All My Children," another soap opera. Her brother comes up from downstairs to borrow some chicken-coating mix. Weeza sends the packet down to her mother. The welfare checks in the family arrive at different times; when Weeza has just received hers, her mother and sister are getting to the end of theirs. As soon as Weeza sits down, there is a timid knocking at the door. The kid from across the hall is standing outside. His mother wants to know if Weeza could lend her some vinegar. Weeza pours half of what she has into a cup and gives it to him. Half an hour later he returns, wanting some more. Weeza gives him half of what remains.

At two o'clock "One Life to Live" begins. Weeza pulls the chicken out of the sink, places it on a wooden chopping board, and begins to chop it up while watching the TV. She tosses the pieces into a white plastic bowl and seasons them with salt, pepper, adobo sauce, and some vinegar, then sets them aside. At a quarter to three, she peels potatoes and cuts them into slices for French fries. She also cuts up a sweet potato for Popeye, who likes it deep-fried. She puts a pan of fat onto the heat and after coating the pieces with a commercial breading drops them into the pan.

She hasn't seen Popeye since he left but is sure he will pick up Paul from school. She must go and get Sita who comes out at 3:00. It is still pouring rain. She finally agrees to borrow my umbrella, even though she says she feels silly with it. I remain to watch the chicken. Her younger brother Juan appears clad in a pair of yellow undershorts. He sits on the floor playing with Paul's roller skates. Neither of the two brothers has been to school today. They have spent most of the time looking very bored, unable to go outside because of the weather. Weeza's mother is clearly less concerned than Weeza about making sure the kids get an education.

Paul, Sita, and Weeza return with Weeza's other brother Carlos. The noise is deafening as the two brothers rush Paul into the bedroom to play with his Alien model. Sita goes into the bedroom and takes off her pink skirt and top, carefully turning them inside out and putting them in the cupboard. She is more reluctant to take off her leather shoes, but eventually, and very slowly, she exchanges them for a pair of sneakers. Weeza wheels the TV into the front room and shoos the kids in there while she cooks. She pulls two chicken livers from the pan and eats them with her fingers as she puts on the French fries.

Sita comes to sit next to me at the kitchen table and begins to read me extracts from her library book. Each page has a different joke, and she giggles noisily as she gets to each punch line. She reads very fluently. Weeza watches all this while eating another piece of chicken by the stove. She then puts the meal on the table for Sita, herself, and me. Sita picks half-heartedly at hers and it takes her nearly half an hour to get through it, by which time Weeza has finished hers and has given Paul his to eat in front of the TV. Weeza explains that the kids get lunch at school and, since she always gives them a cooked breakfast, they often aren't hungry in the evening. Sita produces some multiplication problems that she got wrong and has to do again. Paul comes to watch her, and the two brothers go downstairs to eat their evening meal. Weeza says she can't understand where Popeye is because he always comes back to eat with the kids around 3:00. She puts his food on a plate and places it on the frying pan on the stove.

The kids are now watching "Good Times" in the other room. Weeza sits by the window on a kitchen chair. Paul goes out to the corner store to buy a six-pack of beer for Weeza and me. (Legal age requirements for liquor purchase are not enforced by the corner stores.) Sita climbs onto my armchair and begins to write a story about a dog for school. This proves difficult because she doesn't have enough room to write and keeps dropping her pencil, but she refuses to move and insists that I write in my notebook everything that we do.

It is beginning to get dark and the sky in the west is a luminous purple-pink. The street is filling up with people coming home from work. The rain has eased off to a steady drizzle. Paul wants to go out and try his roller skates now that the rain has stopped, but Weeza says no. The sidewalks are still wet and there are too many cars about at this time of night. At six o'clock, the brothers come back up and the boys run into the bedroom, making a lot of noise. Soon one of them reappears to tell Weeza that the other two are fighting. Weeza gets up, yells at them to stop it, and order is restored.

Popeye is still not back, and Weeza is getting edgy. However, her father's car is also missing, and that probably means they are together somewhere. A couple of weeks ago the two of them stayed out until one o'clock in the morning, drinking. Weeza had waited up for Popeye and they had a big argument when he returned, partly because she had been worried about him but mostly because she felt that since Popeye doesn't like her to go out of the house alone at night, he should at least come back and get her if he is going drinking. Anyway, he promised that he would not do it again, and since it had never happened before, it was forgotten. On the whole, Popeye is very considerate of Weeza, certainly more so than any of the other men with whom she has lived.

Weeza's mother appears and speaks to her in Spanish. The only word I recognize is "Popeye" and Weeza shakes her head. Sita goes into the bedroom to finish writing her story. Weeza gazes out of the window with her mother and sees her father's car pull up outside. Her father gets out alone; Popeye is not with him. Weeza is really beginning to worry about him, even though it is only eight o'clock. We speculate on where he might be. Weeza is sure he isn't in the abandoned buildings at this time of night. She guesses that he probably met up with some of the Sex Boys and is getting high somewhere. Paul makes himself a peanut butter sandwich and sits in the armchair to eat it. Weeza's concern is catching; the kids can hardly sit still. The conversation becomes sporadic as her eyes keep turning to the window.

In the kitchen there is a rustling every now and again from behind the garbage bag. Paul points as a mouse appears in the center of the kitchen floor, then darts into the bedroom. The radiators have suddenly decided to work and they give off long hisses of escaping steam. Weeza has left the oven on to warm up the room and it soon becomes very hot, but she makes no move to switch the oven off. She sighs and moves into an armchair as we watch "The Incredible Hulk." Her eyes keep closing, weary from the heat, the food, and the day's early start, but she doesn't fall asleep. Her mother comes and goes, shaking her head. I tell Weeza that she is worrying too much although the neighborhood is not a safe one. She tells me to watch out for myself when I leave. I say I will be back tomorrow and not to give Popeye too hard a time when he gets back.

Weeza's Biography

Because Weeza can neither read nor write, the exact dates of specific events in her life were often hazily recalled and frequently contradicted, making it difficult for me to reconstruct her biography. Accepting literally the number of years she spent in a given place would put her age nearer to thirty-eight than to twenty-six. The lengths of time she reports for relationships have been left unaltered in the text, however.

Weeza was born in Puerto Rico in 1954. She had an older sister and brother who at ages three and five went to live with their maternal grandmother and received a stricter and more traditional upbringing than did Weeza. Two years after Weeza's birth, her mother had a son, Afro. Her mother had no more children for several years – in fact, not until Weeza was seventeen and pregnant with her first child. Mother and daughter went through their pregnancies together, resulting in daughter Sita for Weeza and a son for her mother. Two years later her mother had another son.

The family in which Weeza grew up was composed only of her

mother and father and younger brother. Weeza does not know how old her mother was when she was born but does know that her mother had been with her father since the age of twelve. They had remained together for thirty years, although the marriage was never a very happy one.

Can you remember the house you lived in in Puerto Rico?
There was this house in the country, right? It was in the front on the street like over here. It was a big house. It got two trees in front, a gate, and out the back my father had fruits – all kinds of fruit. And the house had three rooms – a kitchen, a living room, no bathroom – you didn't use no bathroom, only a house and a hole.
What was school like?
I don't remember because I hardly every go.
Did you always have enough to eat?
Sometimes my grandmother used to help us – my mother's mother, we used to go over to her house. Sometimes my mother, she didn't have and my father, he was always in the street – never bring money to the house. He used to work with smoke – one day he went out, you know, and he just went to jail and everything, when we were small.
Why did he go to jail?
Hanging out with womans – those women on the street.
Did he get in a fight?
Yeah, in fights.
So your father was in jail part of the time?
Yeah. Almost all the time he was away. Sometimes he was living with us, but when we was real small, he used to work. My mother used to tell us this – he used to work when we was small. When we got about six or seven, he used to going out, stay out, hit my mother, we always got to be moving, hiding, you know, late in the night and everything.
Were you frightened of him?
No, I wasn't scared because he never hit us – he never bothered us, only my mother. He never bring food to the house and he used to come and say, "I want food. Give me some food." This and that. "But I don't bring no food," like that. But I never frightened but, yeah, we had to be running because when he come home high, he used to take the machete to hit my mother, to kill her.
Did you understand why your mother and father were fighting?
I guess because my father was out with another woman.
Did you understand that then?

Yeah. I understand. I was young but not in my heart.

Did you see him with other women?

No. Not that I remember. I never seen him, but he bring a woman one day to my mother's house. I don't know who it was. I don't remember, but my mother told me about it.

Were you happy?

When I was a kid, yeah. I wasn't happy when they were fighting. They never stopped fighting. Now they fight too.

Do yo think Puerto Rican women put up with more than they should?

Yeah. Puerto Rican women – they have a lot. Some woman they hurt *a lot*. They suffer a lot because of the man. Or because of their kids, I don't know. They suffer a lot. Like my mother – I say, "Mommy, why you don't leave Poppy?" And then we talk and she told me, "When I was younger and you people was younger (I was about seven or six, something like that) I left him." My mother say, "And I went back with him." And I say, "Why you left him and you went back with him? You had me and Afro already. Why you left him and you went back?" "Ah, because I love him at the time and I don't want you to have a stepfather." I used to tell her, "Oh man, sometimes – you're stupid."

We was raised without no father. Let's say like that, without no father – only my mother. She used to work in the American people's house – Italian house. Over there in Puerto Rico they got some place for white people to live over there – beautiful houses. So my mother used to leave and work over there for them – iron, cooking for them, you know, something like that. They used to pay her twelve dollars. At that time, twelve dollars.

Then my father used to come drunk, ask my mother for food. He never even bring no food to the house – no money. All hickeys over here, his shirt all full of lipstick, and my mother had to hold that. Sometimes I had to be running. Me and Afro behind my mother running. Hiding. Shit. I say, "Shit, what kind of life is that?" And I watch all day because I'm the oldest in the house. He hit her one day with a stick and he broke all this over here with a stick. He hitting her. He brought some woman to my house when we was small. She stole two dresses from my mother's house in Puerto Rico. She stole two dresses. Whores on the street. My father took them to my mother's house, my mother's working. Over here nobody have to give me clothes, but in Puerto Rico I remember this man, he was a cop, his name was Blackie. He was Puerto Rican guy I remember him. He was kind of fat, he was tall, and one day my mother and my father had a big argument. My father came real drunk and my father had a blade in his hand. He cut her on the back. And my mother ran. She ran, she fell, and my father didn't have no chance to cut her. My mother fell. So then – I was the big one – I got Afro. (I used to call him, Pito, I call him that name, Pito.) I took Pito, I said, "Come on, let's go." And I went to behind a gate and I had him over here like this. I didn't know what to do – what I could do? I was small. I was hiding like this. Then the cop came and he opened the gate and he seen me and my brother like this [crouched down] and he told me, "Why are you hiding?" And I said, "Because my father and my mother is fighting." I told him in Spanish. And he told me, "Why?" And I say, "I don't know – they're fighting but why I don't know." So he came. And the next day he brings me a box of clothes like this. He brought me a pink dress with a lot of little bows – little bows, yellow bows and everything.

When Weeza was eleven, she moved to New York. Her father had gone ahead to find accommodation and work and the rest of the family came later. Her father's attempt to straighten out his life and responsibilities was not successful.

Did you come to New York on an airplane?
Mm-mmm. My father was here first – he was here first and then he sent for us.
Did you go to school?
Yeah, we went to school. We went to school, then we went to welfare. We came from Puerto Rico without no clothes. Hardly had no clothes. When we was here, we had no coat. We came here, we thought my father had a job, a nice apartment for us, but he really had no apartment, he had no money – drunk. He went to the airport, he was drunk. My brother he only had a jacket – a little light, light jacket.
So you had nothing?
Nothing. The welfare helped us, you know – my mother got us clothes and we went to school.
You really went?
Yeah, I went for a while. Since I was fourteen, I went. Playing hooky, you know. Most of the time playing hooky.
Did anything particular happen at that time?
Nothing changed. It was the same. My father fighting, getting high. But then he came in with a gun, he shot, he almost killed me.
Did he mean to?
No. He was shooting and I went to take the gun away from him.

I did take it away, but he almost shoot it. Always the same, never change. That's how come I dropped out. At fourteen – I never went to school again. [When] I ran away with my boyfriend [Tito], I was going to be fifteen.

Tell me about that.

I was fourteen, going to fifteen. My father never trust me – I don't know what happened, I guess I'm the only girl – he never trust me. So I was getting tired, tired staying home, so then one day I decided to run away with my boyfriend, and me and him talked all about it. He went to school and picked me up. We went to a park and we were talking and he told me, "Yeah, let's go." Then we went to New Jersey to his father's house all the way over there to New Jersey – to Connecticut, New Jersey. All the way down there.

It must have been exciting.

Yeah. Then my father was looking for me. My father had a picture of me. He went to the [police] precinct. He was mad. When he catch me, he was going to hit me. But he never do nothing. He just worried, you know, and he went into my father-in-law's house and he find me over there. And I was real scared. I went to the roof. And I was only fifteen and I say, "If my father comes over there and tries to hit me, I'm going to jump." He [Tito] told me, "OK, I jump with you," but he didn't tell me nothing [to dissuade her].

How long were you away for?

About a month.

Did he make you go home?

No, he didn't make me go home. He gave me money – I went to buy clothes, you know. So I stayed with Tito, about a couple of days, and then we used to fight a lot. He didn't let me go out or nothing. He just wanted me to stay home, home, home. He used to hit me for nothing. And that's when I came out pregnant. Then I came back to my mother. When I was eight month, I went back with him.

How did you mother feel when you were pregnant? Was she mad?

Yeah, in a way, but in a way she understand, yeah. Not my father. He went to the hospital, and see me – nothing. He was angry. I'm the only daughter he got. So he was angry with me. I don't care.

Weeza's pregnancy sealed her schooldays and her childhood, but it did not change her stormy relationship with Tito. She left him only six days after the birth, although now she looks back on that time as a period before disillusionment. Though they went their separate ways and there is now little bitterness, she has not forgotten her introduction to the emotional suffering that characterized many of her relationships from then on.

Did it change your life?

Not really. In a way it changed my life because I hat Sita and I forgot everything. Her father, I had always had him on my mind. And she made me forget everything – a lot of things. I used to buy her clothes, dress her as if she was a toy. Yeah. I was alright. Then about six days, I was in a house with Sita. Sita was six days, he hit me again and I was bleeding and everything. He hit me. I ran outside with my gown. And his mother got to call the cops for him and everything. So when the cops came, I tell him I want to go home with my mother. And I had five dollars. And I tell the cop, "Give me some change," and he told me, "I don't have none," and he give me a token and I catch the bus and I went to my mother's house. I left him when Sita was six days born. Yeah. I was crying a lot. I thought like I left him, I got a kid, I never going to find another man. That's the way I used to feel. Because I wasn't a woman, so I used to think that way. Now I don't think like that. You know. When I was about eighteen, I realized it's not like that no more. It's not like that, even though you're a woman and this kid don't belong to this man. You know, they help you and they get together with you. Nothing matters. But for me I thought he was the only man. I never going to find another man.

Returning to live with her mother meant that Weeza went on welfare. Because she was under eighteen, her allowance was paid to her mother, who administered it to her. After only a few days, her mother sent her to Puerto Rico for a variety of reasons: to give her a vacation, to ease the domestic congestion, and to get her away from the "bad" influence of New York that had been indirectly responsible for her pregnancy. In this last respect, the plan completely backfired.

I stayed at my sister's about a couple of months. Then I went to my aunt's house – to Saliera. My sister used to live in Wyama. And my aunt she used to live in Saliera. But I used to live with my sister, you know, back and forth. Then I knew Misa. He lived near. And my cousin he said, "Weeza, this is Misa." This and that. And, you know,he was the one – he liked me, but I didn't like him, you know, but he was alright. Like he used to buy me milk for Sita – he used to

buy me milk. This and that. You know, he used to buy me milk.
Then he told my aunt that he wanted to live with me. This and
that. And my aunt said, "Yes, it's alright," because he was alright
and everything. He was working. He was working when I knew
him. He was working on those big machines, the construction
machines in Puerto Rico, he was working and then I went out with
him.

How long did you stay there?

In Puerto Rico? Seven months, that's it. Seven months. Then I
was tired to live in that little house and I was tired to live in Puerto
Rico. Same faces – that was boring and I told my mother to send
me my ticket, I want to come back home. And then Misa came
back.

Was he sad when you left?

Yeah. Then he came back. I was already pregnant. I came
pregnant about six months.

How did you feel when you found you were pregnant? Were you upset?

Yeah. The second one? Yeah. I wanted to make an abortion. The
lady told me that's no good for God to kill a baby. Then I say, "Oh,
my God. OK, OK, OK, I ain't going to do it." I ain't going to do it,
so I had it. He's eight.

So Misa came to New York? How old were you?

I was seventeen. Still seventeen. And then Misa went to Manhattan. And started dealing. He was dealing dope, coke. And I was
over here and he find me an apartment over there and I went over
to Manhattan with the kids.

So he went ahead.

He came to get me. I went over there with the two kids. Paul was
about two months and Sita was about a year – almost about a year
and a half or two.

How did you get on with Misa?

He was alright. He used to give me everything I wanted, you
know. I didn't want him to do whatever he wanted to do.

How old was he?

He was older – about twenty-seven, twenty-five.

So you got on well?

He was alright. Sometimes I used to have arguments with him
because sometimes he used to come to the house all sleepy.

Did you think he was shooting dope?

Yeah. Then one day I was taking a bath and I was finished and I
went into the room – watch TV. When he went into the bathroom,
he was taking so long. I'm curious though – "Why's he taking so

long?" Then I went to the bathroom, he was taking it. I stood crying. I never seen nobody – I'd known people, a lot of people who had taken it but I never seen nobody like that. I say, "Oh yeah, – that's what you're doing." I told him, "I'm going home." I start dressing the kids – two o'clock in the morning I was going to Brooklyn.

Did he stop?

He keep using it. Until he went to jail. I left him when I was about twenty, nineteen. I left him. I came over here to my mother. He was a junkie and everything, but he always look after the children. I ain't got no complaints. The only thing he used to use – not no more, he don't use it no more. He used to deal it. Now he be locked up again.

You said you tried all that stuff? Was it with Misa?

No. When I was with him, I was curious, you know, why he went to the house all sleepy, you know. Why that stuff do that to him, this and that. But I never used it with him because he never let me use it – never in my life. Even for my nose. Nothing. No. He didn't want to. So then when I left him, I was living with Lito, I living with this guy and he give me a skin – not to my veins, to the skin – and I went and I told Misa. He [Misa] was a junkie, he was all messed up, right? Living in a basement, all messed up. Then I went to tell him, you know, he's going to feel proud that I did it. I wasn't thinking, you know, and he went and he smacked me in front of the kids. He smacked me and he told me, "Look, you don't see how I live? Look, I look like a dog, you know, like junkie. I'm no good, you see, and you're a woman, you got two kids." He told me just like that. He told me, "You know, I don't kick your ass because your two kids here." Like that. He didn't like it.

When Weeza returned to Brooklyn, the family was living at the intersection of Pitkin and Essex street, at the very corner where the Sex Boys hung out. Her youngest brother Afro had begun to spend time with them, and through him Weeza met them. They had only been in existence for a year or so, and at that time there were "dozens" of girls who hung with them and took the name Sex Girls. The leader was Ralphie. Weeza became involved with a boy called Lefty. When Lefty was killed in 1976 by a rival gang, the Bikers, his death had a much greater impact on Booby, his current girlfriend, than on Weeza. But Weeza, although by this time living in Manhattan again, could not bear to return and watch the elaborate funeral in which his open casket, draped in gang colors, was walked by the gang through the streets of East New York.

After breaking up with Lefty, Weeza had moved back to the Lower East Side in Manhattan. At the same time her entire family – her parents, Afro, and her sister and her family – moved back to Puerto Rico, leaving Weeza, who refused to go, alone. The move was to be permanent, although in fact they returned en masse three years later. Weeza's few years in Manhattan were a testing time for her, living on welfare and raising her two children. In desperation, she sent both children to Puerto Rico for a year with her parents. Meanwhile, she had brief relationships with men, some of whom supported her.

What happened to Sita and Paul in Puerto Rico has left a rift in her relationship with her parents that will probably never be rectified. It also drew her much closer to both of her children and to her brother Afro.

My kids, you know, I send them to Puerto Rico with my father and my mother. They stayed there about a year with them. So I thought they were going to take care of them real good, you know, like their grandson, but my sister went over there to Puerto Rico. My sister came back and she told me that they were starving, they hardly don't give them food, this and that. You know, they don't treat them right, they didn't have shoes, their hair all messed up. I never had them like that – they always be dressed with shoes and everything and their hair combed. My baby she almost die – my daughter.

Really?

It was Afro. Afro came one day from work and she was sick, you know, and nobody noticed about it because my mother don't notice or nothing. So then my brother came and she was eating – you know kids, they eat anything – some little thing there in the street. I don't know how you call that. And she was kind of poisoned already. So she was on the sofa. Then my brother Afro he went over there to her and he told her, "Sita what happened?" "Ah, I don't feel good." She said to him in Spanish, "I don't feel good." So then he touch her and he said, "This kid have fever." He took her to the hospital – he rent a car – he took her to the hospital. They give her a needle and everything and, thank God, she's alright. Thanks to Afro, she's alright. Thanks to God, she's alright, you know. But if it was my mother, I think she would have died. My mother used to send me a letter and tell me, ah, this and that, she got palsy and this and that.

But a lot of things happened to her. My father used to treat her bad, he used to hit her. That's like when something – they're my parents alright, but I'm angry with them. I angry because of what happened and at Christmas I used to send them toys, clothes, and everything. When I went over there to Puerto Rico – no clothes, no toys, nothing. And the clothes all messed up, they didn't have no clothes. To now, when they got everything. I hardly don't buy me clothes – I got clothes, but I hardly don't buy me clothes – I buy *them* clothes. I buy them everything they want. As long as I could, I buy them everything they want.

During her stay on the Lower East Side, Weeza came back often to East New York to hang out with the Sex Boys. It was on the corner that she met Chico, who had just been released from prison for killing a member of a rival gang who was responsible for the stabbing of Danny, the Sex Boys' leader and Chico's brother.

How did you meet Chico? You knew him already?
No, I knew Danny, his brother, he used to talk about him a lot. Chico, Chico, Chico. I say, "I wonder who's Chico." Then once I was coming from Manhattan. I was walking down the corner. He was in the corner and I see this guy with shades and nicely dressed and I said, "Oh my God, what a fine guy. I wonder who's that." Then I say, "I bet you he's going to be mine." I said inside of me, "I bet you he's going to be mine." I went over there and they told me, "This is Chico. This is Weeza – Afro's sister." The guys tell him and we met like that and then he start rapping to me.
Was it a happy time?
It was a happy time. Happy. We was good. We had a nice apartment, bar and everything. It was nice. Better than this one.
You were both still hanging out?
Hanging out with the Sex Boys. It was nice.
Did he have a job?
He had no job. He used to get around hustling, looking for money, you know. He used to be cool. We were together all the time. All the time. With him – forget it!
What did the kids think of him?
They said he was nice, but the only thing they don't like because he got a big mouth. And my daughter tell me, "The only things I don't like he used to call you a whore. He used to tell you names. I don't like that." She used to tell me. Paul he never say nothing. Like he's mad but he was afraid of him – not afraid. We used to be

fighting – Paul knew, so he used to be afraid.

What did you fight about?

He was jealous. He didn't like the way I dress – my hot pants. This and that. Forget it.

How come you bust up?

Really, I was tired of fighting. I really loved him, and I think if it wasn't for Popeye we'd be together, fighting and everything. I think we'd be together – maybe. In a way but in a way not. The kids don't like him back. I throw him out and Sita told me, "Don't bring him back." And I say, "Alright." Then Popeye get involved in a way – he was in the middle – and Chico find out that I was going out with Popeye. One day, Popeye came and told me, "Weeza, Chico was with this morena [black girl]." Popeye told me and I said, "What?" And I told him [Chico], "What? You was fighting with me last night that I was with Popeye? And you was with this negra? This morena? Right." And he told me, "No. Who told you that?" And I said, "Nobody told me that. You was with this morena." Then he told me, "No."

The morena was in the clubhouse the next day. That was Friday, Saturday she was there. I really forgot. I had that in my mind that he was with *another* morena. And me and him was fighting. I hit him with a stick. So I went the next day and I see the morena in the room and I was nervous. And I said, "Oh shit, that's her." I didn't tell her that I was Chico's woman. I tell her, "What you doing here?" And she told me, "I'm waiting for Chico." And I was shaking. I explained to the morena. I said, "What? You're waiting for Chico?" She told me "Yeah. I'm waiting for Chico." Then I say, "Why you waiting for Chico?" "He told me to wait here." And I said, "Yeah? You was with Chico last night?" And she told me, "Yeah" – and she told me. "You get down with Chico last night?" And she told me, "Yeah," and I went blah. And I kicked her, boy, I hit her, took her outside and ripped her blouse off. I make her run through the streets with no shoes, without no bra, no blouse, nothing only her pants. She don't give me the chance to take it off. She was running and I almost caught her with a knife and Popeye hold me and she was running. I hit her. I hit her, forget it. Then I told him [Chico], "Don't worry. I'm going to do it with one of your friends and you going to find out who." And I did it with Popeye. I know it was wrong, it bothered me a lot. Sometimes it bothers me, I think about it.

Why did it bother you?

It bother me because I know I did it wrong really when I went with one of his friends. He don't care about me or nothing. But in a way, I think I did it wrong going out with his friend, you know. His own boy – going out with him. That's a bad thing.

So you been with Popeye how long?

Five months, six months.

Was all this last summer?

Last summer. 1980. Yeah.

So in some ways you like Chico?

When I'm alone by myself, I think all that. Even though sometimes I'm with Popeye, I think that.

Does Popeye know?

I don't know if he knows. Sometimes I stare like this and I start thinking. "Tell me what? What you thinking about?" I say, "Nothing, nothing."

Weeza: Family and Lovers

Although Weeza and her parents never got along very well, they continued to live under the same roof. They had the downstairs apartment, she the upstairs. The noise rose from below and it was possible to follow whole arguments from Weeza's kitchen. Sometimes, when I arrived to find that Weeza was out, I would hammer vainly at her parents' door, behind which a great deal of yelling and banging clearly indicated that someone was home. Sometimes no one answered, and I was never sure if it was because they did not hear me, or because they were so unused to people bothering to knock, they assumed a knock on the door meant a visit from the welfare office or the police. Inside their apartment, the kitchen always looked chaotic, the sink piled with dirty dishes and the table covered with a collection of dirty utensils, crumbs, and spills from the last meal. Off the kitchen were the bedrooms. Two of the three rooms had mattresses on the floor, strewn with sheets and pillows of different colors. Every available inch of floor space was occupied by the boys' toys, which seemed to make the already tiny apartment totally impassable.

Neither of Weeza's parents spoke English, although her father could manage a few phrases. Her father knew all the Sex Boys well, and he and Popeye would go off together some mornings looking for ways to make money. They would come home with perhaps fifteen or twenty dollars from selling what they had stripped from abandoned buildings or from other activities about which they were more enigmatic, except that they had "sold some stuff."

Much of Weeza's bad feeling toward her parents arose out of the issues of money and her children – often interrelated. An informal credit system operated in the family and with other residents of the building that allowed them all to get from one welfare check to the next. The same system was used with food. Small quantities of bread, eggs, or flour were exchanged back and forth, and if someone else's kids were playing in your apartment, they were fed with your children in return for a like favor at a later date. Naturally, such a system could only work if it was not abused by any particular member and, in Weeza's opinion, it was her mother who usually took out more than she gave. This led to much bad feeling, since even within a family generosity has to have limits when resources are scarce.

How do you get on with your parents now?
It's different. Because you see something – most of the time I have food in the house. I never say I don't have no food in the house. Because the welfare, I got. They send food stamps. You know. I go out shopping and for now Popeye help me, you know, a little that he do. He help me. You need something? You got to go down there and knock at the door. "Give me this, I need this, I don't got this." And we don't like to ask – especially me, I don't like to go. I never lived like this, with my father and my mother down here and me up here – never. I used to live in Manhattan. Far away. Never like this.
It's better when you're far away?
Yeah. Especially when my two little brothers always fighting with my kids. So when my kids don't got nothing to eat in the morning – but they always got, you know, I didn't say that – but sometimes they didn't have nothing to eat in the *morning* – no cereal, no egg, or nothing – and they have, they [my parents] don't call my kids to give them no breakfast. But when their kids don't got, they always come over here and knock.

Her parents' treatment of her children in Puerto Rico has led to a great distrust of them and a sense of shock at their betrayal which neither she nor her sister can fully understand.

Were you really angry with your parents?
Yeah. Now I don't want them to touch my kids, not even my mother. Sometimes when they scream at my kids, I scream at my mother. I'm not supposed to scream at my mother, but why she don't get along with my kids? They never do nothing to her. *They*

got to be angry with that. Not her with them 'cos they never do nothing with her, you know. I don't know why they don't like them. I don't know.

It's strange.

I don't know. It's strange, yeah. Me and my sister sometimes we talk – I go to my sister's house, talk with my sister's kids, the same. She went over there to live, my sister went over there – from here to Puerto Rico to live – and my father throw my sister out and her five kids that she's got. Throw her out.

To Weeza, it is clear that her father has never loved her. She feels that her mother cares for her but is so weak that she dares not express any affection against her husband's wishes. Often our conversation would turn to her father's behavior, which came to represent more and more all that was bad about men. At the same time, her mother's passivity grates on her, and, as evidence of her own assertiveness, she points to the fact that she would leave such a man. On the other hand, to leave too many men is to be in danger of acquiring a reputation for being loose. Weeza veers between repudiating anyone's right to label her and at the same time documenting the long periods of time she has spent with her boyfriends to show fundamental monogamy.

Did your parents love you?

[Pause] I don't know. I never tell it because when I was small, my father used to be in the street with whores – a lot of girls, whores. My mother used to suffer.

You think your mother took too much from your father?

Yeah. Too much. Thirty years. Thirty years of it. Too much.

What would you do?

I would left him a long time ago. I don't care about my kids or nothing – I would left. I really care for them, but, you know, I ain't going to suffer like that. Only for my kids? I ain't going to be suffering in the house. Only because my kids, I got to be suffering? You know, like that? Uh-uh. I just walk away.

Kids feel when parents aren't happy.

Yeah. They feel it.

Weeza tells what she believes to be a prophetic story about the whore whom her father knifed. In retribution, the woman swore that her father's daughter would become a whore. When she is in an aggressive mood, Weeza claims to have become not only more independent but emotionally tougher than the whore too. On the other hand, well aware that her parents view the number of men she has lived with as excessive, she protests that she doesn't care what they think. Weeza views all aspects of her assertiveness – her aggression, her independence, and her sexuality – as part of what sets her apart from her family. She was the only one that "came out crazy."

She [the whore] tell my father, "Look, you did this to me but I hope you pay with your own daughter you're going to have." The lady tell him, "And your daughter she's going to be like me. She didn't going to be happy with no man." She tell him just like that to my father. My father knew that and my mother knew that, so they told me and I think, I say, "Uh-uh. I'm going to be stronger than her." 'Cos she ain't going to see me like a whore like she was. And she ain't going to see me on the street. And I changed men? It's because *I* feel like it. I live with a man – I could live with him four months, four years, or whatever time I feel like it, especially he treat me right and my kids. But I ain't to be like her. I say inside me, "I'm going to be stronger than her." And that's the way I think she wanted it. She was like me. She like to wear makeup, she like to wear a lot of bracelets, jewelry – a real freak like me. Real freak – get dressed, go outside, like that. But I say, "I ain't going to be like her." 'Cos she was on the street going with this man now, now. They used to pay her for her body – not me. I'm going to show her that I'm stronger than her. I tell my mother, you know. That's the way I am now. I'm stronger than her. I'm not taking any man because I feel like taking one. Because I took Chico and I lived four years with him. Four years straight, and he did so many shit to me. Not that he played dirty 'cos he only did it once – that's how come I play him dirty with Popeye. So – other man – Sita's father, I lived five years with him. Yes, five years with him, and Lito I took five years too.

Do your parents think it's bad that you've lived with different men?

No, they didn't say *real* bad, but they say – like, they don't tell *me*. I knew they tell somebody else, but they don't tell *me* 'cos I always tell them, "This man, I don't like him. The way he treat me and the way he treat my kids, I left him." I don't care. And I find me a better one. I keep that one and that don't mean I'm a whore.

While her parents may not be happy about the life-style Weeza has adopted, they have not made any real attempt to discourage it. Weeza's father often smokes and drinks with the Sex Boys, and both parents apparently have always tolerated her brother Afro's involvement with the gang, if not always Weeza's.

While Weeza's father's behavior toward her might be the result of his protective attitude toward her sexuality, he apparently feels no compunction about making sexual advances to her girlfriends.

Can you describe that fight with your father?
What happened then? Because my father he was drunk and it was my girlfriend here – two girlfriends – and he's the kind of man when he drunk . . . When he's sober, he's straight, but when he drunk, he get real, a little bit nasty. It was my two girlfriends here, you know Joan? They was alright. So he just came to her and slap her because she don't want to pay no attention to him because she don't like him, so he just came to her and smack her and I tell him, "You don't do that." That was in the street. Then she came up and he came up knocking on the door. My kid was here and he came to the living room and he start saying, "You're a whore," in Spanish and I tell him, "Look, stop that. This is my house. You don't do that in my house. She's in my house. You want to say that, you wait for her to go outside. Don't say that in my house because my kids are here." He told me, "You're another one." He told me and that big knife I got there? I just grab it, and, I don't know, I stab him over here. And he grab the bar? The bar chair I have, he grabbed that to throw it at me and I say, "Go ahead, throw it to me and I'm going to stab you." And I tell him, "Get out of my house. I don't want you no more in my house." And he went.

The relationship between her family and the gang (and its activities) is quite a close one. One day, Weeza, Booby, and I were sitting in her kitchen talking when Weeza's younger brother Juan rushed into the room, out of breath, screaming in Spanish. Weeza explained that the police had got Popeye. Weeza and Booby ran out of the room and down the stairs with me in pursuit. We ran four blocks, led by Juan, to an abandoned building where Popeye was standing with Weeza's father, smiling and talking. Popeye had been stripping copper piping out of the building while Weeza's father loaded it into the trunk of his old and unreliable car. A squad car had pulled up, and two officers had come over to investigate. It was at this point that Juan, who had been playing nearby, had run home. Apparently, the officers had cautioned the two men and told them to clear out. We arrived to find them loading up and laughing about the scare. A second later, Weeza's mother and sister, who had been downstairs, appeared amid much laughing and back-slapping. Then the eight of us struggled into the car, with Popeye riding on the trunk, and drove home.

The nearby community considers Weeza's father almost part of the gang. In spite of Weeza's rejection of her father, neither she nor the rest of the gang hesitates to enter a barroom dispute on his side.

Me and Booby? Over here in the restaurant? My father was over there, he get drunk, he start being a little bit crazy. We was in the corner hanging out – all the guys and the girls and there was this restaurant right here on Pitkin and Essex, right there? We used to go over there hanging out and drink beer, hear music. So there was this man drinking and there was my father. I know my father is a troublemaker when he's drunk. So Booby – she's another one – I don't know what happened. I'm telling you, I don't know what happened that day. I'm sitting down, drinking a beer, then Booby started arguing with this man. "If you're going to hit him, you have to hit me," this and that and "he's going to hit your father." I say, "Yeah?" Booby and I hit him with a bottle. Then Booby hit him with another bottle. Cashews flying. Oh, everything. Then we had the man on the floor. Me and the man, we was on the floor and I was hitting the man and Booby . . . He was all messed up. And then he went outside and the Sex Boys got him and they messed him up and then Cat came, then Popeye, my brother. They pulled me up and took me to the clubhouse. 'Cos the cops came. So I never get hurt, I never get hurt. I don't know. I never get blood or nothing.

Weeza has never had a shortage of male suitors, yet she views herself as a loser in romantic relationships. Love remains mysterious to her, perhaps because of an idealized view gathered from soap operas and popular songs. The relationships she has had seem to happen to her, rather than being chosen by her, and, with two children, having a man around to help out emotionally and financially is often an advantage. Whether or not relationships benefit Weeza, they do seem to offer stability to the men with whom she becomes involved.

When she was with Chico, her friends thought he was no good for her. He had a background of persistent trouble with the law and had been in and out of prison frequently. He encouraged Weeza to hang out on the corner to panhandle for money for drink and marijuana. After they broke up, Chico moved to the South Side (Williamsburg), where he lived with a thirteen-year-old girl

Some members of the Sex Boys. From left to right: Popeye, the author, Afro, Cuiso, Trouble, Ex and Officer John Galea

(he is twenty-eight) and became seriously involved with heroin. Weeza visited him a couple of times and was shocked at the squalor of his apartment. He had lost a lot of weight and was lying on an unmade mattress, panicked because he had no money for heroin. Weeza gave him a couple of dollars to buy food, but she knew as well as he did that he would use it for drugs.

What kind of life did Chico have?
The kind of life he have. He used to hang out with morenos, Negroes. He used to hang out with them. He used to rob people – snatching people's pocketbooks. He get locked up with the morenos. He used to go out with this morena. He had a baby girl. Morena, she left. He was locked up, he was fourteen. And then, when I met the Sex Boys, he wasn't there, he wasn't around. He was locked up.
What for?
Robbery. He be with a gun. Stickups.
Is he still doing that stuff?
He need to stay out of trouble. He used to get locked up with the Sex Boys a lot. But now I haven't heard he be locked up. On the South Side I think he's doing the same thing – robbery. Maybe he'll go one day. In a way I'm not sure about him.

Popeye was only eighteen and had been with the Sex Boys since he was ten or eleven years old. His stepmother had thrown him out of the house at eleven, and from that time until he was seventeen he had lived with the parents of Big L and Cat (both Sex Boys). He had been adopted into the family as an unofficial stepson. Popeye was quieter than Chico, always present, usually smiling. Popeye had had skirmishes with the law together with other members of the Sex Boys. In 1979, he had been arrested five times: twice for robbery, once for burglary, once for auto theft, and once for threatening the life of the leader of the Montauk Chestbreakers. In 1980 he was arrested with four other Sex Boys for harassment and intimidation of a witness. None of these arrests had resulted in more than a few nights in jail. Weeza had known him since he was a kid. She had watched him grow up and felt strongly protective toward him.

Maybe it's good for Popeye to live with you?
Yeah. He told me, "If I don't be together with you, I'd be locked up." And he by himself, he's going to be locked up.
Has he been locked up already?
Mmmm. A lot of times with the guys.
For what? Different things?
Really for fighting, but never for something serious. Not stealing, not burglary. Nothing serious like that. Only for fights. Be fighting with a cop, you know, gang trouble with the cops to lock him up, this and that. Smart talking back to cops. Something like that. Nothing serious like drugs.
What about Popeye? He's got a weird background, right? Where are his parents?
He's another one. He never was loved. His father never loved him. But to me Popeye *says* that he hates his father, but for me he don't hate his father. Because, you know, he talk and the way he talk, he don't hate him. For me, I say he love his father, you know, but he say that because he's angry with his father, you know. His mother she died. Popeye take Social Security. His father take everything, never give him a penny. When he seen him on the street, he always give him three dollars, two dollars, that's it. That's the most he give him – three dollars. Now he's eighteen. The other day he give him five dollars. Five dollars – that's it. That's how come Popeye's angry – he talk that way, but, like, I don't think he hates his father. I think he loves his father. Yeah. His mother died when she was twenty-three. Yes, twenty-three.

His father got married again?
To this old bastard lady. [Laughs.] I never met her. And I don't
want to do it.

One of the most pervasive themes that emerges in Weeza's
discussion of relationships is that of male control over her. Although the restrictions placed on her by boyfriends are a frequent
source of frustration and arguments, they are seen as the inevitable
alternative to being "on the streets." A good man, one who values a
woman enough to keep her well cared for and to protect her
reputation, consequently must deny her some of the pleasures of
street life, however immediately attractive they may be for her.
"Hanging out" offers a girl many possibilities: getting high, gossiping, flirting, partying, fighting, and excitement. But a girl who
hangs out too much is seen as irresponsible (especially if she has
children) and even "bad." In her more reflective moments Weeza
accepts this. Given what she has suffered from men in her life,
however, she, sometimes refuses to adopt the madonna role. At
times, her streak of independence reasserts itself, and she sees the
streets as a positive rejection of control. She believes she has earned
the right to please herself, since men inevitably deny her those
pleasures without offering stability and security in return.

Chico was less restrictive than Popeye in terms of Weeza's being
on the streets, and many of her friends felt that he allowed her too
much access to them. On the other hand, he never allowed her to
roam without him being there to supervise her activities. In the
end, as the relationship deteriorated, Weeza accepted his control
less and less.

Did Chico see his old friends?
No. Never go out. He never go out. He never let me go out. He
didn't go out with his friends. He go to the corner – I go to the
corner. We be together.
Why did you break up with him?
'Cos I was tired of him. He got me tired already. He used to tell
me, "Oh man, you're a whore." I never been with no guys. No. He
used to tell me, "You got this guy. You got this guy."
Maybe because he was in prison before.
Yeah, he never had a woman like that. All the time – forget it.
Nobody see me with him now. They see me with Popeye – they
think it's better. Some of them tell me, it's better to be with Popeye
because you're alright now. You don't be on the street. When I was

with Chico, I was on the corner: "Give me a quarter." Sometimes we used to make ten, fifteen, five dollars asking for a quarter. Fifteen dollars on the corner. People give me a dollar, three dollars, two dollars, like that. I used to ask with Chico. With Popeye it's different.

Are the guys you know very controlling?

Yeah. They always tell me how to dress, don't go out, don't do this, I don't want you with this friend. I don't want you here. Everything.

Like a father?

Yeah. Forget it.

What about the way you dress?

About the way I dress? They don't like me to wear short pants, blouses, tight pants, like that.

Do you think Puerto Rican men are very macho?

Some of them. Some of them. They want to be men. Some of them, they are. If they say something, they stay with it, but some of them – *bendejos* [jerks]. [Laughs]

Do you still believe other people know what's best for you?

I know best. They could *tell* me, you know, I listen to them, but *I* know what's best for me.

Weeza was the victim of a brutal attempted rape while I was with the Sex Boys, and she was well aware that the situation might have been averted had she listened to Popeye, rather than defied him. The incident certainly reminded her that male protectiveness and control may indeed be "for her own good," and that the streets are no place for a woman alone.

So I was walking home, I was crossing the street to go to turn around ready to my house on Linwood. So right there, I don't know, some men came and they just grabbed me like that. Just grabbed me. They was pulling me and I was screaming and screaming.

Did you know what they wanted?

No. I didn't think they wanted the money. They say they want pussy. As they was pulling me, they say they want pussy. And my earring got lost. I had a trey bag [three dollars' worth of drugs] it disappeared – I ain't had it no more. So then I start fighting with them, they keep dragging me to the empty building. I say, "No, no." I start fighting with them. I said, "Please don't do nothing to me – I got kids." And they told me, "Shut up, shut up." They used to tell me that. So then two of them ran and they went. So one of them put the chain to my neck. He kept pulling me to the empty building. So I keep fighting with him, but in the end he had me too tight and I can't scream no more. So he pulled me and he took me to the floor and he grabbed me to the empty building, like a garage, it had a gate. He dragged me there, he closed the gate, but he didn't close it real good. He told me, "Shut up. Don't scream, don't scream."

Was it dark?

Yeah. It was dark. Dark. He held me next to the wall like that with my throat like that, and I said, "OK, OK, I ain't going to scream." He told me, "Take your clothes off. I want pussy." He told me, "Take your clothes off." I say, "No, no." Then in the end he had me too much and I can't talk. Then I tell him, "Alright, I am going to take my clothes off. Let me loose – 'cos I can't talk. Let me loose. I ain't going to scream or nothing." Then he told me, "Alright," and he let me go. He let me go – I push him. When I push him, I ran. When I ran, I fell again. When I fell again, I get up again and I ran. I opened the gate and I ran and ran and ran to the street. When I was on the street, I thought I was screaming and screaming. So then I see this guy and this girl in a car. And I told them, "Help me. Please help me. Somebody tried to rape me." And the guy he didn't want to open the door – people are like that, they could be afraid. They don't want to open the door, they think, you know, it's a set up – to give them a holdup or something. So I told them, "Help me, please help me." I was bleeding, all messed up. And then the girl say, "Alright, open the door." She put me in the car and she took me to my mother's house. And I was screaming and screaming. I didn't want Popeye to touch me. I was afraid.

The need for control over her often arises, she believes, from a tremendous jealousy and insecurity among men, notably Chico. This insecurity extends to Weeza's female friends, whom Chico believed shared her affection and led her astray. Weeza rejects this last implication most forcibly since it clashes with her own strong sense of autonomy.

It's a big difference between Popeye and Chico?

Yeah. You see Chico is twenty-eight, but he didn't act like Popeye. Popeye acts like a real man, even though he's nineteen. Chico used to act like a kid. You know, like a kid. He always – like a kid you always got to have them like this, kissing, kissing. He always wanted to be like this, you know. Suppose you're my friend and you come over here and I be with you, talking with you. "What? You like your friend more than me? You give attention more to your friend than me?" You know. Talks shit. I used to get mad, I said, "Oh man, shut up." Then a little thing like that? We used to fight. A little thing like that. Always my friends. I want to go out and I stay late. "What, you went to your friend? Your friend told you to stay late?" This and that. Always my friend, never me. Always friend. You never see *me* do anythng – always my friend made me do this. I tell him, "Look, I'm not a kid. I'm a woman. And I don't want to do this? Nobody could force me to do nothing, you know. I do it because I *feel* like it. It's late and I came out this time because I feel like it. Nobody told me to do it. They don't put a knife in my chest to do nothing, you know."

Fights have been a part of most of Weeza's relationships, although they were most frequent and violent when she was with Chico. He frequently called her a whore, an epithet that she resents more than any other since it once again challenges her independence, forcing her back into the passivity of her mother's traditional role.

All the guys I have – really *all* of them – hit me. Chico used to hit me, I used to hit him back. Lito used to hit me, I used to hit him back. And Popeye, no, he never hit me.
What's the worst thing somebody could say to your face?
They call me a whore, or they talk bad about my kids. You know. Especially my mother like that, but you know about my mother. You know, kiss my mother's ass. Talking bad about my kids. They call you a whore just like that. I don't like that word. Chico used to tell me when I fight with him, he used to call me a whore. The next day he would tell me, "Oh, I called you that? I'm sorry. Because that's the worst thing you don't like." He told me, you know. I tell him, "You know I don't like it – how come you call me that? Even on the street, you know. The people don't know that. You call me a whore, everybody going to think I'm a whore. And you tell me I fuck with all the Sex Boys, they're going to think I fuck with all the Sex Boys."

Weeza does not see her life as atypical. The suffering she has experienced she sees as common to Puerto Rican women in general. She does sometimes distance herself from them, however, believing that she has exercised more autonomy and possibly suffered for it.

But the stresses of infidelity, male control, children, and poverty seem to weigh heavily on her.

Sounds like Puerto Rican women really suffer.
They does. Suffer a lot. Like my mother, see like my mother. She was raised in Puerto Rico, she was born in Puerto Rico, everything. She come over here when she was already old, we was big already. Not when she was a kid like me. In Puerto Rico those ladies, boy, they have to suffer a lot. Those men, they play you dirty. All having a bunch of kids. All dirty and shit. And you see a man like that, why you going to keep having kids? For the same fucking man? Having, four, six, seven kids like women do in Puerto Rico? I say, "Uh-uh, that's not me." I do me an abortion. And like I tell you, I do four abortion already, but why? Because I ain't going to bring no kids to suffer. I got two already and that's enough.
Why do Puerto Rican women have so many kids?
I don't know why. Because the men. The man say you can't have abortion. You can't have an abortion.

The role in which Weeza's boyfriends are most critically assessed is as providers. Providing need not be done through a legitimate job, for it is not social status that Weeza seeks. Legitimate work carries the advantages of alleviating the constant worries about arrests and trouble and of guaranteeing a secure income, but a man who brings money into the house, whatever its source, is respected and valued.

I could stay with Popeye. Stay with him because he's alright. He alright, he care for my kids. When they need something, they say, "There's no milk," and he go out and he gets milk. He alright. He's eighteen but he's got a mind like a grown man, he ain't like a kid. That's how come I like him, you know. But, like I say, I'm not that old but I can say he's younger than me, you know. He say he really want to work and he want me to give him a baby. And I want one myself because I feel lonely right now. I'm over here all by myself. But he say he want to stay with me, he want woman, he want to move to New Jersey. It would be good. This is the first time, and for his time, he's doing alright. Yeah. For his first time, he's doing alright.

Aside from the turbulence of Weeza's relationships with men, her children put real constraints on her life and are critical in many of her decisions. Sita is talkative, curious, and bright. Paul is quieter, more serious. Their behavior, in contrast to that of Weeza's two younger brothers, is exemplary. Weeza places great emphasis on their schooling and goes each term to talk to the teachers about their progress. As a veteran truant, she is wise to any attempt on their part to avoid doing homework.

Especially Sita she speak real English, straight English? Yeah. She doesn't get messed up or nothing. Not like me – I get confused sometimes. I never went to school real good, but, like, she's going to school almost every day.
When she's older, if she skips school will you be angry?
Yeah. I'll be angry in a way. I tell her, "You go to school." I be checking her out. You see, I used to play hooky but my mother never went to school to check on me. She used to beat me and leave me there, that's it. She never knew if I went to school. One day they sent my mother a letter, but she never got it – I took it out from the mailbox. I seen it first and I say, "Oh, there's my name." And I took it out my mail and I read it – ninety-two days I was absent and my mother never knew. She never knew, she never went to the school, you know, check me or nothing. Talk to the teachers? Nothing. I'm telling you, nothing. I used to play hooky.
Now do you wish she had checked?
Yeah.

Weeza decided to have a third and final child with Popeye. Six months before I met her she had gone to the doctor to find out why she was unable to become pregnant. The doctor was surprised to learn that Weeza had no idea that she had been fitted with "something to stop babies" (presumably an IUD). No one had ever told her. It had been done automatically after her last abortion, and whether or not she had been told, she had clearly not understood. The doctor removed it at her request, and she and Popeye decided to have a child and move to New Jersey, where Weeza had some relatives. Still Weeza had not become pregnant. She began to suspect that something was wrong, possible as a result of the final abortion.

I used nothing and I haven't come out pregnant yet and I use nothing – no pills, nothing.
Does it worry you?
Yeah, it worries me. I ask, "Why?" I want to go to the doctor.

I'm going to go. I was supposed to go today. But I didn't have no money to go.

You think something is the matter?

Yeah. I think something's the matter. I don't know why, but I think. I don't feel nothing 'cos I feel great, but I think something is the matter just like that.

But Popeye was to die before she went to the doctor.

Weeza and the Sex Girls

The Sex Girls were a part of the Sex Boys from the start of the club in 1972. They always had their own special identity with their own leaders and rules. Talking about the club with members of both sexes suggested frequent discrepancies both in the information given by different members and between talk and action. One of the first stumbling blocks was the size of the girls' club.

How many girls were there at the beginning?

(Big L)   A lot. At the beginning there was about eight.

(Weeza)   When?

(Big L)   In the beginning.

(Weeza)   Girls?

(Big L)   Yeah. About eight.

(Booby)   There was more.

(Big L)   Mains, I means mains. Originals. About eight or twelve.

And it grew?

(Big L)   Like fire.

How many girls were there in 1972?

(Weeza)   There was a lot. I couldn't count them all. There was a lot.

Twenty? Thirty?

(Weeza)   More. There was a lot. Girls from all over – other addresses used to come over here and hang out in the building. The Sex Girls? There was a lot. Now there's only a couple of them, they're not much now. There was a lot.

(Booby)   There were so many of them.

(Weeza)   More than fifty.

(Booby)   We didn't count because we had them all scattered. Like we would go to a rumble, then all of them would show up.

(Weeza)   Um-hum.

(Booby)   Then when we used to have our meetings, we never used to fit in the basement.

Part of the confusion obviously relates to the time period under discussion. Big L's comment also suggests that there was a distinction between core and fringe members: when a fight was on, the full complement would arrive, numbering perhaps fifty girls. Available police reports suggest that the male membership was between seventy-five and 100 in 1976–1977 and 100 to 105 by 1978, which would put the percentage of female members at about 33 percent. Girls who hung out did not need to be fully-fledged members – some were prospects.

The girls, right?
(Big L)   Yeah. They have their own rules and regulations, their own laws.
Do the girls have to be going out with a guy?
(Big L)   Not really.
(Popeye)   Just friends. They could be friends or they could just be living in the neighborhood. And they like to hang out, party.
(Big L)   Some of them could be called prospects too.
Can you explain?
(Big L)   A prospect is a thing – you're just hanging out. You're not a member. You're just hanging out with us. A lot of people that hang out with us were never members.
(Popeye)   Just friends.
(Big L)   They're prospects.
(Weeza)   They want to be members, but they don't want to be members. They don't know if they're sure.
(Popeye)   They don't know if they want to get involved.
(Weeza)   They don't know what they want to do.
(Popeye)   So they would just like to hang out.
(Big L)   To say "I hang out."
(Popeye)   They like the way we hang out. They like our style, but they don't really want to be members because they don't want to get involved.

Some of the girls were simply temporary girlfriends of male members. They were tolerated by the females but never became part of the club.

If a guy brings a girl, does she automatically get in the Sex Girls?
(Weeza)   No.

(Booby)   No.
(Weeza)   No. She can hang out with the guys.
Unless she wanted?
(Weeza)   Not even if she wanted. We don't let her. No.
(Booby)   Because really the ones that we have now are the main ones. You have to learn too that he probably picked her up from over there. Meanwhile, we don't know – she could be from another clique, trying to take our things from us. Meanwhile, the guy doesn't know it. Like when we used to have meetings – like, we all used to go to just one room, but she didn't go. She had to stay out.

To be fully accepted into the female gang, a prospective member was expected to have a fair fight with one selected full member in order to prove her courage and her worthiness to be in the club. This initiation effectively deterred freeloaders who wanted to take advantage of the protection offered by the club without being willing to fight for others.

Did girls have to get initiated?
(Booby)   Well, when we started, it was like initiating people – when you take them to the park, like, to see. Like, there's some girls that like to join, like "I get in trouble, I got backup." Now for us, this wasn't that. We used to take a new girl to the park. Now that girl had to pick one of our girls, and whoever she wanted, she had to fight that girl to see that she could take punches. Now if she couldn't, she wouldn't fight. Then we wouldn't take her. Because then we knew that someday – you know, somewhere in the streets – she's going to wind up getting hurt, so we knew that she could fight her battles and we used to let her join. She had to fight first. Without crying.

Like the boys, the girls had their own colors. Wearing them was not required at all times, but if a major rumble was on, then all members were expected to "dress outlaw." Weeza didn't seem to enjoy this aspect of the gang, however.

Did you wear your club jacket?
No, we used to wear dungarees, blouse. Summer, sometimes without no bra. Like summer blouse, short pants, sandals. You know, if we was going to a rumble, we wear boots, dungarees, you know. Sticks.

Did you have colors?

No, I didn't have no colors, only boots, jacket, like that, but no colors.

You never wore them?

No. Just jacket, boots, sometimes boots, but I never liked it too much.

Why?

I never like to dress all outlaw. Sometimes, when I was going to rumbles and fights. But wear boots every day, every day, every day, like some girls? They got another gang wear boots every day. No. I got to dress every day, change my pants every day and everything. I never used to wear the same clothes. The same jacket, nothing, you know, not like that. And the boots – I don't ever like to wear the boots.

Why?

I don't know. They looks nice, but really it's for men, you know. They for men and I think for me, I think when I put those boots on and walk around, the people going to think I'm gay – they all think I'm gay. You know – my jacket, my clothes. I never like to wear them. Only when I'm going to fight or rumble something like that. I never like to wear them.

The girls had sweatshirts emblazoned with SEX GIRLS and the individual's name. These were preferred to the full outfit, which was considered to look too masculine. The girls were very fussy about their appearance, and their clothes were always scrupulously laundered and ironed. Their hair was washed almost daily and the little makeup that was worn was sparingly applied. Perhaps this preoccupation with cleanliness was a way of defending themselves against the "dirty" image of the girl who hangs out with a gang.

The girls were responsible for the discipline of female members who broke club rules. In this matter, the males stayed well out.

Are the girls' laws pretty much the same?

(Big L) Their laws are like similar to ours, but except we can't get involved. If Weeza says, "This girl is going to court, she did something wrong, she broke one of the rules," we cannot get involved.

(Popeye) They take care of it on their own. It's their own rules.

(Big L) We cannot say, "We'll take over, Weeza." We cannot say that. Weeza has to pass judgment. Weeza has to pick a jury,

Weeza has to pick a prosecuting attorney, a lawyer, whatever, and then she must take care of that.

What would I have to do to get a court?

(Popeye)   Sniff glue, you'd get punished.

(Big L)   You don't mess with anybody else's man. That's like . . . I seen a lot of girls go to court for that. And a guy should never mess around with somebody else's girl neither. Vice versa. It's like similar to the same rules we have. You don't lie, you don't steal to each other. This is not done. To us, it's not a gang because we don't consider ourselves a gang. We see ourselves as family. And once you become a member of the family, that's it. You must obey the laws, the rules of the family. You break one of those rules, you're gonna pay.

What kind of deterrent would you use?

(Big L)   Deterrent is like lashes.

(Popeye)   The girls have their own Apache lines. They have their own lashes too, but before, it's like years back when there used to be a crowd of girls. They used to have their own lashes. Apache line. Their own fighting.

Ever had a girl to go through an Apache line?

(Big L)   Yes. Booby, a couple of girls. A bunch of girls – India. Carmen once. I remember one day Blondie – she was a Godmother [leader] by this time – I remember she got this girl. I don't know why, the girl was fighting with another girl's clique. And then she lose. Blondie didn't like it – the way she was fighting. And she whoop her. About sixty-nine lashes.

What?

(Weeza)   With a belt. We used to whoop them if they do something wrong – punish them.

An Apache line is when the members line up in a double column, armed with belts, or (more usually) fists, and the offender must run the line, accepting, without retaliation, punishment from all members. It was sometimes used by the girls but more often by the men, where the injury inflicted tended to be more severe. Lashes could be given to a girl for a number of reasons. One was as an injunction against involvement with other girls' boyfriends. The function was to prevent internal eruptions of jealousy, which would be divisive to the club. The other reason related to a general level of self-respect, which demanded moderation by girl members in the number of male partners they took within the club. "Loose" women were no more tolerated within the gang than they would be among adolescent groups in general. In these situation, it was always the girl's fault, not the boy's. The consensus seemed to be that men by nature could not be expected to turn down a female who willingly offered herself to them. This arose out of their general view of a man as the "rogue male," whose sex drive was naturally strong and often threatened to lead him away from his partner. Also, at least on the girls' part, it arose from the fact that even if a male wanted to refuse a girl's advance, to do so might (if it became public) tend to imply that he was something less than fully male. A girl who behaved promiscuously would be taken aside by the other girls and warned off, as Weeza described.

If a girl slept around, would that be OK?
No. We think that she's a whore. She's a tramp. We just call her and we tell her, "You got to get down with that one. But don't let everyone go to you." You're going to play with one, play with one, but the other ones, they're like friends. We stop her. There was one in our group. I ain't going to say her name, but there was one in our group. And she was like that – we stop her. We talk to her and she listened.

Did she want a lot of attention?
Yeah. The guys, you know. She wanted to be more friendly with the guys than with the girls. But she used to put herself down because the guys used to talk about her. With us. They used to talk about her. We used to tell her, "Look, they talk about you – this and that. You think you're doing it right, but you doing it wrong. Because they're talking about you like a dog." She cool out in the end. She said, "Oh." She feel bad. But that's the way it is.

Friction arising from sexual relationships was a particularly prominent problem among the girls. Female members were expected to behave with restraint, and this could be enforced through peer pressure or, if necessary, through disciplinary measures. Often, however, friction was caused not by female members but by other neighborhood women, who came around to talk to the men and threatened the unity of the males and females in the gang. The males assumed a rather sanguine view of the situation. The girls, however, viewed outside females as a constant threat. The males naturally wanted to make new sexual conquests, and the girls strongly resented the attention they paid to nongang girls. If a girl was going to become a prospect, then she had to make it clear that her interest was as much in friendship with the girls as in sex with the boys.

What about fights with girls?

Girls? Yeah, we used. I had a fight with this girl, her name is Sugar, right? So, she was new on the block. She just came to the block, right, and you know how the guys are. I used to be going out with Chico? And the guys, they see a new girl? This guy – our guys when they see a new girl, they be checking her out, you know. We don't like that. So she came to the block, but she didn't come to make friends with us, she just came to make friends with the guys, you know? She met the guys first, then us. And we was in the clubhouse – me and Booby – I was sleeping and I seen Chico when he get up. I didn't know there was the girl in the living room because my door was closed. It was right here in the clubhouse, so Booby told me, "Weeza, Weeza, Chico's going off with this chick." And I said, "Oh yeah?" And I went to the sofa and he told me, "What? You want to go to the room?" And I say, "No. You could go to the room, I don't want to go to the room." So then we stood, you know, away. So Chico went to the room with the girl – I didn't know what they was doing, you know – he went to the room with the girl. But by that time, I don't give a fuck because we weren't living together, we were just making out and that's it.

So then one day we was in the corner and Big L was in the corner with her, and she was over there real, you know, flashy, and everything, like nothing happened. And I had that in my mind and then I was in the corner and Booby was in the corner and Booby's talking and we was laughing. And I see *her* laughing and I tell Booby, "I bet you I'll go over there and slap her in the face." I tell Booby and Booby tell me, "Go ahead, Weeza." I went over there and I almost going to hit her and Big L get in my way. He goes, "Hey, Weeza, you hit her? I'm going to hit you," and I say, "Yeah? You're going to hit me?" And I grab a stick and I hit her. And I hit her right here and I tell Big L, "Go ahead, Big L, hit me. If you're going to hit me, hit me now." And he didn't do nothing and then he took her to his house like always. To his house, right? And I stood on the corner and – nothing right? Everything was going to happen.

Then she came with a sweatshirt, her hair was all grease like she was ready to fight me. So I don't know what happened. Big L said, "OK, Weeza, she's ready for you." And I tell her, "Oh yeah? She's ready for me?" And I took my shoes off and I rolled my pants up and I said, "Oh yeah? Come on. You ready for me?" I just hit her once. The fight only last three minutes. That's it. I just hit her and I bit her over here. I was biting her and biting her and my chest, it was all out because my blouse . . . My brother stopped the fight.

When I spit, I spit only blood. That's it. They got to take her to the hospital. She used to go with them all. That was finished.

Discipline was usually harsher among the males. One of the laws of the gang was a taboo against stealing from fellow members or from the local community. This latter rule seemed to be only sporadically enforced though. Gang members told stories of robbing bar customers on a Saturday night as they stumbled out of the local bar, and no one suggested that it was in contravention of their own code of conduct. Once when Danny was leader, however, Weeza and one of the Sex Boys, Little Man, did get in trouble for a local robbery. Little Man came off considerably worse than did Weeza.

What kinds of things could get you in trouble?
Hardly the girls never do something wrong. Only the guys. Like they do it once to Little Man. Danny do it to Little Man because Little Man – you know, there was me, Little Man, Benito. It was this old lady, she had a bunch of money in her pocket and we was on the corner, you know. We seen the money and I told Little Man, "Come on, Little Man, you want to do it? Let's take the money." So this old lady we know for the long time. She was a little bit crazy. I said, "Come on, Little Man, let's do it." Then she walked to the corner and we walked to the corner, right? And then we grab her and took the money, but it was on the same block. The cops came and everything, but we did it wrong because it was on the same block, so then Danny didn't like it. He started to scream at me, but he can't do nothing because he wasn't my leader. He can't do nothing. He scream at me, "Man, Weeza." This and that and I tell him, "Hey, man, don't scream at me," and I just walk away. So he had to whoop Little Man about ten on his back. They didn't do anything to me.

There was certainly a disjunction between the expressed philosophy of the club and their actual behavior. The Sex Boys presented themselves as guardians of law and order and defenders of the local population. But their crime statistics and anecdotes suggested that on occasion it was probably their neighbors who were the victims of many of their crimes.

(Weeza)   People in the neighborhood used to give us cold cuts, beer, food.

(Popeye)   Yeah, money.

(Big L)   When we were there, we was a form of what they call themselves now – the – what the hell they call themselves? The train? These clowns – the Guardian Angels? [The Guardian Angels are a group of urban youths who patrol subways to deter crime.] Well, we were the neighborhood's Guardian Angels, that's what we were. Like, a lot of times we've caught people trying to snatch pocketbooks and believe me they didn't *walk* away. They crawled away. If they got to crawl away, they were good. There's one thing you didn't mess with it was somebody's pocketbook. Some old lady, some old man. All of us have parents. All of us have parents.

At the same time, police records indicate that in 1979 and the first six months of 1980 there were thirty-seven arrests in the gang for robbery, twenty-four arrests for auto thefts, and eighty-four arrests for assault; most were perpetrated in the neighborhood. It was an attack on a local woman that brought Weeza face-to-face with the criminal justice system for the first time.

Only I caught this lady over here – the one I told you – I had a fight right here on Linwood.

Tell me again.

You see, Chico and Chico's friend, we was passing by and me and my girlfriend, and these guys start talking bad to us. Dirty words. And we start talking back to them. We start throwing bottles to them. Then Chico chase this guy with a knife and he this lady's son – we didn't even know it was the lady's son. Then I hears Chico had the son in the car with a knife. Then his mother came to hit me with a shoe over here. She hit me with a shoe and I had a blade. And I just took it and I had it right there in the car, ready to hit her, and her son came and he pushed me, hit me. Then Benito, my friend, he came and hit him with a bat. Then we had a fight, we start throwing bottles, this and that, and the cops came. We was in a lot of shit. We was high. But we didn't start it. Yeah, we was high, but we didn't start it that day.

How did you wind up in Riker's? [Riker's Island is a New York jail where suspects awaiting trial are housed.]

She [the lady] was scared. Because she don't belong to a gang, she was scared. So she took me to court and all four went. It was me, Chico, Benito, and my girlfriend – all four. For my girlfriend and Benito, they don't got no case. Me and Chico had a case already. So me and Chico had six days – waiting for the case, waiting to go back to court. They put me bail – one thousand dollars of bail. I haven't do nothing only I caught the lady, but it wasn't much 'cos she ran. Only a little. She just had a Band-Aid.

What was Riker's like?

When they took me there, I was sent to Brooklyn, Central Booking. They put me in a bus with another girl and she was a prostitute. Then we went to Riker's Island about three o'clock in the morning. They give me a big plate of food – cold food at three o'clock in the morning – and I say, "I don't want that shit," and I didn't took it. So they told me, "Take all your jewelry, everything you got in your purse, your shoelaces," and then they passed me into another room. Take me to this room and I got to shake my head – see if I got something. All naked and they give me a towel. Into a shower and we all took a bath, then dry ourselves. They give us our clothes, took us to a room. In the room they took me, there was about six beds altogether, you know, six beds, yeah. The girls in the room, they was alright, never mess around with me, never had to fight. I was crying, crying, that was the only thing to do.

What did you do all day?

Nothing. Sometimes I went to the room and watched TV. Sometimes I go in my bed and cry. When it was time, I start thinking about my kids. Not afraid to be inside because I know I did something and I deserve to be there, and that's alright, but, you know, I was thinking about my kids. My mother ain't going to take care of them good, you know? I was thinking a lot and I was missing them. The next day I was supposed to go to court, but I didn't see the judge or nothing. And they told me, "You're going out." And I said, "Yeah? I'm going out just like that?" They told me, "Yeah." I say, "Oh ay, ay," and I told them, "Chico too?" and they told me, "Yeah, him too." And we went out. We didn't see the judge or nothing. And the bail we had? They dropped it. I don't know.

Leadership among the girls proved difficult to pin down. Several girls' names were mentioned in connection with the role of leader or "Godmother": Weeza, Booby, Maria, and Blondie. The title seemed unofficial and not very stable, but clearly there was a core of girls whose opinion carried more weight than others. Also, as time went by, it became dangerous to announce leaders' names publicly as it made them easy targets for the police and for other gangs. Booby told of a challenge to her position as Godmother that ended with an almost ritual fight, but this degree of formality seemed the exception rather than the rule.

It sounds like you were the leader.

(Weeza)   Not really. All the guys never made the other girls leader and they didn't make me leader because I didn't want to do it. But when they need something, they come to me and say, "This is not right." And I used to say, "Right. Do this, do this." And even though I was little they used to follow me. The girls, they'd ask me. Like Booby told me, "Weeza, let's do this." I tell her, "No it's not right." She didn't do it.

(Booby)   Well, they had put me as the leader, then, like, Lefty didn't want me to be the leader. They say they don't want no leaders making them a target. So then they had switched me and made this other girl the leader.

(Weeza)   Blondie?

(Booby)   Blondie or Maria.

(Weeza)   Blondie, I think, and she whipped this girl.

(Booby)   Then Blondie, then they put Maria. So then the other girls started to say, "No." They ain't going to listen to them because they don't want them as the leader. They wanted me. And I said I didn't want to be the leader no more. I said I'll hang out with them, whenever there's problems I'll go down with them, but I didn't want to be the leader no more.

So you were really leader but didn't have the name.

(Booby)   They used to call me the Godmother. I become the Godmother because I fought Isabelle. This girl named Isabelle, she started saying, "I'm going to be the Godmother." So, you know, I didn't say nothing. I wasn't even worried about it. So us guys were like practicing, you know, so she comes out of nowhere, she goes, "I'm going to be the leader," and she smacked me. So when she smacked me, I said, "Come here." I didn't tell her nothing, but I took her to the other side of the park and said, "Come here . . . You want to be the leader? I'm going to prove to you that I *am* better than you. Alright?" And right there we ended up start fighting. So the guys came, so my old man had to hold me. So she was coming towards me, but he was holding me, so the first thing that I could use was me feet, so I held myself back like that and she went right on the floor. That's how I became Godmother. Because they said, "We don't need that." Look she already messed this one up and the other one was bigger then, because I was like this – I was a toothpick.

(Weeza)   It's true.

(Booby)   She was husky. The other one. I was like a toothpick.

The clubhouse was the center of activity. Some members lived there full-time, but most used it as a surrogate daytime home. The gang had taken over one of the many abandoned buildings and had somehow brought in electricity, apparently without the utility company's knowledge since they never paid any bills. A stereo and refrigerator had been installed and mattresses moved in, providing three bedrooms. The members came in and out. During the summer they built evening fires in front of the house in old oil drums and held parties. Occasionally, members would return home to shower and change, then go back for another few days. Marijuana was in easy supply, food was stolen from supermarkets, and money was panhandled or "acquired." Memories of the earlier days, around 1976, are happy ones.

Why did girls want to get involved? Same reason as the guys?
(Weeza)   Yeah.
(Popeye)   They like to hang out. They like to party. Like to get high, have fun.
(Big L)   We throw parties. We DJ [put stereo speakers in] the streets. We buy beer. We have block parties in the summer.
(Popeye)   In the winter we stand in the pouring rain.
What was the club like? A lot of people?
(Weeza)   A lot of them. A lot of girls. It was nice. All the stores was open and we used to hang round on the corner – playing handball all night, all night getting high till the next day. We used to go home, take a bath, bunch of girls in the bathroom taking a bath, getting dressed, ironing in my mother's house, everything. Then I'd go out again, getting high again. And I used to go home, dress the kids, give them a bath, food, stay with them a little while till it's time for them to go to bed, put them in bed. My brothers used to go round the corner – I was on the corner. We used to have good times.
What was the clubhouse like?
(Weeza)   The building on the corner? It looked really nice. Had curtains, lots of posters, a private room here, a private room there. It has like a living room there. We had sofas, light, water, everything.

Whenever the good days were recalled, fighting took a prominent place. Most of the stories were about feuds with other gangs, notably their neighbors, the Montauk Chestbreakers. However, fights also occurred between members of the Sex Girls. Many involved jealousies and flirtations with male members. Usually they erupted quickly and were just as soon forgotten. It was not uncommon for even very close friends to come to blows, but the anger soon wore off and friendships were resumed.

When was the last time you had a fight?
The last time I had a fight was 1979. That was my last one. It was with this girl on the beach, Rockaway Beach.
What happened?
We all went to the beach – Cat, you know, a whole bunch of guys – we went to the beach. Popeye and everybody – Chico. We went to the beach – Booby, Willie, Carmen, everybody, all the girls. It was this misunderstanding, you know. So by that time Carmen and Booby, they was having an argument – they was enemy.
Why were they arguing?
Because of Popeye. Booby used to like Popeye and Carmen did too.
Oh yeah? And you wound up with him?
No, but I never used to like him because he was a kid back then. I used to let him pass by. That's it. To now. And we get along. We never used to be like that. So they was fighting. And they had a fight, right. Because of that Booby and Carmen at the beach. And Booby's bigger than Carmen – she messed Carmen. And I said, "Booby, why? You want to fight with me? You know she can't fight, so fight me." You know Booby. And Booby didn't tell me nothing. Then her cousin, Booby's cousin – Lilly. She came and told me, "What Weeza? You want a fight?" You know, I wasn't in the way, but she told me, "You want to fight, Weeza?" And I say, "Yeah. I want a fight. What?" And I grab her and we fighting. We roll all over the dirt and everything. I bit her finger. I bit her. She used to scream, "Ralphie, Ralphie – tell her to let me go. Tell her to let me go." Like that. Then I used to hit her and hit her in her face. All messed up with the dirt and everything. They broke it up. After she was all messed up on the floor, they broke it up. That was the last one. I didn't look for it – she was – she came and said, "Weeza, you want to fight?" Like that – it wasn't her business, it wasn't my business either. I just told Booby. She just came like that.

Within the gang there were individual loyalties to lovers that sometimes led to conflicts. Chico was often incapacitated because of drink and drugs and Weeza would defend him, escalating the conflict to involve the girls as well as the boys.

Then I had a fight with Nellie. She was one of our girls, you know. Once I used to live with Chico, right? And Nellie's old man, he hit Chico, right? Chico was all drunk, all high, he don't know how to defend himself. They went to the house and get me. Then I told Willie, "When I catch your woman, I'm going to kick her ass." Because he hit Chico, you know, I said I'm going to kick her ass. He says, "So? Go ahead. I don't care." I said, "Alright." Then she came around the other day – the next day – she came around, right? And I tell her, "What?" Because they hadn't told her. She was on the floor and she was laughing and everything. And I went to her and I tell her, "You was laughing when Chico was on the floor, right?" And she tell me, "No." I smack her and she pulled my blouse. She wanted to hit me with a bottle. And I grabbed her and my father break the fight.

The next day she came around and I was in my house eating and my brother said, "Come on, sister. You're going to the block. Nellie's waiting for you. She wants to fight you." And I say, "Oh yeah. Come on." I went over there. And I fight her and I fuck her up. She only scratched my face, that's it. I fuck her ass right all over the floor. I was punching her, hitting her. I had my boots by that time. But then, we fight about four times. The Sunday? Four times. Then the last one, she wanted to fight no more and she was so tired and so fucked up she didn't want to fight no more. Then, like that. Then she came on be friends with me.

So you were friends?

Yeah.

Weeza and Booby developed something of a reputation as being "crazy." Often the trouble they started was a way to end the boredom of another day on the same block. Being "crazy" also had certain advantages in a neighborhood like theirs. It warded off a lot of trouble because they were perceived as fearless and unpredictable, not people to be provoked. It also gained the respect of the boys. Booby and Weeza encouraged this reputation by taking money to beat people up – though they claim they never lived up to their part of the bargain.

What's it like to have that tough reputation?

(Booby) Makes me feel the same, but you can't always act tough because there's always one tougher than you. You be walking down the street, that person going to wind up kicking your ass.

(Weeza)   We ain't really tough. We don't consider ourselves tough – not me.

(Booby)   Because we try to communicate with people. But when they don't want to communicate with us, then that's their problem, not ours.

Isn't it a good thing around here? Do you get respect?

(Weeza)   We have, even the guys.

(Booby)   Um-hum. We have respect around here.

(Weeza)   We crazy. "They're crazy."

(Booby)   "They're retarded, man, I don't know. We don't have to go fight, we just have to give them anything. The gun."

(Weeza)   "Weeza is crazy. Booby? She's crazy." You don't know. Forget it. Yeah. They call us wise guys.

(Booby)   They don't call us girls. They call us wise guys.

(Weeza)   They come to us, they tell us, "We'll pay you. Let's do this." They come to us because they know we're down. So they say, "I'll pay you this."

To do what?

(Weeza)   To kick her ass or tell her something.

What did people ask you to do?

(Weeza)   Go over there and kick her ass, but we never used to do it.

You didn't?

(Booby)   We do, "Yeah, we'll go." Let them fight their own battle.

(Weeza)   They give us the money, we never used to do it.

(Booby)   And they never came back for the money. We used to take the money and get high. 'Cos they know us already. They say, "Here, I'll give you the money. Go get high, then come over here and do this." "OK." We used to get high, go hang out, then go to sleep.

(Weeza)   The next day they say, "What happened?"

(Booby)   Let them fight their own battles.

People should look out for themselves?

(Weeza)   Then *we* get locked up. We fight for them. We getting paid. But how about the cops take us? We going to be locked up and they're going to be in their house, all cooling out. And we be locked up for nothing – some stupid thing.

(Booby)   We can't go around doing those things no more. They got our pictures over there. They already know who we are and everything. Probably go, "The little short one that's always with the tall one." Oh, OK. They'll come here, go to my house. "OK. Come on. The both of yous under arrest."

Accounts of fights were mostly recalled with amusement and pride, which was all the more surprising in the light of the fact that several of the girls had seen lovers and brothers die because of their involvement with the Sex Boys. Nor were the girls immune: Weeza was shot at by rival gang members and T-Bone died because her boyfriend had been playing with a gun. Many of them lived with imminent death as a possibility and accepted with a fatalistic detachment that it might be them next.

Didn't you worry about getting hurt or killed?
(Booby) Sometimes. They always say that's one thing you cannot avoid. Death. Because if it's going to happen, it's going to happen one way or the other. You could be in bed and it could happen there. You can't hide from it. Suppose someone is looking for you. I live over here with my mother. Now they find out where I live. I wouldn't want that person to knock on the door and the person that opens it is my mother – God bless her – and she gets it. So I say, "Fuck it." I be in the streets. That way if they want me, they catch me in the streets, but don't go hurt my family.

Ralphie, Booby's brother and the first leader of the Sex Boys after they split from the Ghetto Brothers, confessed in 1973 to the murder of a rival gang member in a bar and the shooting of two bystanders, only to have the confession thrown out because he was under sixteen and had made it without his parents present. Later, however, he was jailed for the killing of a social-club owner who attempted to intervene in the robbery of his customers. It was while Ralphie was in prison that Lefty became leader in 1973. Booby, then seventeen years old, was his girlfriend. When she was thirteen, she had run away from home to live with him. In 1976, he was murdered – stabbed to death at a swimming pool by members of the Bikers.

On Christmas Eve 1980 the house in which Cat lived with his wife and two children caught fire. The fire appeared to have begun in the ground-floor hallway, spreading up the stairs to where the family was sleeping. The only survivor was Cat's wife, Marilyn. She told how Cat had pushed her out of the window to the street, telling her to catch the children he would throw down to her. She looked up from the sidewalk, badly burned but safe, and saw him turn away from the window toward the children's bedroom. The three bodies were found huddled together in an upstairs room. They had been unable to get out through the flames, which by then had engulfed the upstairs hall.

Although no formal investigation was ever made, the Sex Boys firmly believe the fire was no accident. It began not in a living room or kitchen but in a hallway, and spread so fast that they can only believe gasoline was used. A few months before, Cat and Weeza's families had both received letters threatening their lives. It was commonly believed that they had been sent by a group of white drug dealers who operated a few blocks away. The motives of this group were thought to be twofold: to avenge the death of one of their family (T-Bone), who had died because of a Sex Boy, and to prevent members of the gang from dealing drugs in their territory. Marilyn still carried disfiguring scars on both her hands and her face, despite plastic surgery. But the burns she had learned to live with more easily than the loss of her family. Cat and his children's deaths also had a devastating effect on Cat's parents as well as on his brothers (Big L and Victor) and on his adopted brother (Popeye) all of whom were in the Sex Boys.

T-Bone's death, which lay behind the threatening letters, had added fuel to the racial hostility in the area too. T-Bone was white, the only white member of the Sex Girls. Her death triggered the war with "the white guys" and seems to have confirmed, in Weeza's mind at least, the dangers of mixed-race gangs.

What if a black guy wanted to join?
The wouldn't take him.
A white boy?
They wouldn't take him. They don't like him. They hate them. They had a war with the white guys already. The white guys, their girl – T-Bone. The one that Trouble kill? They white people, you know, Italian people. Lush people. And they don't like us and the guys don't like them, none of the white men.
What happened that night?
I wasn't there. It was in my girlfriend's house. Here on Essex. They was playing cards, and Popeye and another girl was playing cards. It was really an accident – the gun was all messed up. And Trouble, he show off in front of another girl. He tried to show her [T-Bone] how he'd kill her. "I bet you, I kill you. Boom. Boom." And T-Bone say, "Come on, Trouble, don't play like that. You know. That thing could go off and kill me, don't play like that." She

say that, it went boom and get her right in the head. And she fell.
He say, "Oh, T-Bone, T-Bone." He was crazy, he went crazy. "T-
Bone, T-Bone, talk to me, talk to me." The police came and one of
them almost killed him with the gun.

Did he know there was a bullet in the gun?

He knew it was loaded. And he know the gun it was no good and
then the gun went off.

He thought it was jammed.

Yes, he think that. He didn't have it, like, on the thing [safety
catch], he had it like he was going to shoot it. I think the gun, it was
so messed up that it shoot. He was shaking. He was nervous. He
was crying. Everything.

Who else was there?

Popeye. In the girl's house. I wasn't there.

What did Popeye do?

Well. Trouble ran out and then he tell Popeye what happened
and they ran out and they was bringing T-Bone out to get her in the
car to take her to the hospital. When they was in the corner, the
cops came. And then they say that the Cheeseburgers did it. The
other guys didn't want to say that he [Trouble] did it.

How come the police came? Did they hear the shot?

No, they didn't hear the shot – somebody call them. They was
dragging T-Bone, taking her out of the apartment to the corner –
the cops came.

Did Trouble admit it?

No. Yeah. He didn't admit he *killed* her. He say he was there.
"The Cheeseburger passing by, they got her." He was so nervous
and so confused that they took him to the precinct. He was so
nervous – he was the only one. You could know it was him. But the
guys said, "Look, Trouble, you'd better tell them that you did it by
accident. And you go tell them you did it by accident, it's better.
Then you do less time. If you don't go, in the end they find out."
They gave him a little bit because he had some witnesses – Popeye
and this other girl witnesses – so they gave him only seven years.

The bullet went through her head?

Right. It went through her nose, brain, everything.

Did you know her?

Mm-hmm. She was T-Bone, she was one of our girls.

I thought she was from outside.

She was white. She was Italian. But she was one of our own girls.
She used to hang out with Puerto Ricans, with us. She used to live
on Crescent. The guys used to know her brother. Then she used to

hang out on Crescent. She decided to hang out right here on Essex. She was kind of nice. We always get along with her. We used to go over there and hang out over there. So then the guys know her, so we let her hang out with us. And she stayed with us.

What about her parents?

Her mother, she live right here. She's skinny. Suffering for her.

Were they angry with Trouble?

Yeah. Her brother came one day, he wanted to kill Popeye.

Why? Because he was there?

'Cos Popeye was there, yeah. Real angry. Her mother too. Her mother too. Her mother used to like Trouble a lot. When she find out it was him, she went crazy. She was the only daughter they had. They had two mans and she's the only girl. She had a small baby. She was about nineteen.

The relationship between the males and females in the gang was a mixture of traditional Puerto Rican male protectiveness and an attempt by the girls to be full participants in the fights. The boys seemed to take pride in their girls' toughness while still encouraging rather traditional pursuits like sewing, grooming, and child rearing. The girls lived with an uneasy ambivalence in respect to their children, wanting to protect them from the streets but unwilling to give up the streets themselves. They felt the same ambivalence about their gang membership, proud of their "heart" while also aware that it carried, to many outsiders, connotations of street life and promiscuity.

What do people think of girls in gangs? Bad?

Yeah, some of them. Some of them say it's alright. Long as they know what they're doing. Some of them say bad.

What? Sex and stuff?

Yeah. Gangs and getting high, getting locked up, fighting, like that.

While the boys made gestures to stop the girls from attending rumbles or becoming involved with the police, they seemed to have offered only token resistance to their participation.

(Weeza) We were hanging out with the Sex Boys, fighting together. We used to go to rumbles with them. To a fight? When they was locked up, we used to go to the precinct. All the girls. We cursed at all the cops and everything. And then when it was time to go to court, we used to go. A bunch of girls, a bunch of guys. All of us to court.

Was there a lot of fights?

(Weeza)   Not really, man.

Mostly the guys?

(Weeza)   The guys, yeah. But we used to go with the guys. They wouldn't allow us, but we used to follow.

Did the girls go to rumbles?

(Weeza)   Sometimes.

(Booby)   Hotheaded. [Laughs] Hotheaded. Because they used to tell us not to go. We used to go, OK? They used to get there, we were already there before them.

(Weeza)   Hiding. "Come on, let's get them with a stick or something."

(Booby)   Whatever fights they used to be in, we always used to help them out.

Does fighting make you feel unfeminine? What do the guys say?

(Booby)   They say that we try to act like men.

(Weeza)   In a way, sometimes. But we like to fight. When they go, we like to go.

They treat you like girls? They protect you?

(Booby)   They do.

(Weeza)   Sometimes there's a bunch of guys and we there and they say something nasty – one of them say, "Look, man, watch it, Weeza and Booby are here. The girls are here, you know."

(Booby)   They defend us. They respect the females.

You like that?

(Weeza)   It's alright.

If you went to a rumble, they'd tell you to stay to make sure you didn't get hurt?

(Weeza)   Uh-huh.

You like that?

(Weeza)   Yeah.

In other ways, the girls' behavior was controlled not only by the boys but by their own acceptance of the appropriate behaviors and demeanor of women. Most of the girls could cook and, from an early age, took care of younger siblings. They often organized the food and drink for parties and remained in the background when police or reporters appeared. Whenever male members were present, the girls would stay quiet and I would find myself talking with the boys. On issues such as politics, the girls never ventured an opinion that contradicted the males' position, and often they allowed the boys to explain aspects of the Sex Girls' club without

Graffiti emblazons the exterior of the Sex Boys' old clubhouse

interruption, simply nodding their agreement. When alone, however, the girls often joked about the boys as if they were overgrown
and somewhat irresponsible children.

The Sex Girls were only a pale reflection of what they had been
in the gang's heyday of 1973–78. The remaining girls – Weeza,
Booby, Marilyn, Mimi, Lilly, Blondie – were united more by family
bonds than by the gang. The gang's disintegration began when
their clubhouse burned down.

When did it begin to die out?

(Booby) When the cops burned the clubhouse down. They
couldn't stand us. They went up there and broke everybody's
things. They were the ones who burned the clubhouse.

Did they ever admit they burned the clubhouse?

(Booby) Yes. Because they got snagged. OK, like I wasn't there,
but there was one of our girls and she used to live right here on
Shepherd and Pitkin. So she went to the store. The clubhouse is

catching fire. They thought I was in there. Because they didn't know
I took my things out of there, right? I was already in my house. So the
girl is standing there and she goes, "Oh, look." So the cop say, "Look
at the clubhouse, I wonder who did that? Do you have any marshmallows?" Like you heat them up by the fire? "Do you have any
marshmallows?" He goes, "Man, they shouldn't have done that."
So Marissa said, "Anyway, I don't care – they did us a favor
because now we don't have to paint it." So then the cops came out
and said, "Ah, we should have done that a long time ago instead of
now."
   They admitted it?
   (Booby)   They got caught in a lie.

At the same time, the arrests and the deaths that they had
tolerated and even romanticized in their teenage years, began to
wear them out. The members were getting old and battle-fatigued.
Most were in their early and mid-twenties, too old to be ganging.

   *Do you think that you've grown out of the club? Do you feel too old to be
hanging out?*
   Yeah. I wouldn't say I'm too old, but I feel that I got to be
straight 'cos I got two kids, you know, and at that time I was going
crazy. I used to think about that, going crazy on the street, this and
that, so by now I'm a little bit older. I say, you know, I better cool
out for a while. And I feel I'm a little bit old to be hanging out.

Weeza believed that having children should mean the end of
hanging out, in spite of the fact that she herself did both. She was
able to do so because her mother would look after the kids overnight, and Weeza would make a point of coming home regularly to
feed and bathe them. Often, however, she saw children neglected
by girls whose life with the gang came first.

   Do you think when they have babies, the girls don't hang out so much?
   Some of them hang out with their own kids. Some of them take
them to the park and they hang out day and night. Some of them
they stay home and take care of the kids. Sometimes they want to
go out, they go out by themselves and the mother stays with the
baby. Baby-sitter or something. Sometimes they hang out and they
don't care about the baby – they hang out and getting high with the
guys, you know, some of them don't care.
   You think it's bad?

Yeah, it's bad. You hang out on the street about – you get out the house about eleven o'clock or by nine o'clock, eight o'clock that early – you're going to be on the street one o'clock, three o'clock, and that baby in a carriage – cold, hungry, crying. I think it's bad. My kids never been through that. Never. I hang out by myself. Not with them. I make my mother stay with them, go out, like that.

The Sex Boys' turf was surrounded by other gangs. At any given time, chances were that they would be feuding with one of them. Their most enduring feud was with the Montauk Chestbreakers (the "Cheeseburgers"), who were formerly a branch of the Crazy Homicides. They also had a long-lasting skirmish with the Bikers, a group from Williamsburg, several miles away. Talk of rumbles, shootings, deaths, and war were common and conducted with a bravado and humor that belied the very real dangers.

What was the worst summer that you had?
(Big L)   They were all bad.
(Popeye)   You can't really say. They were all bad. Always fighting.
With who? The cops?
(Big L)   With everybody.
(Popeye)   The niggers from Shepherd Avenue. The Montauk Cheeseburgers. The Pitkin Boys. The Elton Boys. Bikers. It was always a fight between us.
(Big L)   We're in the middle of it all. We have all the clubs around us.
(Weeza)   We're number one here.
(Big L)   That's it.
So if they can take you?
(Big L)   But, see, they can't take us. That's it. They can't take us. You see, the only way you could kill, really demolish, Sex Boys is – the only way is like clip them one by one and that's like very rare because once you kill a boy, that's going to be a whole clique on to you then.
It's going to come down?
(Big L)   Yes. It's going to come down to a showdown. And that's what they're asking for and that's what they eventually will get. A showdown.
Who were the biggest enemies you had?
(Big L)   We don't consider anyone the biggest enemy. The biggest enemies that are out there? We consider the biggest enemies

to us is us. They ain't no better than us. That's it, that's the way we feel. And we don't go out there looking for static, we do what we have to do. We had a big thing with the Bikers, right? We'd always go into their neighborhood and do our thing. But they never come down here.

(Weeza) No, never.

(Big L) And the Bikers are supposed to be the baddest. They consider the Bikers the baddest.

(Popeye) Out there on the South Side.

(Big L) They consider them the baddest, but how bad are you?

They wouldn't come here?

(Big L) No.

(Popeye) But really all of them are a bunch of glue sniffers. They all sniff glue – all of them.

(Weeza) Get souped up.

(Big L) Rape old ladies. Rape young girls. Kick people out of their homes. Steal. Vandalize the whole neighborhood. Burn cars and all this. And they're bad. That's why they consider them bad. They're bad.

How bad are they? When it comes down to it.

(Popeye) They ain't really number one.

(Big L) Every time we go to court for one of the guys, we find two or three of them – fire them up.

You've been going for a long time – seven years, eight years? What was the nearest it ever came to ending?

(Big L) For us?

(Popeye) I don't think it's ever come that near.

(Big L) We've gotten locked up all together. Really. Incarcerated us, but we've always managed to get out. Get away. When he was a kid and the Tomahawks came over here Pitkin Avenue and Essex Street and tried to shoot it out with us? I mean there were a *lot* of them.

How many?

(Big L) [Whistles] I mean, don't shoot till you see the whites of their eyes. Here you are, I mean, a bunch of black people shooting at you and we just chased them right back where they came from. A lot of poeple have tried. A lot of people have come out here. See, they say, they say to themselves, "Well look there's only about five of them hanging out." But see, don't let something happen, because then you have five hundred. The five will turn out to be five hundred. And they just keep going on and on and on.

They had guns?

(Big L)   Oh man, guns, shotguns, cocktails.
(Popeye)   Bottles.
(Big L)   Bats, everything.
(Popeye)   Garbage cans.
(Big L)   Lot of gasoline.
(Weeza)   Rifles.
(Big L)   We made the Iranians rich!
Was anybody really hurt?
(Big L)   A lot of people got hurt. Both sides. Stabbed. Cracked head. Broken arm, ribs. A lot of people got hurt. Weeza was out there, throwing bricks, bottles.
Did they have girls with them?
(Big L)   The Tomahawks had girls, but they didn't have that many girls. There wasn't that many. Not like us. Like when they came out here to start some shit with us and they saw the girls out there, they said, "There's more girls than guys, what the hell is this, man?" You know?
How many people have gotten hurt?
(Popeye)   A lot of the guys have got hurt. Shot.
(Big L)   Trouble? He got shot once.
(Popeye)   Little Man got shot.
(Big L)   Willie, right?
(Popeye)   Willie got shot.
(Big L)   Little Man.
(Popeye)   Little Man got shot.
(Big L)   Ralphie.
(Popeye)   Ralphie got shot. Chico got shot.
(Big L)   Willie got shot in the neck.
(Popeye)   Willie got shot in the neck.
You been lucky, you two?
(Popeye)   I never got shot.
You neither?
(Big L)   No.

Attempting to construct a chronology of the Sex Boys' gang feuds was an overwhelming task. Stories were told and retold, each time with different dates and often with different protagonists. Information from the Gang Intelligence Unit helped to structure some of the events, but the police themselves had only scattered information furnished by rival gangs and neighbors, which may not have been accurate. There were also events of which the police knew nothing. Take, for example, Weeza's almost incomprehensible account of a homicide committed by one of the Sex Boys on a group of blacks (*morenos*) from a nearby block.

Danny hate black people. He hate black people because of one of the morenos. So he got locked up, but he's crazy now. He hung himself. Crazy. He was in a rumble with this moreno one day. Afro sent Chico to the store. They're always passing by, never do nothing. So one day Chico went to the store about twelve o'clock over here? Over here it's closed, but over there it's open. So he went over there to the store and a moreno shot him. He got it over here.
How come they shot him?
They know he was from the Sex Boys. They need a fight with them – Chico's brother killed one of them.
How did it begin?
Because he went on our boys. They hit him – he's a Negro. They hit him. So then all the guys went over there and the morenos start arguing and they start going mad. They got to start fighting with them, you know. They start fighting. They start shooting. Guy shoots them – they shoot Little Man, they shoot Ralphie.
Did they come by in cars?
No, they wait till we pass their block, then they shoot.
So Danny went down and shot one of them?
Yeah. He killed him. No, they don't like us.
Is that why Danny got locked up?
Yeah . . . They got Danny in jail, beat him up, they hit him and he hanged himself.
The cops?
No. Some other clique. They know he's a Sex Boy. He hanged himself.

By matching this and other accounts with police data, the story of the escalation that resulted in Danny's admission to Kings County Hospital appeared to be this: A group of blacks were selling marijuana on a nearby block. Four members of the Sex Boys bought some but felt they had gotten a "bum deal." There was an argument and a fight, but some other blacks who were passing by intervened and drove the Sex Boys away. The Sex Boys returned half an hour later and the blacks were waiting for them with guns. The police report only one injury in this fight, but the Sex Boys maintain that Little Man and Ralphie were both injured. The next night, four of the Sex Boys stole a van and drove back to the apartment where they had purchased the marijuana. They threw kerosene bombs in the building, shouting "Fire!" The blacks ran from the building and one was killed and another badly injured as the Sex Boys opened fire on them. Eyewitnesses could only identify one of the Sex Boys – Danny – who was sent to Riker's Island detention facility to await trial. While in jail, he was threatened by a rival gang that was aware that he was the Sex Boys' leader. He tried to hang himself but was cut down. He did, however, suffer brain damage which affected his memory. When I was with the gang, he was still in the hospital and only sporadically recognized his friends. His last memory was of Lefty's death. He did not recollect any of the events that had led to his incarceration. Meanwhile, Chico (who had strong ties to the black community) was shot by the blacks as he was walking through their territory on his way to a late-night store.

When Weeza and Booby and Cuiso, a Sex Boys member, talked about the Chestbreakers, they attributed almost every gang "deviance" to them. They were accused of using guns against unarmed opponents, of using "hit" tactics over fair fights, of shooting girl members, of being punks and drug addicts, and of having girl members who would not fight and only wanted sex.

What are the Cheeseburger girls like?
(Booby)   Tramps. All they think is about screwing. It's true. It's true, shit.
(Weeza)   They don't fight. They don't go rumble with the guys. Nothing.
(Booby)   Sometimes they lie. "Oh yeah, the Sex Boys did this." When you come to see – you just hanging out. You could have peace and they come and they take a cap at you.
Are they tough?
(Weeza)   They're punks. They're a bunch of punks. Cuiso, right? The Cheeseburgers are a bunch of punks. They're not tough?
(Booby)   They're a bunch of dope fiends. The guys are a bunch of dope fiends.
(Weeza)   Ivan he's supposed to be the leader. He's not tough. He's the one wants to make peace.
(Cuiso)   I know *I* ain't got peace with *them*, they sent me to the hospital not so long ago. I think they were involved in it too.
What happened?
(Cuiso)   Fifteen guys they jumped me.
(Weeza)   He got a mark.
(Cuiso)   I was in hospital about two weeks.
What did they do?
(Cuiso)   They beat me down with a bat. It was supposed to

be the Elton Boys, but I think the Cheeseburgers was down with it too. They both together, you know.

Girls were often accused of precipitating gang feuds by getting involved with guys from other clubs. In fact, there were quite rigorous taboos on a girl becoming involved with a male from a rival club. The same did not hold true for the boys, and their frequent involvement with outside girls not only affronted the collective pride of the Sex Girls, but also represented a threat to the security of the gang.

(Booby) We would fight for our respect. Because those girls would know that the dude was going out with us, they would come out like they was better than us. Like, OK, they put their shit in the guy's face. The guy ain't going to be dumb – he's going to take it, you know. So then after that, we hear about it. Because they be thinking that we sleeping and these guys talk so loud that they wake us up and they think that we sleeping. We got our eyes closed, listening to everything. But meanwhile, they're trying to find out how the hell did *we* find out. And, of course, they don't know it was them. They was the one who told us. Because, right – they talk, whatever they do to anybody out there. "Oh yeah, I got this girl. This girl just put it right there in my face, so I took it."

On some occasions, the girls who slept with Sex Boys had been sent from other clubs as spies. When T-Bone was shot, the police believed she had been shot as a spy, since she had a baby by one of the Chestbreakers and was also from the family of some drug dealers who were at war with the Sex Boys. The Sex Boys totally rejected this idea. And certainly, had they wanted to kill T-Bone, it was most unlikely that they would have done it in one of their own apartments.

These sexual betrayals by the male members perpetuated feuds between the female factions of various gangs. In early 1981, a peace treaty had been effected by the Gang Intelligence Unit between the Sex Boys and the Chestbreakers. The Sex Girls, however, refused to be part of it and continued their hostility toward all female Chestbreakers.

What are the Chestbreaker girls like?
What are they like? I don't know, I never heard they went to rumble with the guys. I never heard nothing like that. They like to

be in disco, dance, party, getting high. Maybe some of them they dress outlaw because they feel we going to let them go to rumble – nothing.

Did you take weapons to the rumble?

Knives, stick. I never used a knife. I never stick nobody.

Did you ever fight with other clubs?

Really other clubs with girls? Never because the Montauk Cheeseburgers, the TB Outlaw [another gang], all the girls, they never want to come over here fight with us. Maybe they talk shit behind our back, but they never tell us nothing, you know? And they never come to our block, look for trouble. We walk all over East New York – everywhere. We go everywhere. Manhattan everywhere. Bus, in cars, in trains, walking, you know. And they see us, but they never tell us nothing. We just pass by and we never tell them nothing either because we're not troublemakers, you know? And they say something, we go back, but they never tell us nothing. Like that really.

What about the guys?

When they used to go rumble, we'd go and the guys used to say, "No, you stay here, you're girls. No girls over there, only guys." And we say, "We don't care. We want to go." We grab a stick or knife or something, we had a chance to hit them with. But we never had a chance because they used to defend us, but sometimes we used to do it. We used to hit over here on the block. They used to fight a lot. But they used to have fights far away, they never want to take us. Like a lot of times in the summer, we used to be on the corner and the Cheeseburgers used to be hanging out and getting high and drunk. Drinking and everything. And the Cheeseburgers used to pass by and shoot at us. You know, take a shot and everything. In cars. And we used to say, "Motherfuckers. Come back." We used to tell them and the girls. One day they shoot Carmen and Booby – yeah. One day they shoot them – one of the Cheeseburger gang. But they always say they're going to get Booby and Carmen and everything. They never did, so now they got peace. But we got no peace with that clique – the girls. Only guys. We don't talk to none of the girls.

Some fights were begun by the girls and involved only females, although the Sex Boys went along in case the opposing males became involved. One such fight began when a single Sex Girl was surrounded by four black girls and beaten. When the Sex Girls found out, they went armed with bats to retaliate, but the black girls had withdrawn into a house and refused to come out.

Because, you see these morenas hit one of our girls. They hit her. About four morenas hit her. Then one of the girls come over here and tell us. All the girls went over there with bats and everything. And then the Sex Boys in the back. Just in case men jump in, they was going to jump in too. We went over there and we talked. They didn't want to come down, only to the window. "All you mother-fuckers, you Puerto Ricans," this and that, "you're full of shit." And we used to tell them, "Come down, come down and you'll see – you'll see we full of shit. We're going to kick your ass." We used to tell them, but they never wanted to come down. Like that, start everything. Something like that.

Among the gang's enemies were the "white boys," the drug dealers from Crescent to whom T-Bone was related. One summer, they had come to the clubhouse in a car, shooting at any Sex Boy or Girl they saw. Booby was on the street and as Weeza yelled out the window to warn her, they shot up at Weeza, narrowly missing her head. When Booby told the story, she said that they "never came back." The Sex Boys now believe that they did return twice. Once to kill Cat and his family. And once to kill Popeye.

(Weeza)   Remember I was in the front window to this side of the clubhouse like this, right? It was in the summer. And then this white dude passed in a Cadillac – they shot a shotgun. My afro went swoosh. I went, "Oh shit. They're shooting. They're shooting."

(Booby)   I went to buy a bottle. I'm drunk already – drunk to my face – and I'm going to buy a bottle. I'm high, I'm not suspecting nothing. She goes, "Booby, watch it." They had a gun pointing out at me. So when she had said that, they seen her head. So they confused her with Afro, her brother. Because she looked like this [wearing a strapless top]. So they probably thought she had no shirt, so it had to be a dude. So they left me alone. So when they went, they shot at her.

(Weeza)   If he had a little bit more, he would have got me.

(Booby)   Lucky that she saw him quick.

(Weeza)   I say, "Oh shit, Danny, they're shooting." Danny say, "Go down, Weeza – stay down." And he went out and got the rifle and he went to the roof.

Who were they?

(Booby)   White boys.

What club?

(Booby)   They wasn't in a club. Something that the guys had problems with them. Cat fought one. So that's what happened. So the white dude went and got some more people. They had us like that for two or three weeks.

(Weeza)   Angry, angry.

(Booby)   Until her brother Afro shot the car. Shot the car. Ever since they never came back.

Popeye

When I left Weeza's apartment the night of Friday, February 20, with Popeye still not returned, I had promised to come back the next day. I did return and, as I turned the corner into Weeza's street, I saw her hanging out of her apartment window, gazing down. When she saw me, she shook her head – no Popeye.

I found the apartment in a terrible mess. The used plates from last night's dinner were still piled in the sink, unwashed. On the stove were the chicken and French fries she had cooked for Popeye. She refused to throw them out, feeling superstitiously that if she did, he would not come home. Weeza handed me a piece of paper with some telephone numbers written on it. One was a hospital, the other, criminal court in Manhattan. I didn't know where she had gotten the numbers – perhaps from Big L or Afro, or maybe from the police precinct house. She pulled on a red plastic jacket and we walked to the corner store. I called the hospital first, realizing, when a receptionist in the casualty department asked me, that I didn't even know Popeye's real name. Weeza told me. They had no record of anyone with that name being admitted in the last twenty-four hours. Next I called the Manhattan Criminal Court, which also had no record of him. They told me to try Central Booking, where he would have been taken after an arrest and before indict-ment. I called; they had no listing of him. After an hour of standing and worrying with Weeza, who was on the edge of tears, I sug-gested we go to the police and report him missing. Weeza was not hopeful that they would even listen.

At the precinct, I stepped forward with Weeza behind me and explained that her husband was missing. I knew they weren't legally married, but I felt that the police might take it more seriously if I implied they were. Without asking for any further information, the officer said with open hostility, "What do you want me to do?" I explained Popeye had been gone for twenty-four hours, that he had left the house expecting to be out for only an hour or so, and that he was not the sort of person who regularly disappeared without notice. Finally, the officer asked Popeye's age. I told him he was nineteen. He shrugged his shoulders and announced that he was an adult and there was nothing the police could do. If he had been a minor or in ill health, they could have put out a call. He said that he would try to see what could be done and turned away to use the phone. He turned back and, in apparent response to a question from the person on the other end of the phone, asked if he had a beard. We nodded, yes. Did he have a tattoo of snakes on him? Weeza shook her head. He put down the phone and announced that Popeye was not in the morgue at least. He told us to give it another twenty-four hours and to come back if nothing had happened. Weeza looked shaky and numb. We walked back to the apartment.

Weeza persuaded her father to help us look for Popeye. We drove off with Weeza's father careening through the pockmarked streets, the car's suspension grating and banging. When we approached a dark towering apartment building on the left at an intersection, her father halted the car squarely in the middle of the road. A crowd of guys were standing outside the building, some white and some Hispanic. This was the drug-dealing corner. Her father motioned one of them over. Dodging the traffic and ignoring the beeping of horns from the cars stuck behind us, he came over. They spoke in Spanish, but I understood that her father was asking if the guy knew Popeye. He replied yes and described him. Had he seen him recently? No, no, not for a week or so. Weeza leaned over and said that if he saw Popeye, tell him to come home at once. The guy nodded.

We walked around to Big L's house. He and his wife lived in the basement, his parents on the first floor, and his brother and his wife on the second. Because Popeye had lived with them for so long, they shared Weeza's silent worry. Big L was the most cheerful, insisting that the cops had got him somewhere and recounting stories of the gang's arrests and the unreasonableness of the police. His main concern was whether or not the police had beaten him up.

On Monday night the telephone rang. It was Officer John Galea to tell me that Popeye's body had been found on a patch of abandoned land by Rockaway Beach in Queens. In the local paper that morning there had been a short paragraph stating that the body of a young man had been found wearing jeans and a white ski jacket (the one Weeza had bought him for his birthday). At that time the police had not been able to ascertain the man's identity. Now they knew it was Popeye.

He was found with his hands and feet tied together behind his back. He had been badly beaten, but the actual cause of death seemed to be a deep wound in the back of the neck caused by an axe or similar weapon. Weeza referred often to "they" and "those people" but did not specify exactly who was responsible. She talked of Cat and of the people who had said they would kill all the Sex Boys. They had sent a letter to her father saying his family would all die. She had showed the note to a police officer. It was much later that I saw it and copied it. It was addressed to her father and on the top lefthand side, where the return address should have been, it gave a plot number followed by Evergreen Cemetery, Brooklyn, N.Y. The plot number was that of T-Bone's grave.

It's about time we have decided to deal directly with you. We know that Popeye is hiding in your home. To be Exact in the front Room. We also know that he is living with your daughter.

We know where your Son Afro, his wife and baby live also.

We are AWARE that you have been robbing, stealing from people around Pitkin Ave.

We know that the Sex Boys ARE bring ALL stolen good into your house. We know that you have guns in your house Also.

We have just signed a contract to get rid of ALL of you.

The time will not be very long now before we take Action.

We are Going to blind your wife, daughter, And AFRO's wife.

WE ARE Going to KILL You, Popeye and AFRO. We ALSO know where some of the other boys LIVE. We SWEAR in front of A CROSS that we WILL get even with You.

Then will get EVEN with Ralphie Also Ralphie's mother.

Mama Mia.

This is Warning.

The note had been received several months before and, after a few days of nervousness, seemed to have been forgotten. Only Big L had said the only way to get rid of the Sex Boys was one by one.

When we arrived at the funeral home, there were at least forty people there; from the gang I recognized Afro, Big L, Willie, Victor, Carmen, Johnny, Booby, Maria, Marilyn, and several others whose names I did not know. All of Popeye's adopted family was there, and his own family had come too. They were sitting apart from the others: his father and stepmother, his brother and his brother's wife. There was a clear separation, a quiet hostility between them and the others present. The front of the room was packed with flowers. At the head of the casket was a huge Puerto Rican flag about two feet by four feet and made entirely of flowers which the gang members had bought. People stepped forward from time to time to look at Popeye, closing their eyes and crossing themselves. Weeza kissed him over and over again, touching his hands and kneeling next to him as if she were trying to protect him.

Someone said they were about to close the casket. One by one, each person stepped forward to say goodbye. Weeza did not move. As the last people turned away, Weeza began to scream wildly. Her father and Afro helped her up. She would not go, and the screaming grew worse. They grabbed her arm, and she pushed them away. They dragged her away bodily with brute force and she was kicking, scratching, and screaming. Big L told them to hurry and take her to the bathroom, away from the altar. They carried her out, and the lid was quickly closed.

At the church, the priest blessed the coffin and all the mourners at the doorway. We then sat down inside. The service was in Spanish, and everyone present murmured the responses. Only the gang members and I needed to follow the service from the book.

The chain of cars in the funeral procession moved off. We were to drive to the the cemetery by way of the Sex Boys' turf. At traffic lights, Afro jumped out and ran up the line of cars, giving instructions to each of the drivers as to what to do as we came to Essex Street. The procession moved slowly. The sun was shining from a clear blue sky on the empty lots, the burned-out building shells, the barricaded corner stores. We turned into Essex Street – Sex Street – the place where Popeye had lived most of his life. One by one, each car sounded its horn as it turned the corner. The neighbors stood in front of their houses, silent, watching, some with their heads bowed. There was a deafening cacophony of horns. We moved slowly through Popeye's turf, noisy, belligerent. We were approaching Weeza's house. Her children stood in front of the door, held back by her mother, their fingers in their ears, laughing. As the cars drew closer, they stopped smiling and gazed confusedly at the serious grownups, unable to comprehend what was happening. We turned off the street. One by one, the horns died away.

Popeye's plot at Cypress Hills Cemetery was a few yards away from that of Cat and his children. All the gravestones had Spanish names. Before the coffin was lowered down, Afro opened a can of Budweiser and poured it over the casket. Big L lit a joint and passed it around. We all took a little, then threw it into the grave for Popeye. Weeza was still sobbing, choking, and she was taken back to sit in a car.

A few weeks before, Popeye had worked in this cemetery, digging graves. It was a temporary job. We had talked about it and about death. When I returned home, I found the tape and played it. This is what he said.

What do you think happens to you after you're dead?
(Popeye)   I don't know, I never been there. [Laughs]
Do you believe you go to heaven or hell or something?
I don't know.
I don't want to think about hell and things like that. I'd like to think you're just asleep.
So maybe you go to another world – who knows? You never know.
I don't think I want to go to another world.
Maybe before you was born and came into this world, maybe you was living in another world and you died and you came into this world. You never know. When you die here, you go into another world. Could you like that. Nobody knows.

To date, no one has been charged with Popeye's murder. There is considerable speculation among the Sex Boys as to what happened. One member of the gang came under particular suspicion. A few of the members had been dealing drugs on the corner where T-Bone's family also dealt. It was rumored that a member of the gang had gotten into debt and owed them money for a buy he had made. He could not pay. It was suggested that his life had been threatened, but that he had been given a way out. I expected that the suspected member would be hunted by the gang. He was not. He attended the funeral. No one knew for sure if he was involved, and they decided to leave it to the police. Although he was questioned by the gang, he was not harmed. I also expected that the gang would retaliate against the men they suspected were responsible. They did not. They talked much about it, made angry threats, cursed them.

Weeza stayed in the empty building seven days, each night praying for Popeye's soul, as is customary in Puerto Rico. She then moved in with her sister for a few weeks. Finally, she found an apartment in New Jersey and moved with her children away from the area.

Chapter 5

Sun-Africa and the Five Percent Nation

The Five Percent Nation considers itself a religious and cultural movement directed toward young blacks, aiming to teach them the correct ways of Islamic life. Its name derives from the members' belief that 10 percent of humanity controls and exploits 85 percent of the poor and uninformed; the remaining 5 percent are those "civilized people also known as muslims and muslims' sons," whose task is to educate fellow blacks in their true religion.

However, as far as the New York City Police Department is concerned, the Five Percenters constitute a gang. They were first recognized in 1976 as an alliance of already existing street gangs who had adopted the Nation of Islam's teaching. By 1979, police statistics referred to them as a single youth gang, the Five Percenters. They had been in existence for at least a decade by then. The first public awareness of them came in 1964, when a white Jewish shopkeeper and his wife were robbed and murdered in their store in Harlem. A group of men identified as Five Percenters were arrested and charged with the crime. In 1969, information obtained by the police department led to the arrest of many members. Most received long prison sentences, and for several years little was heard of them on the streets. They were actively recruiting members in prison though, according to police sources. One congressional report on conditions in prisons suggested they had been active in the 1971 Attica prison riot.

By 1975, the New York City police had become aware of a resurgence of Five Percenters on the streets. Members of the Nation were allegedly canvassing street gang members to join the movement. In Brooklyn, they recruited the Tomahawks (with an estimated membership of 300), the Fugitives (100 members), the Ministers (fifty members), and the Together Brothers (forty members). Members of these groups were arrested 141 times in

The hangout corner of the Five Percenters, situated close by a pool hall and a "numbers" operation

1976 and were responsible for 18 percent of Brooklyn gang arrests. By 1978, that number had grown to 418 arrests or 28 percent of all gang member arrests for that year. In 1976, the *Amsterdam News*, a Harlem-based newspaper, ran the following story after a killing attributed to the Five Percenters:

> In an *Amsterdam News* interview, Hamien [a member of the Five Percenters] said that the Five Percenters are a non-violent group now engaged in social work. That, he declared, consists of working with teenagers in Brooklyn and other boroughs.
>
> "We want to make sure kids stay in school and learn. Without an education they've lost.
>
> "We're not a youth gang as many are led to believe. The hope of our race lies in our young acquiring brains and wisdom, for without that they can't hope to eradicate the injustices we face daily."
>
> Admitting that the three alleged killers were members of the group, whose size he refuses to estimate, he said: "We're not responsible for their actions and take the position that if a man does wrong he must pay for sins. They must pay the penalty."
>
> Most new members, he said, are recruited in junior and senior high schools and in Riker's Island prison. The text of their teachings are from the Islamic Koran bible and lessons used by the Black Muslims in their schools.
>
> But from another source, Maliki al-Hadi, it was learned that an internal struggle is raging within the organization. As it now stands, he explained, no leader exists within the Five Percenters as each member is responsible to no one for his actions or judgments.

As late as 1982, newspapers in New York were "rediscovering" the Five Percenters, who were believed to have been involved in a spate of robberies in Queens and other violent crimes throughout the city. They were, at that time, reported to be engaged in a massive recruitment effort in the schools, and there were accusations that students were being terrorized into joining.

When I spoke with Sun-Africa, she was sixteen years old. At fifteen, she had rejected the name she was given at birth (her "government name"), had taken on Sun-Africa and had joined the Five Percenters in Brooklyn. The movement is also active in several other boroughs of the city and on Long Island. Unlike other gangs, the Five Percenters were growing in numbers and in arrests between 1976 and 1979 and were becoming particularly involved in serious or index crimes. Figures from the precincts that covered the territory of Sun-Africa's group show that in 1979, 113 arrests of Five Percenters were made, chiefly for robbery (33 percent), criminal possession of a dangerous weapon (15 percent), auto theft (10 percent), and burglary (9 percent). In that year, there were five arrests for attempted murder and one for murder.

Sun-Africa's Biography

Sun-Africa's family, like those of many of her friends, originally came from Panama. Sun-Africa's mother came to New York first, followed by her father. Her older sister Lila remembers the most about their background because she remained in Panama as a young child, living with her great-grandmother on her mother's side. She was four and in New York when Sun-Africa was born in 1965.

Lila and Sun-Africa had a very close relationship from the beginning. It was particularly close because Lila looked after Sun-Africa after their parents' marriage broke up, their father left home, and their mother began to work full-time. They also have a half brother, Natural, who lives nearby with his mother and their father subsequently had five sons by two other women, all of whom live in the South. But for all intents and purposes, Sun-Africa's basic family unit has been herself, Lila, and their mother. Her grandmother lives nearby and visits often.

So let's go right back to the beginning. Where were you born? Were you born in the States?

I was born in Brooklyn, and my family was born in Panama,

right? That's what makes me be so good in a way too, 'cos you know how people are real, real, extremely bad? I was never really like that. I was bad, like I went to a home before and, I mean, I ran away from home a lot of times, you know. It's like my mother, you know? What I mean, I have her in me as far as "Man, you can't go that far. You know you gotta stand strong. You know you gotta go to school and get a diploma, because that's what you need." You know that I'm bad, but I wouldn't go stupid, you know what I mean? I wouldn't really go stupid and do something and I don't care. I'm just good at heart. I've always been, ever since I was young, and I get it from my sister too you could say. My sister brung me up.

How old is she?

She's nineteen. She'll be twenty in September. We were born in the same month, same sign – Libra. That's why we get along jointly [extremely well]. You know, any problem I have, I can come to my sister and tell her, you know? Just as far as she could tell me too. You could say she brung me up, she used to cook for me, everything. I mean, wow, it got so much that I used to call her Mummy, and we are four years apart.

Sun-Africa recognized the strain of her mother's life, in spite of day-to-day quarrels with her, and admired the way she brought up the two girls.

I want to know how you liked growing up and stuff. You moved here when you were eleven. Was your father living with you then?

I think my father left when I was about, I was about five maybe. Maybe I was a little older than that – yeah, I was about five.

So your mother really brought you both up pretty much on her own?

Yeah, with my sister's help.

She must be a pretty strong person.

She is. And I'd give it to her. Because she made it on her own two feet, and she made her daughters, you know? I got a lot of proper ways about me, you know, that people don't have. Like people out on the street that don't got too many manners and stuff? Well I always have manners. You know what I mean? Even though I like to be bad like the bad crowd too, but I still have manners.

When she was a preschooler, Sun-Africa spent her days with a paid baby-sitter, while her mother worked. Sun-Africa's early memories revolve around events at her sitter's house. Most of these memories are bad ones, of being beaten or involved in fights. They have a common theme of loss and isolation, perhaps not unusual for a four-year-old.

When Sun-Africa began school, apart from normal anxiety over separation from her mother, she performed well in order to gain her teacher's attention. Her older sister remained a very important figure, outside of the classroom, protecting her but also acting as a model for "grownup" behavior, like having boyfriends and smoking reefer.

When I went to school, right, it was nice and everything, but you know it was sad for me to leave my mother. It was real sad for me to leave my mother.
Were you frightened?
No. I started to like it. I started to like school and then what happened? I think when I was – how old was I? My first boyfriend, I'm trying to think. I think me and Steven was about . . . we had to be about seven, maybe eight.
What was Steven like?
He was the joint [the best]. He used to buy me little rings from the bubble-gum machine. For real. He used to get me nice stuff. Yup. I was tongue kissing when I was young. You tongue kiss, right?
Yeah. But five, that's so young.
A girl tried to teach me how to tongue kiss. I told her fat stinky ass off. Her name was Sherell. I was about seven – in the second grade, for real. And she started showing me how to kiss. Spending the night over my house. She used to pee the bed. Yup. She used to pee the damn bed.
You started smoking reefer at seven or eight?
Yeah. I was eight.
Can you remember the first time?
My sister and them was doing it and I was asking for some, so they started blowing it in my face, right? And I was letting it come through my nose. Every time they blow, I go [inhales deeply]. Then I hold it in. Then I let it go. Then when I let it go, I be high, and for a long time we used to do it that way. Then I just started smoking it myself.
Did you like it?
I loved it. I loved it.
Some people feel sick at first.
I loved it. Cigarettes got me dizzy one time. [Laughs] Me and this girl named Oz, she had a baby when she was twelve years old.

Wow.

She was my best friend too. She was my best friend from about nine to ten, or eight to ten. You know, right there. And the guys used to feel her up and stuff. And this one time she had got down with this dude named . . . When I say "got down" you know what I mean, right? I means she had sex with him, right? And this dude named Lee – he fucked her.

I bet her mother went crazy.

Her mother burned her out with a cigarette.

She got pregnant that young?

Twelve. She had the baby when she was twelve.

You grew up real fast.

But in that project [apartment building] you had to be tough 'cos they would eat you for breakfast, lunch, and dinner. They'd have you. I was a bully, 'cos being I was there young, I got to know the ways. Being as I used to hang out with these older people like my sister.

She explained about sex?

When I was little, my sister used to bug me out.

Why?

She used to do a lot of stuff with me. She used to take me places and stuff.

You must have learned a lot from her.

Hell, yes.

Maybe that's why you grew up so quick.

Of course, that's why. Of course.

By the age of ten, when she transferred to a new school, Sun-Africa had begun to rebel. Certainly, a year spent mistakenly assigned to a class designed for Spanish-speaking children did nothing to advance her education, although most of her later school reports suggest she was a bright student but lacking in application. She shared enough time with her older sister to learn very early about the delights of "goofing off," and she was already realizing that she could block communication between the school and her mother by forging notes. After one year, she changed schools again. Briefly, she began to enjoy school, because she had two excellent teachers. One in particular made a deep impression on her and is responsible for her present interest in becoming a teacher herself. When that teacher left the school, however, things began to go wrong. Sun-Africa became disruptive in class, was often involved in fights and was preoccupied with boys.

I don't hardly get along with no teacher. I just get in there and do what I got to do. Claudette and me used to go out to lunch. And when we come back, we be all late and stuff. Mr. Chasworth be breaking, "Where's our late passes?" and stuff. He used to get me sick. Always asking for a late pass. "Where's your late pass? You got to get a late pass." And then we have to get one. Me and Claudette we used to try to get high and stuff and we used to buy reefer and stuff. And then we had to smoke the seeds when we ain't got no more. We used to be desperate, boy. Smoking seeds!

When Sun-Africa was eleven, the family moved to the area in which they now live, in southeast Brooklyn. Sun-Africa began junior high school in a new neighborhood. Lila was by now sixteen and had left school. Sun-Africa suddenly found herself having to go it alone, with no older sister to protect her. Her precocious interest in sex continued, but life became harder as she had to learn, quite literally, to fight her own battles. At junior high, she met a girl named Mimi – two years older than herself – who seemed to fill the void her sister had left. Other girls began to hang around with the two of them, and the group came to be called the Puma Crew, because of their habit of wearing Puma sneakers and clothes. Sun-Africa's agemates resented her association with these older girls and she was excluded from the day-to-day social life in class. She was preoccupied with clothing and appearance. Her references to clothes are part of the self-definition of the Puma Crew, whose members aimed, by dress and manner, to be "too cool."

When did all the trouble start?
When I moved over here and I met up with Mimi, right? We wasn't the Puma Crew yet, but we used to dress alike and we used to go to parties and stuff. I mean they used to have me coming in this house one o'clock, two o'clock. That's kind of bad for an eleven-year-old. I'd be coming in, man, and I used to wear lipstick and everything. Like I started smoking cigarettes when I was about, I'd say I was about twelve and a half going on thirteen and I was smoking reefer ever since I was about nine. I was always getting high, I was a little pothead.
Tell me about meeting Mimi.
This girl named Damaris [who lived across the sreet] and me was walking. And we was behind Damaris's brother and Mimi was smoking reefer. She asked me where I come from. I told her something about her jacket was nice, right? And she said some-

thing, and me and her started hanging out from that day on.

So the Puma Crew started with you and Mimi?

No. Me, Mimi, Angie, and Tammy – not too much Tammy – but me, Mimi, Angie. Who else? Julie. Who else? Big mouth – Chris. Who else – Crystal. Then we all got together. Then it was me, Mimi, Crystal, Angie, and Julie. Who else? Alright – Shatasia, she live upstairs. Me, Tania, the whole crew. We used to get fucked up because I was bad. I used to stick with Mimi. Mimi and them was older than me, and I used to go to jams in the park and come back to school and tell everybody about the jam that I went to. That's why a lot of people in school, they never used to like me 'cos Mimi used to let me hold her clothes.

Anyway, we used to have fun. We used to have fun. Mimi used to come to my school with all the big crew from high school and stuff and they used to come to the seventh grade and stuff. So after I knew them that's when me and her used to go on the bikes and stuff. We used to talk to a lot of dudes, boy. And I was real young. And I used to talk to almost every dude I see, you know. Then after that, we used to get high. Me, her, and Crystal. That's when nickel bags used to roll twelve joints. Nickel bags used to roll twelve skinny joints. And we used to get fucked up. Smoke them joints and stuff, go to the park. They used to play music, and that's when Little Coke was out here, Cool Ray, and all of them. And everybody was on my brother Natural. Every girl in that whole school was on his shit. Every girl. Every girl, and they used to want to stick with me and stuff. But he used to tell me to beat up girls for him – the ones he don't like and stuff. And that's when Mimi used to come up to my school and stuff and we'd get high. Then I'd be off my lunch break, have to go back to school. Then they'd leave and whatnot. And the reason is when I was thirteen, I used to do a lot of stuff, Anne. I think we was even stealing back in McCrory's, them days. We used to go to McCrory's and steal. We used to even go to Fayva's and steal. Fayva shoe store. We had fun.

Needless to say, things were not going well at school for Sun-Africa during this period. At fourteen, she was to graduate to high school, but her conduct had been so poor that she was banned from attending the junior high graduation ceremony. She was clearly upset by this but determined not to let anyone know. The majority of the Puma Crew went on to the local high school, but Angie went to a different school. There she met some older boys who were involved in the Five Percent Nation. Natural (Sun-Africa's half brother) also knew this same group. The Puma Crew continued to associate with different groups of boys but increasingly with the Five Percenters. They also continued to party, drink, and shoplift.

You all went to the same school?
Mimi, myself, Carol, Crystal. Angela used to go to another place. And that's how we got involved with the Five Percent. When I was in the ninth grade, that's when I thought I was too cool. I used to run around my school with my sneakers on. Nobody in that whole school could stand me. There was this girl named Carla – she's having a baby now – she real big. She used to never could stand me. There was this other girl in there named Monica. It was Monica, Carla – who else? Beatie, Bebe, and Shabee and all their girls. We couldn't stand them. We never used to like them.
Why didn't they like you?
'Cos the Puma Crew, that's why. 'Cos they hear about us. And they don't like what they hear. But that's when I was fourteen.
What did they hear about you?
That we could fight and all kinds of stuff. 'Cos, see, the dudes used to soup it up for us. That's real. They used to really tell people stuff about us. You know, they used to say, "Our girls from up our way . . .," you know? 'Cos I know a lot of niggers they used to take up for us like crazy. That's why we wasn't ever scared of nobody. You know we wasn't ever scared. They come up our way, they just get dogged up or shot or whatever, you know.
And we used to have fun together. You know, we just used to all stick together. We used to have parties. We wear our Pumas. Sometimes we used to be shoed down, looking good. I mean people used to be on our shit. That's for real. 'Cos we used to dress the same. I'll talk about when me and Mimi put our hair in the same style. We go outside, we dress the same. Niggers used to say, "Damn, they look like twins." We used to be dressed alike. That's when I had my hair dyed – it was dyed auburn red. Red and brown. Everybody dyed their hair in the seventh grade, right? And when I was twelve, that's when I was real bad. From eleven to twelve to thirteen that's when I was doing stuff on my own. I used to smoke cigarettes. I used to dye up my hair. Come looking with my hair in a different style. That's when we used to wear bands on our heads. 'Cos we used to wear these black plastic jackets and these shiny jackets and black pants. My pants always used to fit so tight. We used to love our pants to fit us tight. Yeah. That's when bellbottoms was out. My pants used to tie in the front. Now me and

Mimi had some nice clothes together. That's when we was down with the Puma Crew. And that's when all them dudes that's big and old and don't go to school now – they all was over there. Shamar [her future boyfriend in the Five Percent Nation]. Angie. Monique. All of us used to go up there, we come from Blue Houses [project buildings] and get all our friends from Blue Houses – Glenda and everybody and come all the way over there. The whole crew of us in the same color and whatnot.

That's when you were lifting out of stores?
Yeah, yeah.

During this time, frictions at home became so intense that Sun-Africa spent three weeks in a group home after running away. She ran away twice but on both occasions returned.

You said you ran away from home. What happened?
The first time I ran away from home was when I got a boyfriend. I'd just turned fourteen and my mother never wanted me to have no boys around, right? I still had company anyway, right? So one time, we was smoking reefer and everything and my grandmother came over here, so we was like busted, right? My grandmother she was saying that I was having sex and everything, you know, even though I wasn't like that. This is just the impression that we gave. So I couldn't really face my mother, that's the first time I ran away. Second time I ran away was 'cos I couldn't have my way, you know. I couldn't go out when I wanted to, you know. When I should have gone according, I went disaccording. I did my own thing, you know? 'Cos like the way she treated us and stuff, you know! I'm not mean. I'm not really mean, but when I look at it now, I say she was looking out for the best. But then I really didn't like her, you know. I couldn't smoke cigarettes and I used to do it anyway. You'd see me right in this house, walking up and down with my little cigarettes, and who care if she saw? I just did what I wanted to do. Wasn't nobody except outsiders that didn't like me for my past, and they still hold a grudge.

Sun-Africa was not the only source of worry to her mother. Her older stepbrother Natural was shot during an attempted robbery and subsequently convicted and imprisoned.

Oh, my brother, here's what happened, right? They used to deal in robbing houses, right, and stuff, and they had diamonds and stuff and everything. Because we used to rob houses too. You know what I'm saying? Kurt was killed and my brother was with him, and my brother got shot six times, but he lived.

Six times!

And the brother that died only got shot twice, but he didn't make it, but my brother did. And the only reason my brother made it was because like he got shot in the back and the behind. Now the other brother, he got shot in the neck, in this area, and I think in his chest or somewhere like that.

Wait a minute, I gotta get the rest of the story, OK? When Natural was shot, how did they get shot?

Because they was in a house, right, and then the man was in his house, right? A man was upstairs waiting for them 'cos, see, they was ringing the bell. They kept on ringing the bell to make sure that no one was there. So they was walking behind the building and he saw them through the window, right, so he waited upstairs with his gun. So they kicked the door down – this is how determined they was to get into that house – they kicked the door down and they went upstairs. So as soon as they got to the top of the stairs by the room, Kurt turned around and said, "Somebody's in there." And then they started running down. As they was running down, they was getting shot. Pow, pow, pow, pow. They was running with their backs turned, so this is how the court case determined whether they was in or out. Everybody got shot in the back, you know, that's why they could determine whether they was in the house, or whether they was coming towards the man. 'Cos if they was coming towards the man, they would have got shot here [in the chest]; being as they was away from the man, they got shot here [in the back]. So what happened is, they made it all the way down-stairs out the house and they was on the floor. Kurt was talking for a little while, then Natural say he died, you know, started foaming white stuff at the mouth. Natural was crying and stuff, trying to wake him up. So the man pulled Natural by the hair, 'cos Natural had got himself a little afro. So the man be pulling his hair back and then put the gun in his mouth. Natural thought there was another bullet in there. He [the man] said, "If I had one more bullet, you black motherfucker, you'd be dead, you know," like that. So what makes it so bad is that the cop then came and got them. Natural know the cop, so that's how he was saved. 'Cos you could believe if it was another cop he'd be laying down for a long while dead, 'cos you know how some cops are. So they took Natural without Kurt. They left Kurt dead for the people from the hospital to come. So a lot of people was seeing him laying on the floor and stuff, 'cos his sheepskin was all wet with blood.

Sun-Africa and her friend Shatasia knew nothing of what had happened until the next day when they were supposed to meet up with Kurt and Natural.

One morning, right, we was supposed to meet. We was in school and we call Kurt's house all day long, all morning long. No answer, no answer, everybody is gone. The only one who answer the phone is his grandmother, right? Shatasia knew something was wrong 'cos there ain't no way in the world that we gonna make arrangements and he didn't make it. You know what I'm saying?

Yeah.

So anyway, we was getting stimulated and stuff. We was getting high. We had a trey bag, a three-dollar bag, something like that. So we was getting high and everything, and everybody was so drowsy, so me and her went to rest, right? We had company, this dude named Jeff was there, so they was talking and stuff. The phone rings, she wants me to get out the bed and answer it. Why I gotta get the bad news first, that's what I want to know? Why me? Why I got to be first? I get on the phone. "Hello, it's Edie." Edie breaking on the phone. "Natural got shot, Natural got shot. Kurt is dead, Kurt is dead."

Where were they when they got shot?

Right up the block, a good four houses down. There's private houses over there. Well, we went to see him in the hospital, right? He was in the bed and he was touching our hands and stuff. We had to go, and he was squeezing our hands. He wouldn't let our hands go, and we had to leave 'cos the lady told us to get out, and he was saying, "Don't leave me, don't leave me. I'm going to die, don't leave me." And we was crying. When we got outside, Revere was outside, Sabrina, Ida, and a lot of people was outside, and they started holding us and stuff and we didn't want to be held. We was holding each other. We was crying together. So we just started hugging each other and rocking, and that's one thing. I don't like too many people involved. The reason they was there was 'cos they was nosy. We said that I was his sister and that she was the guy's girlfriend, that's why they let us in. But they wasn't letting nobody else in 'cos his mother didn't even get there yet, you know? It was a lot of static 'cos we saw her the next day.

So what happened to Natural after that, did he go straight to court?

He got better first, and his mother was going to court for him with his lawyers and stuff.

What happened, what did he get done for?

Oh, for the robbery that he got shot for. 'Cos, seeing as somebody died, somebody had to go to jail for it.

At fifteen, Sun-Africa began a new school term under great pressure to improve her grades and moderate her behavior. That October she became seriously involved with the Five Percent Nation. She already knew many of the members but decided to work hard at "getting knowledge." Becoming part of the movement entailed learning by heart lessons about the history of Islam, symbolic and physical facts about the universe, and, most of all, behaving in a manner appropriate to a good Muslim woman. Each girl who enters is taken on by one of the gods (men), and it was Shamar – whom Sun-Africa already knew – who accepted her as his earth (woman).

You said that after a while you didn't want to steal stuff, you didn't think it was right. What sort of changed you, do you know?

I don't know. I stopped smoking reefer and stuff, you know. Maybe it was my mother pressuring me, it was everybody pressuring me.

How was your mother pressuring you? She didn't like it that you were hanging around with them [the Puma Crew]?

No, 'cos I'd come home too late and stuff.

Right. So in the end you began to drop out of it?

Right.

And then how long after that was it that you got involved in the Five Percent Nation.

When school started, about a month after school started, that's when I joined the Five Percent Nation.

And since then, you've been what?

I've been great. But before, in school and everything, I was really goofing off. 'Cos, like I told you before, when I was dealing with that Puma Crew, like we was a gang and everything together, right? And I mean we had unity amongst us, right? It's just like, you know, you'd like to further yourself, right? Into an education and stuff and I was really messing up in school, my ninth year in high school, right? I was just attracted as far as they [some Five Percenters] was sitting in my lunchroom in school. I went over to a sister that had on her refinement [a full-length dress worn by women in the Nation] and I told her that I wanted to be the earth, you know? And she just kept on talking to me and we just building, and here I am. Yeah, it was just that fast.

So you knew about it, I mean before you got involved you knew a little about . . .

Yeah, 'cos like when I was younger, they was all around. Like, the area I used to live in the whole project was involved, right? They were all over there, you know. And I really like it. In fact, I love it. Being in it, it makes me so happy 'cos there's things that I'm aware of, you know? I'm more secure with my Nation.

Tell me about the whole Nation thing, how it got going, what it believes.

We deal with reality, right?

Right.

We deal with a lot of reality, right? Everything we go by is the truth, you know. We believe in the teachings of the Son of Man, right? We add on to ourselves as far as we teach each other, right? I really couldn't tell you about the gods. You'll have to ask a god. He's supreme, you know what I mean, and there's certain things that he goes through, and I really don't know too much about it. But the earth, we just show a lot of equality to each other and we like to have babies.

Right, what do you mean by the earth?

Alright, we're symbolic to the earth. We believe what's up above is down below, so the sun is man and the moon is me and the stars are the child. Right, just like the earth is up above, and we rotate around the sun, right? So that's why we're symbolic to the earth, so that's what we believe in, right? And we teach each other.

What do you think would have happened to you if you hadn't gotten involved in the Nation?

I probably would have been killed.

Sun-Africa's mother was not very reassured by her daughter's new life-style and did not see eye to eye with Shamar and his philosophy. After four months, Sun-Africa broke up with Shamar and took a new god, Barsun. At the end of six weeks, she returned to Shamar.

You said a couple of times you and Shamar broke up and then went back. What caused the breakup?

See, him and my mother didn't get along, right? One time he was here and he was saying he wasn't going to change and stuff like that. And I took it hard, because like I was saying, "Man, you know you could at least show that to my old earth [mother] so that she wouldn't freak or nothing." Because my mother used to freak in tight. She don't care. "I don't give a fuck what you think you know and everything, 'cos you do what you want to do. This is my house, you know, and everything." 'Cos one time he was here and he was laying on my bed and, being as I was here and was his earth and everything, what's mine is his and everything. So he was just cooling out in my rest and everything, and so mother came home and she just messed up everything. She said, "Excuse me do you live here?" You know. "Did you see me this morning? Why you not say hello?" and all kind of stuff, you know. He say he don't have to listen to that kind of stuff and he left and everything and that's the reason why we broke up. Another reason too is that his lessons too were different from some earths that I knew. Right? And being that his lessons was different, man, I was saying, "Man, I don't know . . ." There's just something strange in me and I was saying, "I don't think he's the right one," you know, and then I went and ended up going back to him, you know?

Yeah.

And when I came back, it was just the joint too because we was together more strangely, you know, and then he just died. I couldn't believe it, man, I was in shock.

On April 11, 1981, Shamar was shot and killed during a burglary. Shortly afterward, his close friend Shasha died also. When I met Sun-Africa in June she was still shocked and confused by Shamar's death. She had recurrent nightmares.

And what happened when he died?

To what I know, it was something like this. Shamar and his brother was going to a man's house and I think it was a burglary or whatever. He was going in and I think he got caught. I'm not sure 'cos I wasn't there, so I really shouldn't be speaking on it, but he got shot in the side, right? And the bullet punctured his lungs, right? And I mean it went straight up and he couldn't really breathe, you know, or nothing 'cos they said they was trying to get air you know, trying to breathe and everything, and it wasn't that easy for him.

So by the time they got him to the hospital he had died?

Yeah, he died on the street. And what makes it so bad, like, they had him draped over the fence, like where he got shot. I guess he walked over to the fence and was over it draped until the ambulance came and they left him there. One of his brothers named Shasha died six weeks later after Shamar.

Sun-Africa's resolve to do better in school did not last the year. When she was with Shamar, she frequently skipped days and after his death she stopped going altogether. Still, her father continued to give her money for college, which she put into a saving account, and she still believed she would one day make it.

Last year, I did good in school, you know. So that's why I'm not behind in my credits – nothing like that. My sister say, "You'd better go to school, you'd better go. I'm going to call in. I'm going to be mad at you." Getting all mad at me. Yup. 'Cos she always wanted me to go to school. This year, I stopped going to school.

How come?

Because I had got my new god and everything. I stopped going. And then 'cos after he died and shit, I was playing dead. So I just stopped going. But I'm still straight 'cos I only failed two classes 'cos I got my report card.

What did the school say?

I told them I was sick – I gave them a letter. I faked the whole shit. I know how to play it off, so I get over.

So there's no problem?

No, no, no. I played it off.

What happens this year?

I go into the next grade.

You'll really go?

Yeah.

Till you finish school, you got two years?

Um-hum.

Then you get the diploma and get out?

Yeah.

Then what?

Go to college.

Where?

New York.

It's all fixed up – in your head?

Yeah.

One year later, however, Sun-Africa left home to live with a new god in the Bronx. She shared the apartment with his first earth and her children. She was seven months pregnant. She planned at some point to obtain a High School Equivalency Diploma.

Sun-Africa's Boyfriends

Boyfriends have been a part of Sun-Africa's life since she was young. Nevertheless, as she sees it, there have been only two of real significance. The first she met when she was fourteen and involved with the Puma Crew. The second – Shamar – coincided with her growing interest in the Five Percent Nation. The relationships seem to typify the change in her view of male-female relationships from a cynical exploitative attitude toward one of submission and humility.

Did you have a boyfriend at that time [with the Puma Crew] or not?
Yes.
Who's that?
Sam.
And what happened to him?
I got tired of him, you know.
You were young, only thirteen or fourteen at the time, right?
Yeah, but he didn't know that.
How old did he think you were?
Sixteen. He didn't know.
Tell me how you met him.
It was through Mimi, and they introduced him to me. One day they was playing music in the park and they introduced me to him. One day he told me to come over to his house and whatnot, so I went to his house and everything, and I guess he liked what he saw. About three days later he told me I was his girl and everything. We was on the phone and I was grinning, you should have saw me, yeah, you know, he was saying, "You're mine now." I was just, you know, like I was a baby. I was fourteen.
Is he nice?
He was real nice, and, like, my mother liked his family a lot and she used to let me go spend a night over there, you know. We had good times together. He used to take me to Coney Island, Great Adventure [an amusement park], take me all over. One Easter he gave me one hundred dollars to buy me a new outfit.
Was he still at school or did he work?
No, he works.
Did he have a job?
No, he was a thief. He used to take me boosting [shoplifting] too.
Where did you go? Manhattan?

Yeah, we both used to be good. He hug on me and take the tag off and stuff. Nobody can't see.

He always had enough money?

He gave me hundred dollars one Easter. And a man never gave me a hundred dollars. She [her mother] would have said, "Where did you get that from?" I slept with that shit under my pillow, you hear me? I slept with a hundred dollars under my damn pillow. I'm serious.

Wow. That's a lot of money. So you had a good time.

Yeah, with him.

How long did you go out with him for?

I recently broke up with him in August, maybe September. I'd say October.

So you were going with him all the time you were hanging around with all the Puma Crew. You were with him, I mean, you were like going out with him?

Yeah.

What about the other girls? Were they going out with guys?

Yeah, they were going out with guys.

You said he was real American, what does that mean?

What do you do with every American man? You use them. You use them American men. You use them.

They're stupid?

Some. Yeah, they're stupid. American men? Sure.

What are they interested in?

They like a wild life. Yeah. They like a wild life. Stupid stuff. Stupid.

What makes you think it's stupid now?

I been always thought it was stupid because it never really meant a lot to me – money and stuff. Look how fast I spent that hundred dollars – in one day. I bought me two pair Gloria Vanderbilt jeans and a top and some shoes and that was it. And I had a good ten dollars to buy me a bag of reefer. All gone.

Money wasn't what you wanted. What did you want?

A nice man that would take care of me. 'Cos to a degree I wanted to have sex with Sam and stuff, you know, but he turned me off.

Why? Not good-looking?

He is very good-looking.

So why did he turn you off?

Because it's the way he talk.

His whole attitude?

Yeah. The way he talked. Stupid. Don't make no damn sense. I tell him everything. Take him to the store, you got to tell him to buy . . . He heard me talking about him like this, he'd want to kick my ass.

But he was good-looking, gave you stuff, thought you were great. Why didn't you like him?

'Cos he gave me everything. A man can't give you everything. 'Cos he spoiled me, that's why. I kicked him in his ass, shit.

So he wasn't much of a man?

No. Down south. Don't even know how to speak proper English, you know? Don't even know how to read, write. Naive motherfucker.

How did he get into stealing?

He's stupid. He follow people. He used to make top dollar.

He never got busted by the police?

He used to get arrested. And then I have to be going to the fucking precinct, man. Shit.

But he never got sent away for long?

He just got out of jail, lover child.

For robbery?

Yeah.

So he made lots of money?

Yeah.

But you weren't very impressed?

No.

Sun-Africa and Sam's involvement in shoplifting paralleled Sun-Africa's similar involvement with the Puma Crew. The crass materialism with which she now charges Sam was just as apparent in the Puma Crew. Her recollections of the crew are mainly in terms of their clothes and their "style." They commanded respect not only for their "toughness," but for their conspicuous consumption of expensive designer jeans and sneakers. By contrast, clothing in the Five Percent Nation is not a major priority and "flashy" women are generally derided, although, as Sun-Africa suggests, some of the gods seem attracted to outside girls with gaudy styles.

Toward the end of her relationship with Sam, Sun-Africa was becoming involved with Shamar and another boy, Dupree, from the Nation. Sam's jealousy finally erupted. He resisted her involvement with the Nation more on romantic than ideological grounds. He also knew Shamar and the other gods and made every attempt to hold onto Sun-Africa's attention. At the same time, perhaps sensing the inevitable, he gave her the money to buy the material for her first refinement or "culture." Sun-Africa is only surprised that

Some members of the Five Percenters with their leader, Father Supreme, on the far right

she was able to fool him for so long.

No, Sam was the only real boyfriend I had before Shamar, 'cos after him it was Shamar.

Were you still going out with Sam when you met Shamar? Or had you broken up with him?

When I was still going with Sam, Shamar put a hickey on my neck.

Poor old Sam.

He didn't see it because I scraped it off.

What with?

A comb. I combed it all. 'Cause once you make that whole area red, it moves. Sometimes Sam, he used to put big ones on me. I used to hate them. Sam was just my money man. I had his ass in big check. Big check. "Yo, Sam, I want some shoes." Yup. He bought me these little rush shoes, he took me to Pitkin. I say, "You bought me those cheap shoes. I don't want them shoes." The shoes he got me was thirty dollars and tax. They was like boys' shoes. He say, "You getting these men's shoes. They're all ugly – you know they are." And I'm saying, "So? So? You going to buy some sneakers?" "I ain't buying any more sneakers. I don't like you in sneakers." Lately, I'm wearing my sneakers.

How long were you with Sam?

About a year. But he was still coming around. He was still buying me stuff because that's how bad he wanted me. He bought me material for my first culture. He ain't even god.

When did you decide to break up with him?
One time he tried to kill me.
What happened?
'Cos this god, right? This god was in jail. Remember I told you
about Dupree and Shamar and Spud? I used to mess with them
three. But Dupree, he called my house. He called my house and
Sam was there. And Sam was on the other line. He was asking me
was I going to come visit him in jail. And I'm up there, "Yeah,
yeah, I'm coming to see you Thursday." Tell him the day, everything. Sam's on the other line. And he came in there. And then Sam
tried to kill me. Sam had me in that corner right over there – see
where the two chairs is at by the table? He had me in the corner,
with his whole hand over my mouth and my nose. And I couldn't
breathe. And I was trying to hold my breath, you know, trying to
play it up, then – my eyes popped open, "Oh shit, he's trying to kill
me." I said, "Get off me, get off me." He was saying, "What kind of
a slut are you?" 'Cos Dupree called. He said, "What kind of a slut
are you?" I said, "Fuck you." I tried to lock his ass out on the
terrace. That's the same day he cried. He said, "Don't leave me." I
did him wrong. I see it. I know I hurt him. I know it for a fact. I
hurt him bad. He was crying. He was so cute too, but he just, I
don't know, he just grew off of me. He was so corny to me. I was
saying, "Get away from me, you American ass." I'm serious.

Of Sun-Africa's three boyfriends – Dupree, Spud, and Shamar,
all from the Five Percent Nation – it was Shamar to whom she was
most attracted. He was a close friend of her step-brother Natural
and of Kurt, who was then going out with Shatasia, a close friend of
hers. Whoever she was with though, she accepted her female status
of subordination, receiving knowledge and rules for living from her
god. When she explains the symbolism of the earth, moon, and sun
to men, women, and children, it is as if she is reciting a catechism,
and, indeed, that is exactly what she is doing. These lessons are
learned verbatim as part of "getting knowledge." Often the rote
answers seem confused and incoherent, at least to an outsider's ear.
Her words seem to make more sense when she discusses her
personal experiences.

'Cos in our nation women submit. That's what really a Muslim
does and a Muslim is one that must learn, right? So that's why we
deal with it, right?
In what way submit?

Submit to our man, you know what I'm saying? What he says goes, man, 'cos he's first, man, we second, and the baby – that's what we created, me and him. We coincide together and we make this baby right like that.

Why do you submit to him, is it because he is nearer the truth and has more understanding or more knowledge than you do?

Yeah, that's why.

So he's like teaching you and you're teaching the children.

Yeah, we teach the children until they are about seven, right? You know, like, if it's a young god – if it's a male – we deal with it until seven. If it's a baby girl, we deal with it for however long until they get their own god, till they get old enough to deal with a man.

What does it mean to be a woman in the Nation?

What it means to be a woman? Got to be strong. 'Cos a woman and a child, I say, is the backbone of a man. You just got to be strong being a woman 'cos you go through a lot of different trials and tribulations, you know, and it's not easy for no woman. You know, some people say it's easy for men, but it's not. You know, but the duty of a woman is to give birth, you know.

Some people think Muslim women are just owned by men.

We are owned by men, yes, that's true, but we play a good part.

You can work?

The gods be *telling* us to get a job. [Laughs]

You have to accept what he says is right?

He ain't going to tell you nothing stupid anyway. He won't tell you nothing stupid.

Sun-Africa does not view herself merely as a mindless follower. If a god makes a decision that he cannot justify, she feels at liberty to query it. Nor is it lost on her that there are many inconsistencies between what a god allows himself and what he allows his earth.

It must be hard to submit, say, if you're with a guy and you think it's wrong, what he's telling you.

If we think it's wrong, we gonna speak about it. We ain't just gonna sit up there and just say, "Well, alright." If it's wrong and we can show and prove that it's wrong, then it's wrong and we don't have to deal with it. 'Cos we supposed to be 100 percent right and exact. Everything got to be right, and if it's not right, we don't want to deal with it.

You don't mind being told what to do?

They don't be bossing you around. They probably say, "Go

upstairs. It's getting too late outside," or they got to say, "Don't smoke cigarettes." It's not like bossing around, like "Go here" or "Go there," "Pick up that." It's like "Don't smoke cigarettes." "It's time to go upstairs."

Is it bad to smoke cigarettes?

It depends if your god lets you smoke. Like if it's necessary. Shamar was my god, right? And just to spite him, I lit up a cigarette, and, you know, I was smoking it and stuff, and he came over and he said, "Put this shit out before I break your fingers." I put it out.

Shamar didn't like you smoking. Did he smoke?

Sometimes. I remember one time he was sitting right on my couch smoking a cigarette, and I say, "You smoking a cigarette?" I couldn't believe it.

During their relationship, Shamar was responsible for Sun-Africa's education and for ensuring that her day-to-day life was lived in accordance with Islam. She was devoted to him as much as to her new life-style and the public persona that she had taken on as a new woman. As she saw it, the days of her youthful rebellion were over and her new demeanor was an outward sign that she was no longer "wild."

According to the Nation, a god may have many earths or girlfriends. Shamar had at least two other girls. One, whose nick-name was Lady, claimed to have been going with him for at least a year before Sun-Africa's arrival. Lady was not in the Nation, and Sun-Africa describes her as "flashy" – cursing, fighting, getting high, and wearing gaudy clothes. Shamar tried to persuade Lady to join the Nation, but she refused. Sun-Africa stresses that she would have welcomed another earth. Lady's sentiments were less altruistic, however, and after Shamar's death the two girls became involved in a jealous and emotional fight. Their relationship since has remained very cool. There was also another girl in Shamar's life named Sandra. She was much quieter than either Sun-Africa or Lady, and, according to Sun-Africa, not particularly attractive. After Shamar's death, she and Sun-Africa became quite close, but eventually Sun-Africa found their meetings too depressing because they inevitably finished with a discussion of their memories of Shamar.

Shamar's death, then, brought the three girls into immediate contact, and emotions tended to run high. Sun-Africa's feelings about the other two seemed to crystalize.

I was walking and then I see this whole crowd of people, right, and they was all sad-faced and stuff. And then this dude named Barsun, he's a god, right? And he said, "Earth, I'm gonna tell you now that your god Shamar got shot," right? So I didn't really think he was dead, so I walked up and down and I kept on going, right? And then this other girl named Ginger, right, said, "Shamar is dead," and I started breaking. I started saying, "No, he not." You know, "You all got to stop doing that." I said, "You all got to cool out because you don't all know," and I was outside for about an hour before I went up to his house. Because I was kind of scared to go to his house, you know what I'm saying? And then Shasha, the brother I told you he was real close to? I went to him 'cos I wasn't really listening to nobody else, and when Shasha told me, that's when I broke down. I was on the floor, I was crying my heart out, I was screaming, and then I just got myself together and I went upstairs to his [Shamar's] house and then I had to listen to his mother. She was breaking. She was screaming, you could feel the pain, man. Every moan, every sound she made, you felt it. You know what I'm saying? Because she was really screaming, really breaking. She was saying, "Somebody suckered my poor child, somebody suckered him out of his life," you know. And I was just sitting up there, and then I went to his room, right? And then I just laid down for a while, you know? And I was thinking about him and everything and I was just talking to myself. "Please, he just going to knock on the door, he going to come home, he going to come home." And he just never come home and everything, you know?

I spent the night there, you know? And I waited, and waited, and waited. And then the next morning when I woke up, that's when we had the fight. Me and the other girl – Lady, you know. Soon as I got up, cleaned myself up, and went outside, there was a whole hallway full of people, talking about him being cremated. And they was arguing and everything, right? And so I had on his crown [a knitted hat worn by the gods to cover their heads out of respect for Allah] right, I had put it on my head and everything 'cos it make me feel a little better. I went outside. And then Lady asked me for it, she asked me for it in the wrong way 'cos she said, "You got Shamar's thing?" And then she just started getting all smart and stuff, and then all her girlfriends started talking 'bout "You ain't giving it up? Then you going to have to get your ass kicked." And all kind of shit. And, you know, I was saying, "Yeah. You all try it 'cos you know I don't play that. That's right." And I was ready for all their little shit. And being that they started it off . . . I finished it for their ass.

And what happened? Tell me what happened in that kind of fight?

She was up in my face, right? Like she was up putting her breasts against me, you know. And I was standing up, and she was saying, "You ain't giving it to me?" And I said, "No!" And I said "No" real smart, you know, right? So she get up in my face and I just punched her. I had to hit her first, you know. I just had to hit her, and like we was fighting and everything and she was pulling my hair, right? And, like, she pulled a whole patch of my hair out, and I felt my hair rip up from my skin and I just broke. I took her head and I started banging it against the concrete. And then they broke it up and everything and I started fixing my hair and everything right, so the guys were saying, "What's wrong, earth? What's wrong?" And I said, "She hit me, she hit me," like that, right? So I fixed up my hair and everything and I was walking and then, like, we went up to Shasha's house, right, and he said, "Don't even worry about it. You're gonna be alright. You got the crown, you gonna be alright," right?

And so as soon as we went back downstairs, right, they was still outside, right? All the girls was still outside, right? So I was going to the cab and everything, and then the fight just started again. I turned around and they was pulling at us and stuff and then we was just fighting again. And then, then we walked 'cos the cab had pulled away. The cabdriver, he was so scared, he pulled off. I'm serious, he pulled off good and strong too. He wasn't letting nobody in his cab, 'cos I was holding on to the door and he just pulled off. So therefore I had to turn round and defend myself, you know what I'm saying? So then we was fighting. And I had this girl on the floor. I was trying to kill her, 'cos she had long hair and I had her on the floor. I was like pulling her hair, like you know, she was down and I was over her, right? And what make it so bad, I had my refinement, you know. I had my refinement. They said that I pulled it up to fight and anything, and I did *not* pull it up. You know, I was just strongly defending myself and everything and that's how everything started.

You know, from then we just took a cab all the way home, and I mean Shatasia was upset. She got up here and she put on her sneakers and her pants and stuff and she was saying, "Fuck it. We're going all the way. We's killing these bitches." Everything, guns was there and we have everything, you know what I'm saying? But we just cooled her out from it, you know? So we ain't even got to deal with it, 'cos we kicked their butts. You know what I'm saying? We already beat them up, so what's we're gonna do back out there? Fight? I can see it where we got all beat up, you know, but we didn't. When I came back here, this whole house was crowded full of people. And they was breaking and I was crying and everything and I was saying, "I want to die, I want to go. I want to go with Shamar. I want to be with him."

The fight takes up as much of Sun-Africa's account as her recollection of her shock and grief. The timing of the fight appears to be so irreverent, so inappropriate, that it suggests that claiming the right to the role of grieving girlfriend was more important than the death of her boyfriend. It echoes the same sentiment she expressed over Natural's shooting, when she felt that others had no right to be involved in the grief.

Within the Nation, it is understood that women will be in the care of a god. There was an expectation therefore that Sun-Africa would find a new god. Indeed, within a few months she had done so. At sixteen, Sun-Africa had no children. It was likely that she would become pregnant, however, since earths are expressly forbidden to use birth control. The following text is part of the question-and-answer lessons to be learned verbatim and "explains" the reason in terms of the need to propagate the Islamic faith and the black race.

Q. Why do women of Islam (blackman nature) teach that birth control and abortion does no good?

A. When the earth separated from the moon all of the wisdom in the moon at its highest form fell into parts that the sun cooled causing it to rotate so that his understanding of culture would be seen by the planet of the universe. So the cooling (teaching) caused the earth to be born the understanding the people may not lose knowledge and wisdom of the sun history (blackman) history means his story knowing the blackman's mind brought about all things in existence . . . He could like to conceal the origin of the birth control occurs when the woman strays away from the root of civilization (blackman) (brings all things about) causing the moon's water to drop to the earth this makes her not able to produce the strongest seed (the black nation). The blackman has no birth record. He is older than the sun, moon and stars. So how could our women accept birth control or control birth unless they are trying to destroy us by the will of Yarob abortion is the modern way to mislead the black-woman. Meaning if you kill the blackman in his stage of being formed Islam is the nature of the blackman which he manifests this body in, therefore the woman must bear Islam (blackman body) in order to exist. Birth control is not good because god will not and cannot fall victim to the devil's civilization.

Sun-Africa expressed little concern about the practical and financial realities of raising children. The Nation expects the father to assume responsibility for the mother and child. Indeed, if the child is a boy, the father should play a major part in his socialization from age seven onward.

And you'd be happy if you got pregnant?
Yeah.
It's a big step, you know. Doesn't it worry you?
No.
Just think about another human being.
But check this out. In the nation of the gods and the earth, once they seven (if it's a boy), once they seven, they their father's responsibility.
Oh yeah. He has to be responsible for bringing them up after that? That's interesting. So it's good if you're with a guy who's kind of responsible. Do any of the guys . . .
Leave their babies stranded? No. 'Cos in this nation, the babies, they the greatest, they the best part. Man, the gods would give anything to have children.
They really want to have children?
Yeah.
It's a big thing for them, is it? Is it better to have a son or a daughter?
It don't make a difference.
They don't care about that. What about if it's a girl, then it stays mainly your responsibility?
Yeah, if it's a girl, I gotta teach it.

In practice, a god may find it just too expensive to maintain several earths and their offspring. Often the women must work to support themselves and their children. Yet if a woman shows any tendency toward favoring a career over her children, the god may simply take the children away from her. Also, it is quite difficult within the Nation for a wife to "divorce" her god, although the converse is not true. In reality, children can bind the woman almost inescapably to her man.

Supposing you wanted to have a career?
No, I don't think I'll be able to do it, leave my baby hanging like that. The father would probably punish me and never let me see my babies again.
'Cos that would be your first responsibility to the children, would it, and what about divorce?
There ain't no such thing as divorce.
It doesn't exist?
No.
If you had a kid, and the father of that kid . . .
You spend your whole life with him, your whole life.

Whether or not the god, earth, and stars will remain together for Sun-Africa's whole life remains to be seen.

Sun-Africa and the Puma Crew

At age twelve, still in junior high, Sun-Africa was one of the founding members of what became known as the Puma Crew. What is noteworthy about this three-year period in her life is that the crew was exclusively female. All-female autonomous gangs are so rare in New York that only six, at most, have been officially recorded in any one year. Yet clearly, adolescent girls do form subcultural groups and, in this case, were substantially involved in crime. As with boys, the group began to destabilize when members became increasingly concerned with heterosexual relationships, which tended to eat into the amount of time available for group activities and also divided emotional loyalties. Whereas among boys this often happens between eighteen and twenty-one, with the Puma Crew it began at a much earlier age. Sun-Africa was fifteen, Mimi seventeen when the crew disintegrated. The movement toward couples replacing the group occurred independent of sexuality, since most members of the crew had been sexually active for several years. Perhaps because the girls tended to date older boys, the age of their boyfriends at that time coincided with the boys' desire to "settle down."
When Sun-Africa describes the crew, it is primarily in terms of a tremendous in-group loyalty resulting from jointly conceived clothing styles and shared activities kept secret from the adult world. In short, the Puma Crew was very much like any other American teenage group. The difference perhaps lies in the extremity of their "rebellion." Aggression, crime, and drugs were intended as much

to shock their peers as their parents. Sun-Africa succeeded better than she had anticipated: many of her schoolmates rejected her and even the Five Percent Nation, whom she knew casually at that time, maintained a certain reserve.

So at the end of the year at the seventh grade, that's when I met up with Mimi. You hear what I'm saying? I met up with them, then we were sticking together and smoking a lot of reefer. When I was in the sixth grade I used to buy reefer and stuff. So I used to get every kind of reefer I could. Her and Crystal first pulled out this nickel bag. They had all these joints in it. And we was getting fucked up, and then Damaris split because she had to go upstairs because it was getting too late for her to be outside. My mother she didn't really put a curfew on me. She still don't, you know. She be saying, "Be in here by eleven." If I come in at two, she won't say nothing, you know what I'm saying? 'Cos she just asked me where I been. I tell her, and then that's just that, you know.

So we was getting high for a long time. I went upstairs, then the next day, I came to her house early the next morning and I had some money. Every day, every morning. I was going. Every morning, every morning. So then we started wearing skips. We started wearing jelly shoes. Started wearing clothes the same, right? We started wearing sneakers. We started off with Pro Keds – 69ers. I had a red pair, Mimi had a green pair. We all had different colors and plus Mimi and me had red – it was just when the sweat suits came out and I had this red sweat suit – a shirt and some pants. And we went to the jam. We went to where they was playing music. Everybody was looking at us, her and me. We was dancing and whatnot – you know how girls are, you know? Two girls going to be outside making a nuisance, so they're going to dance. So me and her was dancing. Then we met these dudes and a lot of dudes were attracted to us, you know. You know, they was talking to us and then girls started looking. And then we got to look out for them. What happened after that? I just started being with her and I started going every place she went.

Where did you used to go?

Sometimes we go to Brownsville, sometimes we go to Fort Greene. You know, every park that they play music, we be there. That's when I started getting dusted [smoking angel dust (PCP)] and all that stuff – started smoking dust. Yeah, 'cos all the way through '80, all the way to '80 from '78, '79. October, I started straightening up.

What was the dust like?

Shit, that stuff get you so high, Anne, you don't know how to hang on to yourself.

You ever had acid?

Yeah. It's like that. Yeah, that's bad. I don't do that no more.

Why? Too strong?

Hell, yes. That shit get you fucked up. I went to this party. And I was dusted, I was practically fighting with the air. I was making noise, I wasn't caring. Anybody come in my way, I beat their ass. Especially the females, you know? I was cool at it. I wasn't just screaming. I was saying, "Oh, oh," to the music. We be dancing. Then I got on the mike and I was rhyming and stuff. But you know how they do, yeah. I was thinking up shit.

Who were the guys you were hanging with?

They live right in this area – they used to be in the Pin Mall. Games was in the Pin Mall. Games room, you shoot dice, numbers spot – play numbers. So I used to be in the Pin Mall every day playing the numbers. Playing games in the game room and stuff. Then the gods used to come in there.

That's where you first started seeing them?

Yeah. But I was real wild when they met me. They were saying, "Damn." I know it. Because I wasn't caring about them. Nobody else. Just my money. I used to whip out my money, you know, tell them I got money. Because a lot of brothers know my past history and that's fucked up too. You know, being that I'm young, it's good. It's good, but it's kind of fucked up. They know my past history. They look at me, they say, "No."

So that was last year?

1980, I was getting dusted. I used to go to parties in spring 1980, boy. Everybody was souping 1980. Plus we cried too because Kurt didn't make it to 1980. That's the brother that died. On New Year's, we felt bad because he died in December.

Sun-Africa was concerned principally with money, which is the key to this period of her life. The drugs, the clothes had to be either stolen or bought. For a twelve-year-old, a weekly allowance just was not enough, and this, as much as anything, contributed to the crew's shoplifting. Although Sam probably also encouraged the activity, Sun-Africa met him after she had already begun "boosting" with the girls. Looking back, Sun-Africa attributes much of it to "greed," since she points out that her mother was ready to buy her the clothes that she needed. One day, she was pulling old articles of clothing out of the cupboard, showing me various styles that had come and gone. She produced a rather expensive fur coat made of different colored rabbit pelts. When I asked if she still wore it, she looked at me with complete disbelief. It had "gone out" over two years ago.

The Puma Crew wore expensive but casual sportswear. They varied in the particular type of sneaker that was in vogue. These fine distinctions between brandnames were not in any way unique to their group, although Sun-Africa contends that they were among the first in the area to wear such things. Whether or not this is true, this fashion was not originated by their group but came from a massive advertising program that sought to impress buyers with the social superiority of one brand over another. The effort was evidently successful.

It was precisely because of this highly consumerist mentality that trips to Bloomingdale's, a trendy department store, became necessary for the crew. When it came to shoplifting, they were very choosy about what they took. They were not wearing "outlaw" clothing or generating an original style. They were every advertiser's dream come true. The items they "needed" for self-definition were expensive and constantly changing. The following suggests the rather fine distinctions that were made.

This is when the Puma Crew came about. Now, I was thirteen. And first we started wearing 69er sneakers, right? And 69ers is the little Pro Keds with the three stripes on the side? They're Pro Keds with three stripes. I had a red pair and a red sweat suit, right? Then we started wearing Pumas. And Pumas is the other shoes with a spade thing? It ain't a spade, but it's a strip coming down. And it say Puma, and it's got the Puma cat on it. We started wearing Pumas. And we was getting big-time high 'cos I used to hang out with this Puerto Rican girl named Winey. And Winey used to dress her ass off. I mean to be a Puerto Rican . . . She used to put makeup on and dress real nice. And, you know, when I was in the eighth grade, I never used to really stay with hardly nobody because at Starrett City, they was all corny.

Sun-Africa and the crew sometimes went on their "shopping" expeditions alone. But they were often accompanied by guys whom they knew from the local amusement arcade. One, of course, was Sam.

You know, the Puma girls, all our stuff we used to wear, like it was really stolen. Like we used to go to Bloomingdale's. Oh, man, we used to pop the things off like with our teeth, or a screwdriver.

Oh, you mean those things that go through the machines?

Yeah. 'Cos there are a lot of grown men out here and they'd look out. They still look out for me, even though I'm with the Five Percent Nation. They used to take us there and act like they our fathers, right? And they'd buy something and we'd steal the rest. We used get Sasson jackets, Adidas suits, sneakers. We really stole a lot, like clothes. Not really too many shoes, 'cos it wasn't as easy 'cos, like, shoe departments always got their eyes on their new shoes and stuff 'cos the shoe department's smaller than clothes department. We used to go all over, Macy's, A&S downtown. We used to go all over flea markets in Queens and stuff.

Tell me about the stuff in the shops, how you did that – pop those plastic things?

I'd pop them. You could do it with a wrench, you know. The thing that squeeze stuff together? You could do it with that, or you could do it with a screwdriver. If you do it with a screwdriver, takes longer, but the wrench is better.

And it doesn't rip the material when you take it off?

Sometimes, sometimes not.

So you'd go and try the stuff on?

Oh, but we don't take them in the dressing room. We do it right there. We don't go in the dressing room.

But how can you do it without being seen?

There are enough people standing around you that you could do it, 'cos the other day I had to steal some underwear 'cos I needed some.

Right. So you get it off. What do you do with it when you get the tag off?

You put it in your bag.

What if somebody asks to see your bag?

We show them. Don't hesitate to show them, 'cos they'll know something is up.

So what if they see the stuff in there?

They won't, not if you put it right. If you've got something in your bag, you just put the stuff on the bottom and put it on the top.

So, on the top you just have like your makeup and . . .

And whatever. Well, they're supposed to pull tags off anyway, so if they see the clothes you could say you was bringing them back.

How much stuff did you get during that time?

A lot of stuff. And we'd, like, sell it and stuff.

What about the guys? Did they get any money? Did you split it with them?

Well, we all take it.
So, did you ever take orders?
Sweatshirts and stuff like that. You could get it if I needed the money real bad.
Mmm.
If I didn't, you'd just have to take what I had.

On at least one occasion, Sun-Africa found that the big department stores offered possibilities other than simply shoplifting. She was lucky to get away with only a caution.

But one time I went in the store and didn't steal nothing. But I was trying to get this lady's pocketbook, right? So everybody was in the changing booth, so I stood on a chair. I looked over and the lady came in and she told me to get out the dressing room. She said, "She's scheming on somebody's pocketbook." She escorted me, you know, out of the store and everything. She escorted me out.
It seems funny, looking back on all that now.
Yeah.
Like a different time in your life.
It's strange, you know, 'cos now I know better.
You wouldn't do that stuff anymore?
It was wrong.
Why, too risky?
It's just not the right thing to do, stealing and all that.
Mmm.
It don't pay.
You never got busted?
Never got busted . . . I got busted one corny time. I wouldn't really call it getting busted 'cos I got off with everything. I had the pants on, so they really couldn't prove that I had stole the pants so they let me go. They called my mother and everything.
Did they charge you?
No, 'cos they didn't catch the stuff on me. At the precinct, they handcuffed me to the wall thing. Yup? The pole on the wall. They put the handcuff around. Put my arm up there. And I was up against there, I was so sad.
They kept you all night?
Uh-huh.
Were you scared?
Yeah. I was smoking cigarettes. My mother came down.
What happened?

She just wanted to know why her daughter was there.

They couldn't charge you?

No. They had to send me home. They just told my mother I'm a little thief and I'm a liar.

She went crazy?

Yeah. She went the fuck off. 'Cos them handcuffs had my hands all fucked up. And when we got outside, she told me, "Serve you right." You know, 'cos I was complaining. Because you know how you is with Mommy. You always be up on her.

Did you ever get busted again?

The last time I told you was when I ran away.

For shoplifting, you never got done again?

No. I always came out safe.

The Puma Crew, with the older guys who were around, became involved in burglary, selling stolen goods, and credit card frauds. Sun-Africa recalls that this was motivated by a desire to emulate the older guys, as well as by greed. By virtue of being younger and female, it was difficult for the girls to be recognized as the guys' equals, but their attempts did gain them a certain notoriety among their peers.

I never really need to steal. What do I need to steal for? My mother always had a few bucks for me, but I was greedy. That's the whole thing, and my being greedy, that's how a lot of my friends is dead to this day, being greedy.

When did that all start. Was that when you were hanging around with the Pumas?

Yeah, plus like I told you, the guys out here. They're older, you know? Like there's a lot of older guys out here. So being that it's like we look up to them, we want to do like they do. But we really can't equal them, you know what I'm saying? But we did try. We used to deal a lot of fights and stuff. Alright, say if we see a house, right? And the guys used to keep a set of keys and stuff, and we used to wash the lock. That's what they called it – "washing."

What's that?

That's when you pick the lock.

Oh yeah?

And like, you know, we used to get together, everybody down there. And, say, there would be about five of us, or four of us, or whatever, and we all got in together, got to stay together. 'Cos we know the chances that we could get shot as well, you know. We could get hurt. But I did change a whole deal, man.

So what would happen? You've got into a house, right, take the stuff, how did you get rid of it? How did you sell it?

Oh, it was easy to sell, 'cos a lot of people live in the projects and stuff. You know, people here, they don't have too much. They ain't rich or nothing. And plus we were giving them a bargain, we giving them a sale, so you know they want it like that. And we ain't definitely getting rich at it, but if we couldn't get rid of it, maybe we'd keep it for ourselves, you know? TVs and if we'd take somebody's pocketbook and we'd find a credit card or something, we'd go charge up and everything. A lot of stuff we used to do. I was a bad little chick.

It really is amazing, you really did manage to stay away from the police, except a couple of times. Mostly you'd get by without getting in too much trouble.

With the police, being as I was so young, they wouldn't expect nothing from me anyhow.

How old were you when you were doing that, fourteen?

Thirteen and fourteen, those were my two worst years.

And you had guns then as well. You were taking night work, you were doing robberies, something like that?

Uh-huh, but, you know, I used to make myself look like a boy. It was easy for a girl to do that, and then I could change back and be, you know, a little feminine girl again. So that's another way I used to get over too.

Yeah, 'cos if anybody saw you they'd say, "Oh there's this young boy."

Never think it was me. Well, I remember, every time we'd do something slick, I used to have to look like a boy.

Useful sometimes.

Put your braids up in your hat, specially wintertime. Boy, Mimi would say, "Better put them braids up, better put them up."

And you thought that if you kept hanging around doing what you were doing, you might have gotten shot one day?

Yeah, I mean I had guns and stuff, you know? Here, alright, in New York City, up here in Manhattan, Brooklyn, Queens, and all that, guns originate from a lot of gang wars and stuff like that. And being that sometimes when you get busted and you have to throw it away, someone can pick up your gun and sell it for any price he wanted to. And there's so many guns out here. That's just what they doing, selling them any price they want. If they need thirty dollars, they just sell you the gun for thirty dollars. They don't really know the value of a gun. 'Cos that can take a life too, you know what I'm saying? I still think I got a pistol, a little .22 pistol. I'm not sure, but it might be in here somewhere. I haven't seen it in a long time. But my brother, he used to hook me up with a lot of stuff. Like I know how to shoot them. I know how to clean them, you know.

Sun-Africa did not manage to remain entirely clear of the police. She was occasionally picked up and returned from areas where she had been hanging out with individuals whom the police thought too old and undesirable for a thirteen-year-old. Her experience of running away from home on two occasions, combined with her three weeks in a group home, seems to have had a salutary effect and, for better or worse, she has not run away since then.

You know the cops picked me up two, three times. They picked me up for getting to know people and stuff like that. Yeah, my little rough future. But the only time I got busted is through my mother 'cos a lot of people seen me get arrested. They thought I was crazy. Everybody saying, "Who getting arrested?" Then they see. I was all alone.

What did you get arrested for?

Told you, the last time I got arrested was 'cos I left my house. They picked me up right in front of another game room.

What happened? This police car screamed up?

Yeah. Showed me my picture. Told me my mother looking for me. There's a warrant on my arrest and I'm in trouble. "You're in trouble, kid. You got a record. Blah, blah." You know how cops are. You be feeling like punching them bastards. You know what they do when they take you to jail? You got to strip all your clothes off there and you got to bend down.

Oh God. Yeah.

And they got to look between your legs and stuff. It's nasty.

Did that ever happen to you?

Yeah. They get thrills out of doing that shit too.

What happened?

That's when my mother was looking for me, and they wanted to see what I had on me.

What, to make sure you didn't have drugs or anything? Guns?

Guns, anything.

So the police did that?

A woman, she worked in the office.

That's a horrible thing to have to do. Didn't you feel awful?
No. I felt like farting right in her damn face.

During that time the Puma Crew was involved in several group
fights. Their most bitter enemies were the Moonlight Crew. The
wild behavior of the Puma Crew had attracted the attention of
some local boys, many of whom were in the Nation. Although
ostensibly disapproving, the boys were clearly fascinated by the
"bad girls" from the projects. This generated a definite rivalry
between the Puma girls and the Moonlight Crew, who clearly
believed that they had first rights to the attention of their local
boys. Tension grew and finally erupted in an all-female group fight,
which Sun-Africa recounted on several occasions.

Now this is the root of it. The guys that be out here, well, the
Moonlight girls used to like them a lot, right? And they used to
come out here and talk about "Puma girls ain't shit" and write it on
the walls and "Pumas are sneakers," right? So the girls really didn't
like us, 'cos the guys, they used to say, "Man, they bad and stuff
and they be dressing," you know? A female say, "Mmm – they
can't dress better than me," or whatever, right? So we just didn't
get on from there. They used to come out here to our gyms and
stuff. And they used to play music in the park, where we did
dancing and everything. They'd be rolling their eyes and sucking
their teeth and all kinds of girlish, childish stuff.

And, you know, we just used to fight a lot. You know, 'cos they
used to talk about us. I don't really know, it's just a grudge that we
held 'cos we really didn't like each other. They lived in that area,
we live in this area. We don't want you here and we don't go out
there. From the start, we didn't go out there, so there wasn't any
real reason for them to come out here.

But also there was a lot of fighting over the guys and stuff. So one
day, they wrote on our wall, "Meet us in the Pin Mall at seven
o'clock." It was on a Monday. I will never forget it, right? So there
was a whole crowd of us and it was time for everybody to go to their
house, right? Well, everybody went in the house except for the ones
that could really hang out late. So I'm in my house, laying down,
resting, when all of a sudden my phone rings: "Come outside, right
now." So I told my mother I was going upstairs to my girlfriend's
house, right? So I went upstairs and I put on her jacket, put on her
shoes and stuff, being as she was sick and wasn't going outside. So I
went outside and there was two girls outside. So we was acting up,

right, and I was breaking on them, 'cos I wanted to know what was going on, right? You can't just come up to me with mystery stories. So anyway, I was saying, "We got to roll, we got to roll out there. We got to go out there and get them." So we went out there, we went out there a whole bunch of us, right? And the gods was there. They wasn't really on the girls' side, they was on *our* side. We was all souped up. I'll tell you who went: Mimi, Angie, Cilica, all different girls. They wanted to take Katzie, Donna, you know? Everybody was up there, so me and Crystal we were the only two left. I said, "Crystal, guess what? Mimi and them left us. They went to roll and they didn't take us with them, so let's get our own crew." We go and we got fifty cents a piece for the bus and stuff.

So we got on the bus and went out there, and what makes it so good is we have her two little brothers with us. So I get off the bus and I'm walking with the little boys and I see a whole crowd of people all around my girls. They was ready to fight. I started running across the street. I was saying, "What the fuck is going on here, you know? What's all your people doing standing around us and stuff?" So this girl, she got a hanger and her clothes on it like she was coming from the cleaners or something. She turned around and she said, "I ain't got nothing to say to you all." And she just turned around and walked, right? And I said, "You ain't going nowhere." And I like pulled her from her collar, and we just started fighting. So anyway, this girl said she had nothing to do with it, right? And she was the main one writing stuff on the walls, so I jumped on her back and started fighting. I said, "Bitch, you ain't going nowhere." I started throwing her down hard and, like, as soon as I attacked this girl, this girl called Noreen who was there too, she jumped her so it was two of us on one girl.

Then everybody started doubling up on one girl. We hurt them up 'cos the girl had to go to the hospital 'cos her teeth were messed up. Noreen had her on the floor. Noreen was over her and I said, "Noreen, I'm going to kick her." Noreen was saying, "Don't kick her in the mouth," you know? I just started kicking her mouth, I wasn't really caring, and she got hurt up by her gums. I guess they were sore and we did see blood. These girls told us that they had to go to the hospital. We had bottles, knives, and everything, 'cos nobody had a gun. We won and it was so bad.

Did the police get involved?

No, they didn't get involved. It looked like a big war or something because we was really going off, man. I'm serious, because we kicked, knocked this girl's teeth out. I was kicking her badly too. I had like her on the floor and I was pulling on her hair and I was just kicking her in her mouth, constantly. I think about three or four of her teeth was out.

Although most of the fights were directed at outsiders, sometimes (more often in the later years of the crew) there were disputes between members. On one occasion, Mimi used the crew's former allies – the Stafford Road Crew – to jeopardize Sun-Africa. The plan backfired and resulted in a confrontation between Sun-Africa and Mimi.

Now this is how me and Mimi broke up. It's the Stafford Road Crew, right, and they live on Stafford, right? She told them that I called them ugly and all of this kind of stuff. One time I was up at her house and she gave me the phone to speak to them, right, and when I was speaking with them, they was getting all smart with me and stuff, talking about "We'll beat your ass" and stuff. All kinds of stuff, all unnecessary. So I asked her why she told them that, being as I didn't say it, and she got all smart with me. 'Cos it was said that I was supposed to go out there to get jumped, right? I asked her and she said, "Did I ever say that?" And I said, "No." She said, "Well then," getting all smart. So I just beat her up totally. Like I had her on the floor and everything. She was bleeding and stuff and then everybody stopped speaking, you know.

As the Puma Crew split up, Sun-Africa naturally gravitated toward her half brother's friends in the Five Percent Nation – Dupree, Spud, and Shamar. She had known them for some years by now. She became more involved with Dupree and, when Dupree was sent to prison, became Shamar's earth.

Before Sam found out about Dupree and fought with her, Dupree knew about Sam and was often jealous. Dupree's temper was considerably more violent than Sam's and, as we shall later see, Sun-Africa was fortunate to escape Dupree with her life.

It all started when me and him [Dupree] was going with each other. So he found out something about Sam, right? 'Cos he was supposed to be my steady boyfriend, but really Sam was my steady boyfriend. So one time we was in a mall and Dupree was teasing me. Then all of a sudden, they mentioned Sam's name and he was telling me to get out of the mall because I was laughing with them, you know? The gods, shoot. And I wouldn't get out the mall, I was still in there – smoking cigarettes and stuff. He didn't like me smoking cigarettes. And I was smoking my cigarette and trying to cool out. You know, you all fourteen, they're up there thinking I'm older than that when I really wasn't. And he was saying, "You'd better get the fuck out the Pin Mall." He was cursing at me. And I was saying, "Alright." I was yelling, "Shatasia, come on." She was talking to her boyfriend. And I was saying, "Come on. We got to go home. I don't want to go home by myself." So she was saying, "Alright, I'm coming. Wait for me, wait for me."

So I just walked outside of the Pin Mall. He came outside. He just grabbed me by my neck. You know how men grab you by your neck, like this? And he was pulling me around, boy. 'Cos I was acting like I wasn't going to be his girl no more. But he tried to kiss me and I snatched away – "Get off me," like. And he just got mad, and then Shatasia came outside and I started hiding behind her, laughing at this guy. He thought I was acting real childish, which I was, you know. I didn't really understand that. He was saying, "See if you can run from this." He took his gun out. And I was crying 'cos everything got serious and shit. I see the gun and I was crying. I was saying, "Shatasia." She was saying, "Don't hide behind me, shit." I was running, shit. Hell, yes. I ran all the way home.

He let you go?

Yeah. And I saw him the next day and we was together again 'cos he called me and told me he wanted me to come with him to Riker's Island to go visit his brother and take him some drugs. 'Cos that's how they deal, you know.

When you were with Dupree, you weren't really with Shamar? They were good friends?

Yeah, they were close.

Didn't they get jealous?

Yeah. They broke, they broke. They couldn't let it be like that.

So what happened?

I went to Sam for a little while, then I came back to Shamar. 'Cos Dupree was in jail. You understand? It was like zigzag, zigzag.

It's so confusing.

I just say I didn't have no business having all them damn men, that's what's confusing. Shit, 'cos one minute I'm submitting to him, then the next minute I'm submitting to somebody else. It's just not easy. I know I can't do that shit with gods. Hell, no. So Dupree he got put in jail.

How come Dupree was in jail?

He killed three people.

My God, what happened?
'Cos they wouldn't let him in this party.
Tell me the story.
I don't really understand it, but what I heard is he used to mess with this girl and she was giving a party and they wouldn't let him in. And he just started shooting.
What did Dupree think of you?
He thought I was young and dumb, too. Like I *was*. I'm serious.

When I talked with her one year later, Sun-Africa no longer believed she was young or dumb. She had a new name and a new knowledge. She believed she had grown up, that the Nation had completely changed her. But elements of the old Sun-Africa still remained.

The Five Percent Nation

IN THE NAME OF ALLAH, PEACE:

The 5% (Five Percent) teaches of righteousness (Islam), teaches the true meaning of the Supreme Wisdom which was brought here to the Shores of North America by Master Wallace Fard Muhammad. It was (Fard) who presented the so-called American negro with the knowledge of Himself and Kind (people of Asia). Showing and proving to the so-called negro that the Blackman was of Divine Origin and not a savage, as he was taught by his former slave masters. Master Fard traveled from the East and delivered the Message of Allah (who is God), to the Blackman who was robbed of the Science and kidnapped and forced into slavery against their will. Master Fard Muhammad was a prophet, and he taught Islam to many. But, he gave birth (Mental) to another prophet whose name was Kareem while being taught. He is known today as the most Honorable Elijah Muhammad, Leader and Teacher of the Black Muslim (Nation of Islam).

The Messenger (Elijah Muhammad) has been teaching Islamic North America for forty years, during which time the majority who called himself (CLARENCE 13X Smith) made his presence known among the Muslim body. Declaring himself as ALLAH the Eternal Savior of the young Black babies (who is the best part). For the babies are the continuity of the Nation, thus all propagative functions must first be applied to them.

In 1964 Malcom X, who was the Minister and Representative of the Messenger at that time at Temple No. 7, expelled Clarence 13X Smith, for his self-styled wisdom had attracted many other Muslims. Upon being expelled from the Mosque, the Blackman known as

Clarence 13X Smith, gave birth to the 5% Nation, and was then recognized as ALLAH. He began to teach Islam in the ghettos manifesting truth in all Degrees of Existence, Borning Understanding that could not be seen, since Fard presented the Blackman with the knowledge of himself. ALLAH showed and proved how and why everything is for real, and there is no mystery GOD everywhere. While teaching, ALLAH's work was heard by many and the people were inquisitive to find out about the Blackman who called himself GOD ALLAH. Mayor Lindsay is among the ones who beared witness to ALLAH being GOD. This is how the 5%, were receiving various grants from the government. We the 5% do not teach Islam as a religion, but as a Divine way of life for the Blackman, but we do not separate ourselves from the Most Honorable Elijah, for we know that he is the last and greatest Messenger of ALLAH. We are not enclosed within his Mosque because we are own leaders and teachers, thus elevating on our own Supreme Intelligence.

Islam is older than the Sun, Moon and Stars, and is composed of mathematics which is everything in life. This is why it may appear to be many phases of the Study of Islam and some may call them Muslim sects. We the 5% are not a Muslim Cons are noted within the 5% cycle. ALLAH made the knowledge of the Blackman (who is GOD) understood.

Many misunderstanding the manifestations of ALLAH, and believing that the Nation was built upon one man who called himself GOD, plotted to destroy the physical composition of ALLAH, and in June 1969, opposing forces were successful in destroying the physical body of CLARENCE 13X Smith. But as you can see today they could not kill ALLAH, because we (THE GODS) are going to be manifesting our culture which is Islam eternally.

We the GOD NATION have never advocated hate teachings, and we are not linked to any so-called religious body. We feel that we should be allowed to exercise our way of life freely and peaceably assemble at least once a week as every other body advocating religion or ideology does. We the 5% can see no reason why we should not be recognized as a NATION.

This account of the origin of the Five Percent Nation, given by a member, is as accurate as any from other available sources. The Nation pursues its way of life within its own membership and does not give information freely to outsiders. New members are required to learn by heart the degrees of knowledge. Precisely what is contained in the total teaching is not fully known, but the following twenty lessons are believed to be required in order to attain 120 degrees of knowledge:

1. The twelve jewels of Islam
2. Supreme Mathematics
3. Lost and Found Muslim Lesson #1 (1–10)
4. Student Enrollment (1–10)
5. Breakdown of the Enrollment (1–10)
6. One to Thirty-Six
7. Applied Mathematics of the Actual Facts
8. Lost and Found Lesson #2 (1–40)
9. Solar Facts
10. Actual Facts
11. Allah World Manifested
12. Four Directions
13. Power and Refinement
14. 5% or the Stages of the Mind
15. Five credits of a Woman
16. Six rules of the Black Woman
17. Allah – 360°
18. Seven Prophets of Allah
19. General Muk, Muk's History
20. The Hog

The basic philosophy of the movement is learned by members in a question-and-answer format. The basic beliefs of the Five Percent are represented in lessons like this one:

Q. What is the 85%

A. The uncivilized people, poison animal eaters. Slaves from mental death and power. People who do not know the true and living God or their Origin in this world and worship that they know not, they are easily led in the wrong direction but hard to be led in the right direction.

Q. Who is the 10%

A. The rich, slave makers of the poor. Who teaches the poor lies to believe that the Almighty true and living God is a spook and cannot be seen by the physical eye, otherwise known as the bloodsuckers of the poor.

Q. Who is the 5% of this poor part of the Planet Earth?

A. They are the poor righteous brothers who do not believe the teachings of the 10% and who is all wise and know the true and living God is, who teach that the true and living God is the Son of Man, Supreme Being, Blackman from Asia, who teaches freedom, justice and equality to all human family of the planet earth. Otherwise known as civilized people also muslims and muslims' sons.

To an outsider, the learned lessons seem tangential to the basic philosophy. Many are concerned with physical facts and numbers related to the solar system and with explanations of meteorological events. Their function seems to be twofold: first, to supply knowledge of "scientific" events to counter animisitic beliefs in a mystery god who makes things happen, and second, to enforce the understanding of the symbolic relation between men (gods, sun), women (earth), and children (stars). Sun-Africa and her friend Shatasia explained some of the lessons.

You know, you call the man god, right? And the woman is called earth, right? But, before you said the moon. How does the moon come into it? What does that represent?

(Sun-Africa)   The moon represent the earth brain. Yeah, alright because being that the moon don't have no life on it, you know, then that's a dead planet. And it, I'll tell you, it tries to take the water from us. Right? That's why, that's why we have rain and everything 'cos the sun and moon they draw up into earth's rotations. That's called gravitation, right? And it's in this fine mist, right, that your eye it really couldn't detect, right? That the moon was trying to observe all this, right? So being that the moon is going to cool, and it still reflects light, that's why we send back to the moon, 'cos it's like our thoughts, it's the earth's thoughts. Know what I'm saying? Only thing, it don't have life on it. That's the only thing, it don't have life.

And what's the symbol of children?

(Sun-Africa)   The stars.

The stars, right. And so the men would be like the sun, right?

(Sun-Africa)   You get it now.

(Shatasia)   How far is the earth from the sun?

(Sun-Africa)   93 million miles away from the sun.

(Shatasia)   How fast does the planet rotate?

(Sun-Africa)   10,030 miles per hour. 66 trillion times.

And the reason you learn all that is because they stand for you and the gods?

(Sun-Africa)   It's like every lesson that we learn has got something to do with earth. It's symbolic to us or something.

(Shatasia)   Everybody should know what the total area of the ocean is.

(Sun-Africa)   And land is 57 million square miles . . .

(Shatasia)   Everybody should know that.

(Sun-Africa)   I mean we live on the face of the earth. That's why, like, the blackman, that we deal with, he know every square inch of the planet Earth. He make his destination all around the earth 'cos he know he's of this earth and the earth belongs to him. Because if it didn't belong to him, he wouldn't be the highest in creation. He's high, he's the most high.

The discipline of learning is mirrored in the discipline of eating and fasting. Pork must be avoided, as it is dirty and contaminated. Similarly, junk foods are suspect, as they contain unnatural chemicals which, Sun-Africa implies, may have a bad effect on human behavior. From time to time, she fasts to discipline her physical body and to purge it of these chemical impurities. She gains a certain amount of satisfaction from these physical and mental disciplines, a satisfaction that she clearly does not experience in relation to her schoolwork. The Nation offers considerably more to her than abstract knowledge. It provides a framework for interpreting her situation both as a black and as a woman. The position of women is stressed in ideological as well as very practical terms. On an abstract level, the role of woman is clearly expressed in one of the Nation's lessons:

SIX RULES OF THE BLACK WOMAN

1. The black woman is not to sell her physical composition for any payment.
2. The black woman is not to destroy or tamper with the god's star by using any form of birth control.
3. The black woman is not to have emotional affects with anyone but her man, regardless if they are devoted to ISLAM.
4. The black woman is to keep and obey the rules and regulation given by her man.
5. The black woman must reflect the light of god and reflect it on her star (child).
6. The black woman must make sure her womb and vagina is clean before permitting her man to plant his seed in her vagina.

In return for her acceptance of subordination, the woman gains the guidance, teaching, and protection of her god. She is taught, both by him and by other women, the practical skills of child rearing, cooking, and sewing.

A god got to protect the earth, you know, he got to keep it

everlasting so that we won't never destruct – self-destruct, you know? He's keeping us in tune, he's teaching us to build and to grow things and to add on to life instead of taking away from life. 'Cos we know that we don't have too much time, you know? 'Cos one of these days one of us going to be gone and then the other one teaches what I taught. Like see, if I taught her to iron a shirt a certain way and I die, she'll remember how to iron the shirt 'cos I taught her, you know? And that's how we add on to each other, by letting each other know the science behind everything, you know? And the science behind everything is just the science of how to do it more better. Knowledge is to know, you know? That's why we build to know, and we could never know everything, but we always moving 'cos if we stay home and we don't study books, we going to learn nothing.

What else do you have to learn – don't you have to learn stuff about the family, about woman, earth, that kind of stuff?

Yeah, we learn about it, like how to sew, cook, clean, right? How to take care of our bodies and stuff, you know? Like the other day I was learning about the nervous system too and the organs in us and stuff. I learned a lot about that too. Yeah, like we breast-feed babies, you know, and we deal with a lot of stuff like nutrition. You know what I'm saying? Things that's natural for us and good for us. You know, we don't deal with nothing that's not too good. You know, like candy with all that artificial flavor in it and stuff. We don't deal with that, 'cos it's not really natural.

A major thrust of the Nation's philosophy is away from passive belief in a mystery god toward a self-consciously active role in creating a better future for black people. For example, this extract from the lessons condemns the old-style god as an agent of oppression.

Q. Why does the devil teach 85% that a mystery god bring all this?

A. To conceal the true and living god which is the Son of Man, and to make slaves out of the 85% by keeping him worshipping something he cannot see (invisible) and he makes himself rich from their labor. The 85% knows that it rains, hails, snows, and hear thunder above their heads, but does not try to learn what is causing all this to happen by letting the 5% teach them. They believe in the 10% on face value.

Q. Who is that mystery God?

A.   There is no mystery God. The Son of Man have searched for that mystery God for trillions of years and was unable to find this so-called mystery god. So they have agreed that the only god is the Son of Man. So they lost no time searching for that, that does not exist.

Q.   Will you sit at home and wait for the mystery God to bring you food?

A.   Emphatically no, me and my people who have been lost from home 379 years have tried this so-called mystery God for bread, clothing, and a home, and received nothing but hard times, hunger, nakedness and out of doors, also beaten and killed by the ones who advocated that king of god. And no relief came to us until the Son of Man came to our City by name of one prophet T. P. FARD.

The importance of learning and specifically *teaching* others is part of the philosophy of actively constructing a better future. Through teaching, experience and knowledge can be passed on to later generations, so that the black man can no longer be "fooled" into ignoring his own history and believing in a false white god. Similarly, it is up to the women to produce and teach children to continue in the Islamic tradition. This is the woman's most important role. Since there is no belief in life after death, the teachings that are left behind constitute the only hope of immortality.

(Sun-Africa)   We know who God is.

(Shatasia)   No, whoever this person . . .

(Sun-Africa)   No, the mystery of it is there is no mysteries. 'Cos we are taught everything we deal with is reality, it can even be dealt with by our five senses. See, hear, touch, smell, you know, like that. You know what I'm saying? That's the science behind it. If we can't smell it, if we can't taste it, if we can't hear it, it's not for real.

This is what I can't understand. You sometimes pray, right?

(Sun-Africa)   We pray every day.

Who do you pray to?

(Sun-Africa)   Allah, and Allah's in us.

Oh, I see. He's inside *all of you.*

(Sun-Africa)   That's right. That's right, 'cos we come as one. We know there's a difference between man and woman, right, so we would say that man's the best creation and he's the creator 'cos he made this planet earth what it is today. It took man to do all this. Didn't nobody come and clap their hands and say, "Ho, we got Eiffel Towers. There's Stuyvesant City." They had to build it. You know what I'm saying? It came about through speaking, through building, and through actions, you know what I'm saying? Through motivations. We can't sit at home and wait for a mystery god that bring us clothing in our homes 'cos we know the only way we gonna get it is if we get up and plant our seeds so that we could have lettuce, so that we could have stuff to eat. But there's the type of person that think, that white man [Ronald] Reagan when he take everything that we got away from us, they think that a god will come in the sky and give it to us. We got to go for self, self-preservation, is that how you say it?

The Nation provides a convenient analysis of the position of blacks in the United States. The division of mankind into "slaves" (the 85%) and the "slave makers" (the 10%) bears an evident similarity to a crude Marxist perspective, as does the Nation's emphasis on historical analysis and particularly the way in which the slave makers used religion as a tool of oppression. However, the interface in Sun-Africa's mind between the Nation and political action is quite complex. She often stresses that the Nation should be seen as a culture, not as a religion. Since there are no mystery gods, the teachings fundamentally are about prescriptions for living. In this sense, she often downplays the religious aspects of her belief. On the other hand, she endorses not a radical change in the status quo, but a separatism, in which the true believers are allowed to pursue their own path. However, since membership is almost entirely black (a few Hispanic members are admitted), this statement becomes political. On some occasions, Sun-Africa expressed views which suggested not that whites were the enemy, but that they were simply irrelevant. They had their "own way" to go. At other times, she was more hostile about the exploitation of blacks, for which whites historically have been responsible. Then she would suggest that whites must be excluded from the Nation as a punishment for what they had done.

In the following account, the black woman is singled out for blame, for having conspired with the whites against the black man. This position can be used to justify the need to protect the black woman from white influence and to punish her treachery by enforcing her subservience to her god.

Why is it that white people can't be part of the earth and the moon?
'Cos all the time they cheated us, they cheated us. They promised

us more gold. We came here to North America. They promised us more gold. We never received our gold. They promise us forty acres of land, I know you studied this. Like in slavery times they told us we was going to have more gold, more than we was earning in our own country, which is Asia. They promised us this gold and we did not receive this gold. So therefore we realize that one who does evil to us is not there with us. You know, that's why we put them down, 'cos they already crossed us.

Right.

They already crossed us up. They don't care.

And they tried to give you all this religion, like believing God's up there and that would make everything all right.

Yeah, tricked again. They try to continue teaching us the wrong things, so he can live in luxury because he desires to make a slave out of all he can.

Sure.

See, that's why we were slaves before, slaves of a mystery death and power. We didn't know our origin was being the earth and being god. We didn't know our origin in this world. When we found out, we began to teach she who was a savage who was the black woman. 'Cos she was living in luxury and she was desiring the white man's luxury and that's how he caught up to the black man, through the woman.

Because she bought it, she fell for it, she wanted it. She wanted it.

She wanted it.

She had to be taught to understand it was only a trick?

Yeah, that's why.

The Nation does not seek formal political power, although police sources suggest it has some involvement in anti-police terrorist acts. It exists separate from the mainstream, teaching its members not only ideological lessons but practical ones – how to build, raise children, eat, and pass on knowledge. The aim of Clarence 13X was, after all, to "Save the babies," the young who will pass on the teachings. The young then have an obligation to live righteously and to contribute positively to their own future.

In spite of this stress on righteous living, the Nation's heavy involvement in crime suggests that the change in Sun-Africa's life from the Puma Crew may not have been as great as it might first appear. The major difference seems to be a cognitive one: Previously, there was no contradiction between Sun-Africa's beliefs and her behavior. She was "wild" and did "crazy things." But now that she

Five Percenters in high spirits

subscribes to a belief in living "right," how does she make sense of the burglaries, the woundings, the drugs?

How many of your friends are dead? How many people do you know who have died?

Um, about six people. This guy he got hit by a truck and he died. He was a really good person, you know, but he used to smoke reefer, you know. That's really a big thing out here, you know, reefer. I mean everybody out here get high.

Sure.

But I don't get high on the street. I'll stay home and smoke me a joint, I'll stay home and deal with that. But I don't really deal with it 'cos I don't really see that I need it.

What does the Nation think of stealing, would they consider it wrong?

Yeah, it is wrong, 'cos that's evilness, man.

So what happened? It seems a big change from what you were doing then. You don't get involved in fighting now, do you?

Not unless someone hit me or really aggravated me to where I had to defend myself. It's just me, 'cos I like to be up. I like to be moving up instead of coming down.

What does the Nation say about fighting, for example? Would they say fighting was wrong?

No.

Or would it depend on what happens?

Yeah, it depends on what happens. We can't really predict what's going to happen. If something happened to you and you get into a fight, I mean, hey, you just have to throw it out, you just have to deal with it.

Is there any stuff the Nation says you shouldn't do?

Shouldn't eat pig, shouldn't do evil 'cos anyone who does evil is just considered by me to be a little devil. You want to do evil, you know, you're a devil, and I don't want any of your little evil teachings. Don't come amongst me and try to be a snake around me. We just don't deal with evilness, 'cos there are soaps that contain pork, there's toothpaste that contains pork. We don't wear makeup – not saying that we can't. If your god lets you wear makeup, hey, you can wear makeup, you know what I'm saying? We really deal with natural things. Everything about us is natural, no imitation stuff, you know? We don't say you must not do this unless it's really, really evil. We don't deal with none of that.

The level of day-to-day violence in the area is high. The massive project complex is filled with unemployed youth standing in basketball courts, outside number spots, on stoops. In the course of just two weeks Sun-Africa and I were both attacked in separate incidents. Sun-Africa was surrounded in a park by some local youths who had a grudge against some members of the Nation. They held her and threw a bottle into her face. The next week, I was robbed by five men on the elevated section of a subway while waiting for a train. They had followed me for three blocks, and when they caught up to me, they held me over the track, threatening to let go if I didn't hand over my pocketbook. Incidents such as these are no longer particularly remarkable in the area. No one is immune. Consequently, there is much discussion of crime and criminals. When Sun-Africa talks about criminals, she clearly does not include in that category either herself or any of her friends (even those with criminal records or who are in prison). She deplores the violence she reads about as much as anyone and takes what measures she can to avoid becoming a victim.

That's why nobody could sucker me out of nothing too tough 'cos I count my change when I leave the store. You don't got no sucker here 'cos I always, like, look two ways before I cross the street. You won't find me flying up in the damn air getting hit by no car somewhere. Look two ways and let's be cool, lest you forget to look.

I don't know, it's like I was saying. A lot of people be wearing tie strings and stuff and bow ties. Suppose somebody strangle your ass to death? You'll wish you didn't have that bow tie on, right? You'll wish you didn't have it on. You can't give people a chance 'cos there's crazy people out there like that. Somebody'll come around and strangle you to death with your own damn necktie.

The inconsistency between her contempt for "crazy" criminals and her own experiences with people who commit crime is highlighted in her account of an event that occurred during my visits with her. One day, when I was not with her, she found herself caught up in sheltering an attempted robber and dealing with the police who arrived looking for him.

Yesterday, this guy named Eric, right, he lives over there and came to my building. He was going to rob this house in my building, right? So anyway, he got in the house and everything and the lady opened her door and she came in and he was caught in the house, right? So he ran out and ran down here, 'cos he had nowhere else to go. And the cops came down here, it was about seven or eight cops. No exaggeration. And they said that they wanted to search the house.

Here?

And I told them, "No," 'cos they didn't have no search warrant or nothing. So then after that, they was getting all smart with me and stuff. They was telling me that he was my boyfriend. All that time he was in the house, so I was real scared, right? He got out. He had to climb down the terrace.

From here to the ground?

Yeah, that's right.

How did he do it?

I don't know. I watched him climb down. He was nervous 'cos the cops was outside.

He got down and they didn't get him?

Right, and they didn't catch him neither. They was all on the building, and staircase, every floor and the cop was right there by the door, trying to hide in case I let him out, you know? He had to run down here, 'cos he didn't have nowhere else to run. When he was scheming on the house, he came here first to let me know, and he told me to go downstairs and watch and he said if I see any security to ring the bell and let him know. But as it happens, I didn't know it was the lady. I didn't know it was her house 'cos I see her go upstairs. I see her go up in the elevator and everything and it was her apartment!

So she walked in and he ran straight past her and out.

And he ran down to the fifth floor and they went to check the house.

Oh my God, have you seen that woman since?

Mmm. I saw her this morning. She tried to get snotty with me and stuff.

He's lucky he made it down, you know?

He fell from the third floor to the first and he sprained his ankle and stuff. I was shitting bricks. I was saying to Eric, "You got to get out of here 'cos the cops they'll try to score you before they go and get a warrant, you know?"

What happened? You went downstairs?

Yeah, to look, to see if the coast was clear for him to get down. He couldn't go through this front door, he couldn't, you know.

Ultimately, the distinction between right and wrong comes down to a very personal level for Sun-Africa. Police who lock up friends and Five Percenters are "Babylon"; police who have knowledge are "for us." Criminals who attack her or her friends are "crazy"; friends who commit crimes are implicitly exonerated as persecuted by the system. Since so much of the local crime is committed by blacks on blacks, it becomes impossible for her to argue only in terms of white oppression. Because some of the crimes of the Nation are against their own members and friends (e.g., Dupree's attack on Sun-Africa and on his other girlfriend), it is equally impossible to justify the actions as "righteous." Insofar as Sun-Africa has a philosophy of crime, it would probably be that there are good and bad people and good and bad actions, and these qualities cut across race and culture. The world in which she lives presents dangers that can only be evaluated on a case-by-case basis. But as a rule of thumb in an anomic world, usually the clever and the selfish prevail.

The moral philosophy of the Nation seems to stress adherence to the more symbolic and undemanding aspects of life (avoidance of pork, wearing refinement) rather than rejection of criminal behavior. Sun-Africa employs a kind of pragmatism that allows for almost anything as long as it is really "necessary." Fighting is apparently necessary from time to time, and joining the Nation has not wiped away old feuds or a strong sense of rivalry between groups. The strict Moslems and the Rastafarians are both rejected as holding incorrect philosophies. There are also clashes based on territoriality. Sun-Africa used to fight with girls who hung out in neighboring Riverdene when she was in the Puma Crew. Although not involved in the Nation, they still continue to fight with Sun-Africa because of her old affiliation.

You know plus Riverdene – I was barred from there and stuff. Because the girls out there, you know, we used to fight them and stuff like that and cut them up, yeah? We used to go through a lot out there. Some people don't have no class. I got class, but when I'm in my house, I just cool out, you know. It's not that I'm different 'cos I ain't no different when I get outside. A lot of people don't have no class. I be seeing a lot of girls like that. Not in my Nation 'cos we all refined black women, you know, but I be seeing a lot of women and they be thinking they too cool. And they saying, "You still the earth?" And I say, "Yes." 'Cos you know they just look tacky.

They give you a bad time?

They know better 'cos I beat their ass if they try to give me a bad time.

Do you ever fight in your refinement?

I had a fight when they jumped me. I wear it every day.

Isn't it difficult to fight back?

Hell no. 'Cos I kicked their ass. That's right. I was with all of them [old friends from the Puma Crew] last night, and they had a .357 gun, and it was big, you should have seen it. I said, "What?" I was all excited you know, 'cos I haven't seen one in a long time and stuff, you know.

Sure.

They're kind of barred from Riverdene, you know what I'm saying? So they have to come strapped or something. They can't just go without nothing 'cos somebody might just try to hurt them.

How come they got barred? Did something happen?

'Cos of a fight we had. It was out there in Riverdene.

Oh. So they have to be careful when they're around there. What about you? Is it safe for you?

Yeah. It's safe for me 'cos I'm the earth and, you know, they don't say nothing to me, so . . .

Right.

I ignore them, but they know who I am as well as I know who they are, you know what I'm saying? 'Cos like the day after Shamar died, they started calling me by my government name and stuff.

Like really trying to get to me and stuff, but I didn't pay them no mind.

Yeah.

Yeah, but I remember it's never going to be forgotten. That's something that's added on to me. I know who they are and what they are really about.

Deaths of Nation members often seem directly related to their involvement in crime. Yet Sun-Africa seems to interpret those who die as victims of oppression or fate. The fact of their criminal lifestyle is more or less ignored. Such an attitude is only really understandable in the light of the area in which she lives. Unemployment is high. Schooling is viewed at best as irrelevant. The streets are filled with people drinking, smoking reefer, playing the numbers. Living on the borderline of legality is widespread. Violence erupts often and is not unexpected, as Sun-Africa and her sister Lila know.

You said that Shasha was killed just after Shamar?

He got shot May 26th, I think it was. He died June the second.

What happened?

(Sun-Africa)   They was on the road and they was arguing. 'Cos it's two numbers spots. At least it *was* two numbers spots – they burned it. The first numbers spot was where the gods hang out. The second one, you know, the man owns it, and they was arguing. Then Shasha told the man something, and the man he just shot him in the neck. He shot him and then they put him in the car and took him to the hospital.

So what happened to the guy who did it?

(Sun-Africa)   To my knowledge, he was in jail, then he got out on bail.

(Lila)   That's not right 'cos he's out, he's out.

(Sun-Africa)   Well, like I told you, somebody got to do that body. It's hard, but somebody got to do that body.

(Lila)   Salat got shot the other night.

(Sun-Africa)   Where at?

(Lila)   Brownsville.

(Sun-Africa)   Is they alright?

(Lila)   Yeah.

(Sun-Africa)   So? If they're alright, tell straight. You know what I'm saying? If they ain't, then we got something to worry about.

Death is dealt with by mysticizing, even romanticizing it. The event becomes reinterpreted in a description which seems to imply a preordained fate, a part of some mystical plan. If death doesn't get you, the police probably will. Somebody always has "to do the body," to serve the time in jail. This is also considered a kind of destiny, with the police acting as agents.

The people over there, I mean, who's over there? Like your Five Percent leader hangs out, right?
(Lila)   They don't like him, they after him.
Who's after him?
(Lila)   We don't know.
(Sun-Africa)   They don't like him. You could know for sure the cops are, you know? Say if he was to get in trouble, the cops would be into it, you know what I'm saying? Like, say he went to the hospital for a bullet wound, 'cos that's like the guy that was with Shamar. If they catch him, he's got to do the bullet, and do the bullet means he's got to go to jail, if he's old enough.

Sun-Africa seems to perceive life as a kind of jungle in which another gang, the police, or a bullet are all likely to stop her in her path. Membership in the Nation cannot prevent these things. They are seen as endemic to the place she lives and the people she knows. These circumstances override anything else. Crime, drugs, aggression are a necessary part of survival. While the Five Percent philosophy may make verbal gestures against them, they are ultimately "necessary."

What the philosophy does provide is an identity that confers some pride and offers hope for a better future. Better still, it does not demand "unrealistic" behavior – no one is expected to be a saint. And for an earth, the Nation offers the chance to throw off a bad reputation and take on a "new" identity, in exchange for submission and maternity.

Now a "refined black woman," Sun-Africa lives with another earth in the Bronx, caring for their children together. Their god is rarely at home, and Sun-Africa is once again in a community of women not unlike the one in which she grew up.

Chapter 6

No Escape

Connie, Weeza, and Sun-Africa are representative of three different kinds of New York City gang. The girls differ in age, in role within their gang, and in cultural background. All, however, have chosen to be involved in a subculture that police and the criminal justice system regard as deviant. So little information on female gang membership is available that it is difficult to assess how representative they may be. In the course of this chapter, data from other girl gang members in New York City with whom I spoke will be offered to substantiate the generality of some of the themes that are common to their experiences. But can we assume that what is true of New York City gangs is equally true of gangs in other major cities?

A comparison, based on aggregated data, of New York City and Brooklyn specifically with other major American cities suggests that in terms of the sex ratio, social background, age distribution, and criminal activities of gang members New York may be considered representative.[1] On the other hand, aggregated data can be misleading, masking important differences between cities. Miller suggests these differences may be great indeed. San Francisco, for example, reports only twenty gangs with a membership of 250, 90 percent of which is Asian. Yet the city's gang problem becomes substantial when it is noted that 72 percent of all juvenile homicides committed in 1974 were gang-related.[2] Experiences in New York City similarly suggest that Chinatown gangs may be small in number but have a high rate of homicide, which has been linked to extortion and drug-trafficking rings that may have strong connections with adult organized crime. Los Angeles may now be experiencing the most severe gang problems. Chicano gangs in the San Fernando Valley and East Los Angeles, which take the names of their *barrios*, have been involved in intergang warfare for decades,

232

resulting in the highest rate of gang-related killings of all major cities.[3] Miller's work in the 1960s focused principally upon young white groups in Boston, where the intergang conflict was far less severe.[4] Gangs as part of a local social matrix wax and wane, changing in the nature of their criminal involvement and their geographical and ethnic location. Clampdowns by police or politicians, surges of community programs may suppress them temporarily. Media attention, economic slumps may revitalize them. Sometimes they simply seem to disappear, as in the South Bronx during the 1970s when arson drove much of the population out of the neighborhood, only to result in an increase in gang membership in Brooklyn.

Trying to pin down the representativeness of any gang is an impossible task. There are no documents on which to rely, and if there were, they would probably become outdated in a matter of one or two years. But we do know that gangs exist and have existed for most of this century. The enigma of the gang member can be approached on at least two levels, which involve different kinds of questions. First, on a general level, how to account for the peculiarly American nature of the gang? How did it come into existence and why did it assume that particular form? Why were girls so marginal to its philosophy and activities? After that, on the level of the individual members, why should a girl choose to become part of a gang?

Youth gangs are not a universal phenomenon. Most cultures have teenagers who form cliques in school, at play, or on the streets – the dependence of the adolescent on the peer group is as true even for primates as it is for people – but these are not gangs. They do not consistently have membership initiation, demarcated roles, rules, names, "colors," territoriality, discipline, a specific philosophy, or feuds with other groups. They are loosely knit collectives of friends who may spend time together for a while but are free to move on to other friendships. Those who have searched for the structured gang in Western societies other than the United States have in general failed to find anything more than such cliques of friends.[5] Some New York gangs do claim international status by virtue of affiliate branches in Puerto Rico, the West Indies, or Mexico, but these are United States exports; they did not spring spontaneously from those cultures. It is in the history of the United States that an answer is to be found.

The earliest gangs in New York were composed of Irish im-

migrants. In Chicago they were made up of Poles, Italians, Irish –
the recently arrived immigrants. As they arrived, they often moved
into neighborhoods populated by their own people who spoke their
language, understood their background, shared their confusions,
supported them as they acclimatized. Within the neighborhoods,
ward bosses rose to power and represented the special interests of
their people: arranging jobs, the immigration of relatives, the social
and political solidarity of their own. New York grew as an amalga-
mation of these groups split by neighborhood and culture, each
fighting politically for themselves.[6] Settlement houses and clubs
tried to acculturate the neighborhoods by encouraging proficiency
in English, diligence in work, and subscription to the American
Dream of material and social success through hard work for all, but
they were only partially successful. They were, after all, trying to
build not only a cultural melting pot, but a middle-class one at
that. Women barely able to feed their families were encouraged to
get up charity boxes, learn embroidery, go to the opera. Boys were
encouraged through sport to compete within the rules and succeed,
to aspire to professional and public success, to become Americans.
A century later in the same city, there is little evidence of the full
realization of that benevolent dream.

In New York, neighborhoods continue to be drawn along ethnic
lines but also by new segregating forces. Huge housing projects
erected in selected areas force those dependent on public assistance
to live together. Systematic arson by landlords demolishes areas,
crowding the former occupants together in neighborhoods of poverty.
The middle class "discover" a new area and move in, renovating
and building, only to squeeze out the former occupants as rents
double and triple. Within every area of poverty, neighborhoods
remain stubbornly intractable. A walk through Brooklyn is a trip
through four or five cultures, each demarcated from the other.
Puerto Rican areas with their *bodegas* and *cerveza* signs sit a block
away from the *trattorias* of the neighboring Italians. In Williamsburg, where Jews and blacks live cheek by jowl, civil violence
erupts often enough to indicate that hostility between groups is
alive and well.

Unlike Europe, America has no history of explicit class conflict.
On the other hand, it is clearly not a classless society. What it has
most noticeably failed to produce is an enduring working-class
political party, philosophy, or culture. The reasons for this spring
from the early immigration patterns of local neighborhoods and
local political struggle. Group vied against group, each concerned

with its own special interests. Each held fast to its own sense of cultural identity. Each accepted the philosophy of the American Dream, which, in its refusal to acknowledge social class, provided no means of understanding the plight of the poor except in terms of personal failure. There were few class confrontations; unions were viewed as evil and corrupt. Those who voiced too much concern about the distribution of wealth or opportunity were denounced as un-American, or, worse, as communists.[7] Until recently, Marx was not taught in schools and the European history of class conflict was seen as a result not of economics, but of corrupt monarchies.

Unlike Europe, where political philosophies specifically embody the interests of the bourgeoisie or the working class, America produced two major political parties, both of which endorsed without hesitation a capitalist system differing only with respect as to how benign the government could afford to be in its welfare system. Politicians diverted attention to America's role in world affairs and dissenting voices on internal economic policy were of secondary importance. So today, as a century ago, legislative and social change comes not from a united working class, but from special-interest groups. In nineteenth-century New York, the populus was divided along neighborhood lines. In this century, society is divided also by sex and race: by the voices of women demanding constitutional amendments, of blacks rejecting segregated schooling, of Puerto Ricans demanding independence, of homosexuals protesting job and housing discrimination. Their causes are just, but there is generally a failure to see the unifying theme behind their grievances. There is no coherent criticism of the negative effects of capitalism and no working-class mouthpiece with which to voice it.

However, in many respects the social and political climate in America has altered drastically since the nineteenth century. When gangs began, they did so in a country that was struggling toward order. Corruption and lawlessness were part of that struggle. It is clear from early accounts that many of the neighborhood bosses were less than scrupulous in their political and business practices. Gangs were employed to fix ballot boxes, lead riots, even murder rival candidates. In return, they were nurtured by the politicians, who gave them money and social legitimacy. Thrasher writes of the power exerted by organized mobsters in Chicago, who controlled police and politicians as well as recruiting from teenage gangs. Growing up in those times, it would have been impossible to conclude that crime did not pay. The businessmen and politicians encouraged the gangs' activities, their disregard for the law, and their belief that one way out of the slums was through crime. The frontier tradition of the right to claim land, to defend it by force, must have added to the belief that power, by whatever means, was the route to success. The failure of the law to control vigilante groups also added to the belief that the violent gang had a legitimate place in society.[8] In the struggle of group against group, violence became a common theme. The gang, its territorial loyalty, and its disregard for the law were passed on through the generations and continue today. It is a hard cycle to break. Where one gang exists and threatens the well-being of its neighboring areas, new gangs arise for protection. When one gang buys a gun, the other must arm itself also. When one member goes to prison, he meets others from different gangs who reinforce his hatred and need for gang protection.[9] It is one neighborhood against another, as the gangs see it. Class solidarity is an alien concept.

The idea of an alliance of gangs, however, is less remote. The "supergangs" of Chicago in the sixties – the Blackstone Rangers and the Latin Kings – were composed of smaller groups. Today in New York, the Inner City Roundtable of Youth tries to unite gang members from different boroughs into a lobbying force for urban youth. These attempts have not met with great success. Feuds between gangs flare up and split the whole into fractions. Members, impatient with the slowness of political change, return to their former activities. Those that become involved at all are in the minority. Many of the gangs have virtually no contact with other groups outside their borough. Some Bronx and Brooklyn gang members view Manhattan as an alien territory. They do not know its geography and fear they might cross into the turf of other gangs by mistake. Police in the Gang Intelligence Unit point out that gang members, even when warrants are out for their arrest, will doggedly remain in the same neighborhood, even on the same street corner. Their whole life is there – their family and friends – and flight into an unknown city is out of the question.[10] With borough divisions of gangs so marked and intractable, the idea of any national sense of unity is remote. It is rare indeed that a New York gang member can name any gang from Chicago, Los Angeles, or even Philadelphia. Gangs remain neighborhood based, divided against each other, fighting for the right to claim an area as their own.

Those who join gangs are from the ranks of those who have the least to gain from the status quo. They are often from backgrounds of poverty, are unemployed, undereducated, and of minority status.

Many have criminal records and most have little to look forward to in terms of economic success. It might be expected that they would form a true counterculture, a rejection of all the social roles, institutions, and values of society at large. Some writers, such as Cohen, have suggested that gangs do indeed invert the middle-class value system. But they do not explicitly exist to challenge the status quo. Crime is not committed for its own sake; it is not a symbol of revolt or a gesture of alienation. Laws are broken as a part of the gangs' life-style and values, but gangs are not composed of potential revolutionaries; in fact, quite the opposite. Their views are often conservative.

The Sandman and the Sandman Ladies:

I'm thirty years old, I'm tired of looking for jobs, and I am not going to let nobody tell me, "There is a job there for you, Gino, you can get it." People tell me, "Gino you can work – you get $150." Why am I going to leave what I got going to work for a place where I am going to make $150 – when I go home and maybe make three, four, five hundred dollars a day? Why? If I can't make it legally, right, if I can't make enough money legally, then the hell, the next best thing for me to do is do it illegal – and I am going to do it.

What about politics?

I don't get into that stuff. I feel no matter what, the world is going to be still running by itself anyway. Most people don't contribute to society, they don't vote, they don't do anything. And it's not just illiterate people. A lot of people just don't want to get involved period. They're just content to let society do what it can do for them, and the rest, they just survive on their own. That's why they have so many crimes, things like that. Because everybody is just trying to survive.

OK, we are talking about New York, just New York. What would you change about New York?

If I am eating a T-bone steak, I would like you to eat a T-bone steak. If I am eating a damn sirloin, I want him to have a sirloin. I don't want to have a sirloin for myself, and have him eat some goddam hamburger meat or something – I want us to have the same. Because, goddam, there is no reason why people have to go without in this goddam society, as rich as this country is. People go with one meal a day, starving, and then have to go onto the streets and find means of getting food for their families because either the welfare won't take them or if they take them, they give you some bullshit. Nobody wants to take bullshit. I would rather have me a good job that is going to pay me good – then I know I don't have to do anything that is against the law. All we are asking for is to have the same that the middle-class people are having. We are not asking for first-class action. The same thing that every middle-class person is having is what we want. We don't want to have what the goddam President has because we know we ain't going to get it, but, damn, give us a break, give us a shot at life – give us a break to be comfortable and to do what we believe in.

Listen, what I want to understand and what I don't understand – if you had control, are you really talking about a revolution in this country? Are you talking about all the poor, all the unemployed just rising up and overthrowing the whole damn system?

No, there is not a revolution that goes without force or without violence – we are not talking about violence. We are just talking about getting ours, whether it's with words or something. They tried to get me to join the Puerto Rican revolutionary whatever. No way. To me, Puerto Rico does not have to be liberated. I like to go and come as I please, instead of having a visa or asking for permission. And then, what the hell, Puerto Rico is only so large, so big. It's always been struggling for survival, one land or another has owned it. If the United States is not owning it, somebody else will. And the United States is the best place. That's why it's the united way, even though the white people came in and took over and said, "We're going to make it united." This is the only place where you can come here and be yourself to an extreme but yet you can still be a faggot – that's an extreme. Or bitch. Dress that way, and I'm not saying it's going to be accepted by everybody, but you can still survive. Feel your identity – whether it be religion or whatever. That's why I say, the United States? I'll never leave and if I have to fight for it, I'll fight for it. I can't stand draft dodgers.

The Sex Boys and the Sex Girls:

America really doesn't want foreigners like me coming in, but right now Puerto Rico isn't foreign.

Yeah. Dominican. Cuban. All those kind of people.

They can come on a boat. They can come on a boat from Santa Domingo to Puerto Rico. A lot of them get caught though, but a lot of them get in. And that's what fucks up the country.

What do you think about freeing Puerto Rico?

Not really.

It's good for them to go over there and listen and explore.
There's some American people living in Puerto Rico. And
they're alright. They're nice. They don't bother nobody.

Where the disenfranchized might be expected to come together
as a separate culture, abandoning the capitalist social structures
that have failed to benefit them, those structures are maintained
intact. Many gangs organize themselves along the lines of business
corporations: they have presidents, vice-presidents, and spokesmen.
Others use paramilitary terminology: sergeant at arms, counselor
of war, and quartermaster. Still others employ the structure of the
family: Moms and Pops who discipline, set limits, allocate resources, buy treats. In comparing American gangs with the subcultures of youth in another Western country, such as England,
their desire for structure is remarkable. In England, neither Punks,
Rockers, nor Skinheads has ever employed such terms, nor has a
power structure of such a kind ever been present.

The Sandman and the Savage Riders:

What about the structure of the gang?
It still exists but in terms of . . .
Some clubs are different . . .
Yeah, right. Sometimes there are clubs that don't want to have a
President, they just want to have a Council . . .
We have a President and a Vice . . . that's the way it is. And some
clubs have Vice-Presidents, they have Warlords, they have every-
thing, they even go as far as Secretary. Some clubs just have a
President and a Sergeant . . .
When we say Sergeant, that means, Sergeant at Arms. That's the
man that keeps track of all the hardware that the club might have,
keeping it in working condition, that's his job. So there is a
structure . . . Like I said again, we have our own laws which we
abide by which is definitely way different from the existing laws in
terms of the system.
And what about gang wars?
The Sergeant at Arms or the War Counselors, they are the ones
to do it. But it's all designated by the President or the Head of the
Council – lots of clubs have got Presidents. In my club we got no
President, we got a Council and then I am the Father Founder. I
am the string, more or less, right? Anything that they decide, I have
the overall word on it. They come to me – I think, I check into my
books, see if it's alright. Then, if it's OK, we do it. If it's not, then I

say we can't do it and they can't say anything. They got to go by what I tell them.

We have groups called Gestapo groups, and they make sure that even the councils in each organization is up to par, is doing what they got to do and if they are not doing it, they themselves get disciplined.

The Savage Outlaws:

If you've got a group, it's supposed to be a family, you're supposed to be together. I can't see why you've gotta beat up on a member. But then maybe so many people come from blood families who deal with all problems by beating up on the kids or other family members, it's the only way they know how to deal with things.

Shadows of Death:

They'd usually have a Committee, the guy's right hand, the Treasurer, and all four of them, standing there and looking tough. And she comes up and says – I want to be the Leader and I can beat her. That's a challenge and they have to fight; and if she wins, she's the Leader.

The pyramidal power structure within the gangs derives from the power structures they see in politics, business, and the military. Climbing the ladder of success may be as important in the gang as in the corporation. The use of initiation rites also generates a sense of exclusivity within the gang, which reflects the "many are called but few are chosen" snobbery of the country club. Not only are structures borrowed from society at large but so are philosophies. Acquisition and ownership are crucial. Turfs are "owned" and "taken" as a tribute to the gang's power or as a means of controlling the economic benefits of drug dealing, extortion, and robbery. Gangs compete with one another in their own area of operation as much as any business corporation.

Why have the gangs chosen to accept so unquestioningly the elitism, the competitiveness, and the materialism of their society? Among gang members, there is a real paucity of political education. Most have never entertained the idea that society might be structured in any other way than through the present system. Given no alternative way of viewing the present social and economic arrangements, the extent of their political unrest becomes a complaint of insufficient welfare programs or a tendency to blame the most recently arrived immigrant group for their plight. Capitalism remains right, their failure within it, wrong. Without a high school education, without a better command of English, they have little hope of success. But with the strength of the gang, they can achieve a measure of status and a means of economic survival. Many try and fail to obtain legitimate work and finally retreat into the safety of the gang; the gang is a small-scale version of society but one in which they can succeed.

Gang members are no less materialist than anyone else. Many hours a day are spent in front of a television. Quiz shows with their promise of instant and effortless wealth, are particularly popular. Numbers are played daily in the hope of a big win. The girls especially are subject to the dictates of fashion and consumer fetishism: substantial sums are spent on the "right" jeans, hair perms – even cigarettes.

The Five Percenters:

You know what? Kool could be the first one before Newport. When I was growing up, everybody smoked Kools like they do Newports now. But I wouldn't say that – I wouldn't be too sure to say that.

You see all the young people, teenagers – Newport. No other cigarette, unless they're white. They smoke Marlboro. Nasty cigarette.

For the white people, it's Marlboro. Yeah, those are strong.

My mother she would take me shopping for the summertime. She took me up to get Calvin Klein and Sasson short sets. Goodness, I used to have so much Jordache, right? All them stuff is my bag, but I gave most of my stuff away. I had Sergio Valente, I had so much stuff.

Wow.

You know everything, and I just gave them all up 'cos I gave Donna my Jordache, I gave Crystal my Sergio Valente, I gave Mimi a pair of Jordache. I gave away a lot of stuff plus stuff they had borrowed from me that never was returned. So you know.

The Sex Girls:

What else do you want?
Something better for my kids. And something better for me – a nice apartment. I would like to have my own house. For me I think marry – I find somebody.

The Sandman Ladies:

Because of advertising, everybody wants to keep up with everything, man. Even children – everything. They make it so hard
for you to live. People ridicule you if you're not really, like, up
with the times. Unless you say "Fuck the world" and you really are
in your own world. Most of the time, even the kids in school. Your
kids might come home and say, "Mom you got to buy me $30.00
sneakers, $2.99 sneakers ain't doing it for me. I just can't stand
criticism anymore. You have to buy me $30.00 sneakers." What do
you do? You go out there and you try to get them for your kids – the
best way you can, the best way you know how or something. A lot
of people – not myself – would have to go through a lot of changes.
It's more like a general feeling.

Clothes are almost worshipped: jeans ironed each morning, boots
oiled, sneakers whitened.

While some writers have argued for the existence of a set of focal
concerns specific to lower-class male life,[11] this should not be
parodied into a simplistic belief that gang members are isolated
from society at large or hermetically sealed in an alien set of norms.
As much as anyone, they are exposed through the media to the
images of a life lived with limitless luxury, in which everyone is
beautiful and relationships are passionate, stormy, superficial, and
ultimately selfish. They subscribe to this as the natural order.
There is no counterculture in the gang, only the rehearsal in
microcosm of an American belief in consumerism, in the equation
of money with power, in competition and success, and in a hierarchy
through which the initiate may climb to power and one day become
president. All are proud to be American, some have fought for their
country and most would do so enthusiastically if the need arose.

In understanding the fundamentally conservative structure and
values of the gang, the position of girls becomes more explicable.
Females must accept the range of roles within the gang that might
be available to them in society at large. The traditional structure of
the nuclear family is firmly duplicated in the gang. In straight
society the central, pivotal figure is the male. His status in the
world of societal and material success is the critical factor, while the
woman supports, nurtures, and sustains him. The gang parodies
this state of affairs without even the economic infrastructure to
sustain it, for the male rarely works and often it is the female who
receives a more stable income through welfare. Nevertheless, the

males constitute the true gang. Gang feuds are begun and continued by males; females take part as a token of their allegiance to the men. Now and again, the females of one gang will sustain a hostility against another female auxillary gang even when the males have ended theirs, but this is tolerated only because of its insignificance. What girls feel toward one another will not cause the males to reengage in war. Their petty quarrels are simply indulged.

Nor are the double standards of morality forgotten by gang members. Hell's Angels distinguish promiscuous "sheep" from wifely "old ladies."[12] Girls who sleep around within the gang are disparaged by the males and disciplined by the females. The Sex Girls discuss the girls of rival gangs as only interested in indiscriminate sex with the boys. At the same time, the sexual adventures of the boys are considered an unremarkable aspect of the male character. The perpetuation of such values keeps the girls very firmly in their place.

The Devil's Rebels (Ladies):

Half of the girls were going out with guys from the gang. For instance, some had made it with all the guys in the gang and they pick their own to stay with.

What did the guys think?

They don't care.

I seen it happen. This girl – you remember Ann? She was a little short girl, light skin. Her and this girl Lillian were the main ones who went all through the gang, even though they denied it. The guys always talk. You kind of hear them. She winded up with one. She slept with four or five of them. And they all knew it. And she's still with one of them. I mean that's crazy.

What do you think of that?

She's got a reputation right there. Say the girl is in love with the guy and they're together and another girl comes, she knows he only wants her for a piece.

So he won't mind?

Of course not.

But then it get a little too much and you see those two girls fighting.

Sure. The girlfriend doesn't mind. Does it work the other way round?

He'll kick your ass.

Once is enough.

So the guys wouldn't put up with it?

No.

But the girls put up?

Yeah. 'Cos, see, once a girl be going all around, she gets a reputation. You know they only want her for that, that's it. That's not a serious thing.

How do the girls feel about that girl?

Some of them probably hate her and some of them probably just get along with her. They know she has a reputation and that's the way she is.

Are they scared of losing their boyfriend or do they really disapprove of her morals?

Both. Most of the girls who does that, they dress sexy. They dress more sophisticated than the regular girl so . . . One of the girls is making goo-goo eyes at the other girl's boyfriend, she's just going to tell her off because she'll be afraid the guy might go with her 'cos she's more pretty and more sophisticated. It works like that too.

The Sex Girls:

Fuck it – I do whatever I please, you know. That's the way I am now, I do whatever I please. Even though I got to live with the people, but I don't care. They don't give me nothing. People say I'm a whore? They got to prove that. They got to prove I'm a whore. They can't say, "You're a whore," just like that. They got to prove a lot of things. Even though they're talking about you, they got to prove that. They could tell you, "You're this, you're that." But they got to prove it. They ain't got no proof, so what's up? Right. So I say, I don't live with the people no more. I live by myself. What the people say. I don't care. You know. Let it go.

Shadows of Death:

I was with one guy and I always stay with him. But there's girls – that's not for me – they go with this guy and this guy. Because all guys want is to get over on you, and once they get over on you, you ain't worth much to them – like you're a tramp on the street.

The Turban Queens:

Do the boys keep pretty strict control over you?

Well, when they're not around, we can do what we want. When they're there, we can't.

We're not allowed.

The Turban Saints would come down hard if you started seeing someone else?
They won't take you back. They just better not catch you on
another turf.

The Devil's Rebels (Ladies):

It ain't nothing to them. They rape a girl, they don't care.
As long as it ain't in their family, if they know them . . .
How do the girls in the gang feel about it.
They say, "As long as it's not us, man." I don't think they mind.
Them themselves set up other girls.
Do they do that because they're frightened?
Probably because the guys ask them to do it, I don't know.

In Gale's account of Bronx gangs it is clear that the girls'
heterosexuality is crucial to their membership because it perpetu-
ates male control.[13] "Dykes," when discovered, are multiply raped
and thrown out of the club. At the same time, male members admit
to engagements with male transsexual prostitutes, and other reports
suggest that male members are not adverse to "turning tricks" for
money.[14] However, the gang girl who dispenses sexual favors too
freely is subject to the same labels as she would be in society at
large.

Another female role is that of mother figure to the males. Connie
is probably the most explicit example of this. She offers advice and
counsel on personal matters to the males. They in turn accord her
the respect due to her maternal role. As female leader, she is clearly
the social and emotional leader. Gino remains in charge of more
public matters relating to income, aggression, and police contact.
In the Five Percenters, the mother figure is clearly embodied in the
term "earth," and her role in the Nation is as guardian of the
children and keeper of the hearth. The separate nature of men and
women is an explicit part of the Nation's philosophy. Not only is
the woman's sexuality controlled by the stigma of cheapness, but
her reproductive functions also become a matter of male decision.
Motherhood and womanhood become almost inseparable and
dictate her role in the structure.

There are tomboys in gangs also, girls who try to succeed on
male terms. They are accepted with the same indulgence accorded
to junior males. If they become too malelike, they acquire nick-
names like "the Hulk" and "Butch," but a sporting attempt at
fighting and stealing is tolerable. Weeza's bout in jail taught her

the folly of emulating males. She cried, she missed her children, she wanted to go home. When times get tough, the girls are just not able to take it.

The Sex Girls:

I'd hate to be locked up.
You know Jodey from the Sex Survivors? He's a moreno too. He used to hang out with the Sex Boys. They say he was drunk and they give him three years for what, I don't know.
What if it was you?
Oh my God. I'd go crazy. The guys are strong. Don't worry, they're strong. I get depressed and I cry. I think in the end I get used to it, I don't know. Take me a long time.

The Turban Queens:

Combat boots, pants rolled up. Hankies all over – I don't do that no more. Because I know it's just putting myself down low. I realized it myself, you're putting yourself down low for no reason.
What do the boys think of the clothes?
My boyfriend didn't like it. But there was a couple of guys that weren't going with girls that would say, "You look bad," you know, but my boyfriend didn't like it. Neither did all the other boyfriends. "You shouldn't be like that. What the fuck you dress like that?" They would beat you up. "Go home and change," or something like that. We used to wear hankies over here, hankies over here. Pockets, on necks, pants, hats, all over. I used to think, "Oh that's bad, that's nice." But then I realized, "Look at me. I'm a girl. That doesn't look right." Besides getting a reputation among older people. Like, "Look at that little tramp or whore."

So the boys let girls play at toughness, knowing it is of no real consequence in the end. The tomboy will grow out of it, have children, and a decent male will provide for her, keep her at home, and save her from the streets.

The fundamentally conservative structure, philosophy, and history of gangs is not something that gang members are apt to recognize or promote. The image they present to the public and the local community is that of the outlaw, the rebel, the persecuted. Gang members are engaged in a tacit, mutually supportive exercise in promoting this rebel image. Their concerted effort does not arise out of an articulated conspiracy nor is it engaged in solely for the purpose of misleading outsiders. At one level, the gang members represent themselves to each other in these terms, and this self-presentation is accepted willingly. At the same time, members offer accounts of their behavior that are clearly at variance with this superimposed reality: they admit to victimizing neighbors and to attacks on single opponents by three or four gang members. They do not appear to be uneasy about the incongruence between their romantic image ("To live above the law you must be honest," as Bob Dylan put it and as the gangs also assert) and their behaviors, which belie any adherence to rebel codes of morality. Many criminal behaviors do not cause dissonance: for instance, gang members (and many other members of society) do not view the selling of soft drugs as an immoral act. They wear this proudly as a symbol of their "rebellion." However, problems appear when gang members engage in the very behaviors they condemn in others and claim to be preventing: robbery, burglary, rape, and assault. But members rarely attempt to justify or excuse their behavior to one another. On the rare occasions that they do offer explanations, it is invariably in terms of necessity: they "needed" the money, they "had to" assault the victim who resisted. Such justifications are seen to legitimate *their* actions but not anyone else's.

Some of the gangs even stress the brotherhood between "out-laws," creating the illusion of a united subculture that is somehow superior to the anemic, middle-class world beyond. Given the prevailing level of inter-gang violence this image is particularly hard to accept. But once again, the gangs appear able to live with the contradictions between the brotherhood of outlaws and the temporary "necessity" of their local inter-gang feud.

The Savage Riders, the Together Brothers, and the Sandman:

An outlaw is a person that enjoys freedom . . .
Yeah, that's the whole point about it, that's his nature, he don't want to go round raping or robbing somebody . . .
They call us outlaws, they say "Hey, rebel, get out of here."
We don't abide by other people's laws, we form our own laws.
We form our own laws but within the law, OK within the law.
Sometimes I would go in my jacket, I would walk in there, men come up to me, "Man, I like what you wear." They would compliment me on the way I was dressed. I got this outfit because I sold all my equipment. And they used to ask me, "How is it out there? Do you get high and all that?" I would say, "We have our

fun," and then they would say, "Sometimes I wish I was out there with you." A lot of lawyers and businessmen and people that own premises, the only thing is, to keep up their image they got to wear that three-piece suit and they got to have that part in that play. They can't do that. They don't have that freedom, they are trapped and they envy us, like we said. Businessmen, they don't have that freedom, they wish they did, but to make that bread off our poor people, they must do what they got to do – and they do that kind of crap without nothing, without no freedom of mind or body. That's no good.

They can't feel the things we feel or the way our life-style is. The [mainstream] Man says, "How can you all be doing this or doing that?" He tries to analyze our life-style. "How do you do this?" and all this kind of shit. We don't want them to get inside us, we don't want them to.

This is my brother right there. If he ain't like that, if he like to be hard with his stuff and he don't want to help another brother, he wanted to be selfish, we put him in check. Because you can't be a brother, you can't be an outlaw, you can't be selfish with your shit. We got to try and help each other, that's the only way to be. He got $1,000 and he got to help his brother out with another $1,000. What kind of brother are you? Together, we can both help out each other, we ain't supposed to be like everybody for themselves, everybody high on their own shit. If I haven't got a place to live and I go to my man's house, and say, "Hey, man, I am out on the street . . ." And he comes over to my house, we eat, we get high, and then we crash out or I get up and go home or I might stay there the whole week if I feel like it. Like he comes over or I go over his place, or we go to a restaurant and he comes over to my place. We are all from different clubs, but that's the way it is.

Gangs draw much on the vigilante image. They claim to keep the streets safe and the neighborhood clean. They defend the area from the lawless evil of adjacent street gangs. In this sense, they feel a deep rivalry with the Guardian Angels – who patrol subways to deter crime – whom they frequently disparage as bums, and they deeply resent the media attention that the Guardian Angels receive. Clad in gang clothes, employing the same structure, the Angels are seen as "good kids," while they themselves are portrayed as "bad." When one of the Guardian Angels was implicated in a highly publicized Manhattan murder, the gangs' suspicions were confirmed. The fine line between vigilante and outlaw had been publicly crossed. Similarly, the police are viewed as just as aggres-

sive and corrupt as any gang. Their behavior, however, is legit-
imated by their badge. Only the gangs have to suffer the stigma of
"badness" for behavior that is tolerated, even applauded, when
performed by others.

The Sex Girls:

How come there are so few white gangs?
Are you kidding? They got the two biggest gangs in this country
– the KKK [Ku Klux Klan] and the cops.
   The cops was coming around, just passing by. We was hanging
out on the corner and they came by and called the Sex Boys
faggots. So the Sex Boys said, "You're faggots." They just get out
and bang everybody against the wall – Popeye, Afro, Willie,
everybody. Then I was passing by and I get in the car – they took
me too – they hit me and everything.
With their fists?
No, they hit me on my behind. Because I had a bunch of change
and I just throw it in his face. And they hit me on my behind, they
lock me up.
Did they hit the guys with their fists?
With fists. With boots. With blackjack. They hit in the mouth. I
was there. The day we got busted. You remember. I told you the
day they hit me in my butt? Popeye in his head, Afro in his balls.
   Who was it? Little Willie. "You want to take my number? Here."
And they hit Little Willie in the face with the badge.

The Sandman and the Savage Riders:

The Guardian Angels got media recognition, they got everything
– now. They say they are this and they are that, that they are
protecting the subway . . .
That's bullshit, man.
That's bullshit, right. They had already gotten busted for ripping somebody off on the subway, with their shit on, with their
berets and with their "Magnificent Thirteen" T-shirts and all their
bullshit. They got arrested for ripping somebody off.
   We patrol the park – there was three rapists in the park two
weeks ago, and we had to take them out of the park. The cops
couldn't find them. We went to the park and we found them, we
found them in 93rd Street. They got a tennis court there and they
were inside the tennis court, and we found them, we dragged them.
Now, they raped this young girl, her mother, and the girl's aunt,

but we got them, we turned them over to the police.

What did you do with them? You didn't touch them, you just turned them over to the police?

Hey, there is so many of us, we don't have to do anything. We just surround them, "Come on, guys, we don't want to fight you. If you want to swing, fine." If they bust up and they take a swing at us, we got our belts and stuff to protect ourselves.

So what you are talking about is community control.

Right. What the community cannot control, I control. What the community cannot get to, I can get to. Sometimes the cops come in and nobody will tell them a goddam thing. Nobody is going to tell them nothing – even to save their hide, they won't tell them – but I will come along and they will tell me. They will open up to me because they know, having gone through that shit, everybody opens up willing. They let me know what's up and that way I bring up what happened. And I have to get some kind of understanding between him and the police, that they won't prosecute him to the fullest or something like that – they will give him a break in some way. And we do it, that's the way I have got it so far in my neighborhood.

We had a couple of homicides that occurred in the neighborhood – they came to us. You guys know, there was a group of guys who did it, everybody got arrested. I came out on bail. I took that same thing and turned it around and I made an investigation of my own. I came up with the guy that did the actual killing. I knew a lot of people that were involved in it and I came up with the whole story, how it started and how it all came about. They didn't believe me, they say, "You did it." Now I had to get citizens to come out and say the same thing. After a while, the story got cleared and they let me out and stuff like that. Then after that we kept a close contact with public relations and working with them. Now we have an edge, you know, we can do things that before they would just jump on us.

There ain't no other area there – no other club – and we control that area as far as drugs, and other crimes go. We make sure that it stays at a minimum – if it is within our help, if we can do it, we do it.

The Sex Boys and the Sex Girls:

Why are there gangs in New York?
That's a million-dollar question, right?

To protect our neighborhood. To protect our people, our family, and somebody to give help. Yeah. Not really to be screaming and killing. To protect the neighborhood.

The Sex Boys did that?

Yeah. Protect the people.

If something happened to me –

You go to them and you tell them, "Look, help me, something happened to me." They go down. Even though they don't know you, they would go down.

They go down.

You're Puerto Rican like us or you're white, you come to them – they'll help you.

The Savage Riders:

The press mention that we exist or whatever, but usually if a club does something good in the neighborhood, we won't get it in the papers. Sometimes, if there was a gang member saving a person from a building, from a fire, or saving somebody's life in a holdup, that's not going to come out in the papers. But if they were doing the opposite, actually doing the act, like putting the fire or robbing a person, then that would come out in the papers. In other words, the press doesn't want to let the people know that we have a good thing on our side, they just want to make us look like a bunch of savage animals and things like that. In civilization we know we have more in our hearts, as human beings, than those that set those laws up. They ain't got no feelings.

The gangs are going to shoot it out and some of them are going to die, and then there are less people for the police to go after . . . and less of their men getting shot up and killed. So then the cops say, "Let them kill themselves, let them go in there." And the thing that they used to do, they used to go to one area and tell these other gangs what's happening in the clubs and, "Man, I heard that these other guys from another club are going to come and do this and do that . . ."

The gangs believe that their efforts go unrewarded. They insist that they are hounded and harassed by the police, who never acknowledge any information or assistance that they provide. The media portrays them as criminals in spite of their attempts to clean up the neighborhood. Street gangs rarely say that they look for trouble – it simply finds them with great regularity.

Shadows of Death:

I'm the type of person, I try to avoid all kinds of fights I can get into, 'cos I was always taught: If anything, try and talk your way out of it first.

The Sandman Ladies:

. . . All I want to do is relax. Why I keep getting violent, I don't know. I guess I just want respect and I want to – just leave me alone. I don't bother anybody. I just mind my own business.

Angels of the Night:

'Cos that girl, you know, she don't like to look for trouble, but they like to look for trouble for her. She's quiet. She's a quiet type.

The Sex Girls:

'Cos I never looked for my fights – they always came to me. I had to fight back because I ain't going to stay with my hands like that, you know. Everybody hitting me, this and that.

Gangs exist only because members must "protect" themselves from another gang. They have been turned against society by incompetent and insensitive teachers and by corrupt police. They have become rebels, rejecting conformity in favor of war with society. A final touch to this public image is their "craziness." Their impulsive, immediate responses against slights or injustices render their behavior unpredictable, uncontrolled. Craziness becomes romantic and frightening, and the term is frequently used in self-descriptions. (At the same time, they clearly recognize that craziness has limits. When one member of the Sex Boys did indeed require psychiatric help, his fellow members were fearful and shocked.) The outlaw image they promote attracts members who believe they will find in the gang a loyal band of rebels living life on their own terms. What is the nature of the particular attraction that this exerts upon girls?

The biographies of Connie, Weeza, and Sun-Africa have many common themes. In them are clues to the personal motivation of girls in gangs.

The instability, both geographic and emotional, in th
girls' lives is noteworthy. Two came as toddlers to the United
to a language and life-style that was new to them. Conn
Weeze changed houses and schools often, rarely remaining
area long enough to make strong friendships. The frequent moves
and failure to form real ties to school friends made truanting more
and more appealing – a cycle that became hard to break. Because
their parents had only a minimal grasp of English, they were able
to truant undetected by forging notes and telling lies. As their
academic performance worsened, the idea of returning to school
became less and less attractive.

Annual uprooting meant that the burden of stability was thrust
onto the family. It alone remained constant in a changing world.
But relationships in the family were stormy and unhappy. In all
cases, the girls watched their parents argue and separate. As
children, they found themselves put in the care of relatives and
baby-sitters. Tensions between mother and father, the sight of their
frequent fights and tears resulted in a rejection of the father
combined with a reluctant and ambivalent alliance with the mother.
Weeza watched her mother's suffering with a combination of
sorrow for the years she had wasted and admiration for the tenacity
with which she determinedly clung to an unhappy marriage. At the
same time, her contempt for her mother's passivity, her surrender
to every abuse she received, engendered in Weeza a resolve never to
do the same. Connie understood her mother's need for a new
husband, loved her for the underpaid work she did to support her,
yet felt angry at her decision to place this new man in such regard
that Connie was sent away to live with relatives. Sun-Africa saw
her mother cope well with her single-parent role. Her mother had a
good administrative job and gave her children a beautiful home.
But she had been left by her husband – perhaps as a punishment
for her independence? In response, Sun-Africa rejected her own
independence, grew to hate herself for controlling Sam, and finally
wanted nothing more than to be a good wife to a strong man.

Violence in the home was not uncommon. Weeza grew up in a
family where physical aggression between her parents was com-
monplace. The instability of her life and the fragile nature of her
parents' marriage were further augmented by fear. Even in the
closest of relationships the danger of physical violence was present:
between spouses, between siblings, by father against daughter.
Weeza saw her father fire a gun at her and watched him make
passes at her friends. Connie waited for her father to die slowly and

stole from her aunt. Trust was eroded, and each of the girls retreated into a fearful independence. It was clear that they were on their own, that intimacy and weakness were the same thing. Yet being alone was not a happy state.

The Sandman Ladies:

Who do you trust most?
Me?
Yeah.
Nobody, nobody. Me? Nobody. A lot of people try to get me to come out of myself and talk to them. And I will tell them something. But I never tell them what I don't want. What is their purpose? Why? I don't trust nobody.

The Sex Girls:

I don't like friends too close because when you meet a friend real good, too close, they stab you to your back. You know.

I don't trust nobody, like I was raised. I don't know why, I don't know how. Like I say, I don't trust nobody. I don't. They got two-face, you know. Hypocrites. Two-face. They give you another one. And they talk behind your back. You know they're not friends. They're not friends. Really, they're not friends. If you had a friend, you don't talk behind her back. You feel something, you call her and tell her. You know, "This and that – I don't like this." That's a friend, you know, but don't be talking behind her back and giving a nice face. Smile friendly and when you go outside, it's a different thing, you know. That's what I change. I change friends like that. And I know I got a couple of them.

Shadows of Death:

Oh, but I could enjoy myself now because my daughter's a little older, and every once in a while, I just turn back into a little kid again, and I love it in a way, because then I think of her like a little sister in a way and I say, "Come on, you're little, you ain't got nobody else neither. You hang out with me, and we'll learn these things together."

Discussing the biographies of the girls can lead to the kind of psychological reductionism that has characterized so much of the literature on female deviance. It is not my intention to paint pictures of clinical disturbance. On the contrary, the very generality of the three major features of their lives – their ambivalence to their mothers' life-styles, their developing sense of isolation, and their fear of being victims of abuse – seem to argue for an analysis in terms of culture rather than of individual deviation.

Connie and Weeza were raised by mothers who exemplified many of the characteristics of Puerto Rican womanhood. Their principal and long-standing relationship was ultimately with their children. Married young, they moved from adolescent to wife swiftly, with all that it implied. Their life was restricted to the home, but their men continued to live in part on the streets. Although Connie's mother was married twice, it was not something of which she was proud, and while she was faithful throughout her second marriage, Connie's stepfather was not. Weeza's mother watched her husband's affairs, unhappy but passive. The roving nature of men was accepted. As wives, the women had gained respectable status, and abuse was tolerated time and again. Their children watched it happen. The poverty of the family meant frequent moves to escape debt, to get into a project house, to pay less rent, to stay with relatives. For the women, such moves were not traumatic because wherever they went, their world was restricted to their family and their kitchen. But the moves did take their toll on their children and their social relationships.

Connie and Weeza watched their mothers victimized by both poverty and cultural role. Each girl also had a sister who accepted her future place in that scheme with equanimity. But for Connie and Weeza, ambivalence was greater. They loved their mothers for their stoic endurance and absorbed many of their mothers' beliefs in love. At the same time, exposed to American culture and values, they would not accept the marianismo role. Yet the instability and uncertainty they saw and experienced in relationships made them long for social attachment, for some sense of belonging. Their anticipation and fear of physical aggression needed to be assuaged also. To be part of a loyal group, to fight for others and in turn be protected by them, offered a new kind of security. In the gang, they would find "sisters," but this time sisters who were like them. And the gang – the outlaws and rebels – would give them equality, stand by them like brothers, treat them with respect. The most important factor in their membership was simply that the gang existed to be joined. Weeza and Sun-Africa were introduced to the group through brothers, Connie through her husband. In becoming part of it, the girls thought they could escape the female stereotype they feared. They declared themselves "deviant," little knowing that the gang would be no escape from the demands of female conformity.

Sun-Africa's experience was different in important ways. Certainly, in a material sense, her home background was far better. There was much more stability and she spent longer at school. Her parents' separation indicates none of the marianismo of female suffering. Her mother coped admirably, working hard and raising her two daughters alone. Her father's new family was accepted. But Sun-Africa was raised in a female, three-generational household composed of her maternal grandmother, mother, and the two sisters. This was true also of many of her friends. The sense of female autonomy and independence from males was strong in her. In her early teens she was part of a female crew, which was associated with various male groups but not exclusively controlled by any. Together, the girls smoked grass, danced, traveled to concerts, fought other girls. Sun-Africa's very strength made her able to dominate males. She would go out with two or three at the same time, playing them off against each other, uncommitted. She stood them up after scheming frantically to secure a date with them. She referred to them often as "niggers" and "fools," conned them into buying her clothes, and tossed them aside when she had had enough. They presented a challenge to the power of her personality, but after her triumph, her interest waned. She had as much equality as she could ask for, and, had things continued as they were, she might have gone on to a future of independence much as her mother had done.

But Sun-Africa chose to reject that uncommitted freedom, just as Connie and Weeza sought it out. She shared with them an ambivalence about her mother's role. In accepting the Nation, she stepped back into a position of female subordination, which offered her a structure and a relationship to males that was absolute. There were no more choices to be made, no more autonomy to exercise. Men were "gods," demanding her respect and unquestioning obedience. She was not required to support herself. Her previous life was a shameful testament to her immorality and need for reform. She felt guilty at the way she had used men, exploited their weakness. Now, in penance, she submitted to their laws and their lessons. The Nation offered the family back to her. A man must take responsibility for his earth and his children. Though he may have more than one wife, he must provide for them all. In this way the disintegration of the black family would be stopped, as would

the matriarchy it generated. In becoming part of it, Sun-Africa
rejected the life of her mother and her generation.

For each of the girls, rejection of the future she faced as a female
came before involvement in the gang. The gang represented a
confirmation of that rejection. Sensing their difference from their
peers, the girls believed that the gang would be a bold public
statement of their rebellion. "Bad girls" hang out on the streets, so
Connie and Weeza declared their badness, even though uncertainty and guilt accompanied that decision. Sun-Africa sewed her
refinement, wrapped her head in a turban, and declared her
reversion to old female values – to the surprise and concern of her
family. Her mother's stress on schooling, the college fund for which
her father gave her money represented her "American" life, which
was past. American too was her crew life: the tacky clothing, the
trivial values, the materialism. But in the groups the girls joined,
they found not a new sense of self nor a new set of values, but the
old ones disguised in a new way.

The boys controlled the gang and the boys continued to live out
the male roles that they had grown up with, casting the girls in
complementary positions – positions that were all too recognizable
to them. Boys were determined to live out the "rogue male" role
that was so dear to their sense of masculinity. In the Sex Boys and
the Sandman, the boys felt free to make out with girls, both within
the club and beyond it. The girls accepted the basic nature of men,
as their mothers had done before them.

The Turban Queens:

Like, when we hang out, all of us got a guy that hangs out with
them. That's her man and that's her boy. Like all of us already had
one of the guys from the Turban Saints. All of us always had one of
them.

We used to fight a lot when they used to cut out and go see other
girls, you know. That's when we really used to go off.

Who did you go for – the boys?

It was the girls.

Girls. Like, say, we'll go to the guy first, we'll go to the guy and
we'll tell them, "Oh, we know you did this and this." "Oh no, I
swear to God." They soup you up. They think you believe them.
We say, "Alright, forget it." Then they make sure the girl won't say
nothing. They tell the girl, "You don't say anything." 'Cos they
know they'll play us dirty but we'll always be their main girls, no

matter how they put it and they know it. That's why I'm still going with him – the same with all of us.

They go to where they think we ain't gonna find out. No matter how far they do it, there's always somebody so scared of us that they'll come running and tell us.

We'll still find out. We'll always find out. They'll swear on their mother, their father, their sister, their brother, "I didn't do it, I didn't do it with that bitch. I wouldn't make good with that bitch." Then try to soup. But I already know the deal with them. "Alright, yeah, yeah, yeah." And that's when I go. Then I go up to the girl. And they don't even bother hitting us 'cos they know the're gonna get worse. I would just go up, "Hey, I hear you made it with my old man." This and that. And blat, and that's it. The whole thing is over 'cos they don't even raise their hands. They put their head down and they cut out fast. 'Cos they know – like if I was hitting a girl and they hit me back and all *these* girls see it, they're all gonna get in, you know? And she's going to get a worse beating. So she takes a slap or two and goes home and cries.

Angels of the Night:

And they [the girls] fight for any little thing. For a guy, they'll fight. Because my sister was going out with this guy named Eddie and these other girls was going out with him too but she had broke up with him. My sister-in-law took him away from her. So she was walking and four girls came up to her – all of them had sticks. When she went to swing, my cousin went like that [punched her] – hit her right here [in the nose] and this was swollen. Real hard, man. Right there, she got the girl – four girls, man. She beat up those girls. She scraped their face. She was chasing the one – she couldn't get her. She took away the stick from another girl – she started banging her.

That happened to me once. I didn't get to meet the girl. I was talking to this guy and he was a popular guy, and the next thing I know he's coming up and telling me his girlfriend is looking for me 'cos she don't know who I am. 'Cos I was just talking to the guy, yeah. I told him that he'd better tell his girl to chill out beause she's going to start getting in trouble. She's going to get it. Because I'm not going to let myself get beat up.

A man cannot be expected to turn down an offer of sexual relations; indeed, to do so might cast severe doubt on his masculinity. The way the story was told, it was always stray and wicked females who had "pushed it in his face" and he could do nothing but oblige. This implicit blame set the girls against one another. Within the gang, they regulated the divisive effects of such a situation by agreeing not to take each other's men. But with other clubs, or with errant females within the gang, arguments and fights frequently erupted. Acceptance of male promiscuity, in fact, became a strategy of both saving face and indirectly asserting female superiority. A girl need not interpret a boyfriend's infidelity as an insult to her own seductive powers as long as it was pointed out that he had no choice but to go along with the adventure. At the same time, the girls were able to treat the males as gullible children, pulled this way and that by female charms, unable to exercise control over their own behavior. They used the same value structure as their mothers. They suffered at the hands of men but also were able to assert themselves through their stoic endurance and motherly concern to keep them on the straight and narrow.

The shifting and unstable quality of romantic relationships is most clear in Weeza. But even Connie, whose marriage has survived many threats, lives daily in a state of uncertainty. There is little sense of an enduring commitment, and virtually no discussion of a joint future. Relationships are lived day-to-day, subject to violent and unpredictable eruptions. Much has been written on the effects of poverty upon intimate relationships; that it fosters temporary liaisons that are often broken by issues of jealousy and unemployment and that lack in long-term planning for the future.[15]

Among gang girls, television also has an impact. The girls followed soap operas closely, with little apparent concern for the vast economic and social disparities between the characters they watched and themselves. The universality of emotion seemed to transcend these completely. Issues of infidelity, love, pregnancy, divorce, and death were of great interest to gang girls, and from these programs they fostered an expectation that normal life was a series of dramas. The Puerto Rican temperament fed this belief plentifully. Emotions, however extreme, were very short-lived. The girl Weeza pulled a knife on yesterday may be one of her best friends today. The bottle-smashing argument of the night before seemed forgotten in the morning. The superficiality of emotions was often striking and probably highly adaptive. It was as if the capacity for being hurt had been exhausted and what one witnessed was the running through of a performance, a charade of feeling. Like addicts who become habituated to a dosage, the girls needed and sometimes generated increasingly extreme emotional stimuli. Connie threatened to jump from windows. Sun-Africa's response to a friend's escape and fall from her apartment was not much more extreme than to a soap opera drama. Weeza's response to Danny's brain damage or T-Bone's death dwelled surprisingly little upon the real emotional suffering caused by such events. In intimate relationships, emotions simmered and exploded. Other women lured men away, and ultimately attachments were fragile and fleeting affairs. Again the girls duplicated precisely the pattern of behavior of their mothers.

For Sun-Africa within the Nation, the pattern was different. She had been weary of female independence, and the Five Percenters seemed to offer a haven of male protectiveness and family values. The reality was not so simple. Males did not always confine themselves to their earths. In fact, their presence in the home was often short-lived and highly irregular. Taking on a new earth, renaming her, giving her lessons and instructions seemed to provide a temporary boost to the men's self-esteem and to occupy them for a few months at least. But later, when they had tired of the novelty, they often disappeared for days and weeks. While the earths were enjoined to remain in the home, cleaning and serving, the gods hung out together on street corners or in arcades. Apart from their crowns, it would be hard to distinguish them from any of the other local youths.

Meanwhile, the girls accepted the right of the "rogue male" to take on new wives as he felt inclined. These women moved into the apartment, previously the domain of this first earth, with surprisingly little difficulty. Peace and love took precedence over jealousy and possessiveness. The earths came to get along well together in the long periods when their god was not around. His irregular financial contribution to the home, exacerbated sometimes by his absences while serving prison sentences, also generated a paradoxical situation where, contrary to religious teaching, he might instruct them to work. The previous months of education on the woman's centrality in the home, her need for restraint, modesty, and secrecy would be washed away with a new dictate that she must wear the "devil's" clothes and find a job. Thus, a year after I met Sun-Africa, she was living with a new god in a Bronx apartment, pregnant but planning as soon as the baby was born to work and share child rearing with his first earth, who already had three children. So in the end, Sun-Africa found herself in an all-female household, raising the children alone while her "husband" remained at liberty on the streets – the very situation she had sought to escape.

For all the girls, as for their mothers, the most enduring bond in their lives was with their children. While men might come and go, children would remain throughout. Correspondingly, children occupied an important place in the girls' priorities. Yet the nature of their lives, the poverty and instability, could not fail to take their effects on the children. Weeza's son had to be moved from one school to another because of his aggressiveness. Even Sita's teachers were concerned that for all her superior intelligence she was seriously underperforming in math. The effects of Chico's aggressive presence and of Popeye's death on both children may not be evident for years to come. Connie's sons, a year after I was in contact with her, were moved into special classes, diagnosed by educational psychologists in one case as having emotional problems and in the other as showing learning disabilities. While Connie nor Weeza would knowingly tolerate the truancy they themselves had experienced, the changes of home, the violence, and the instability from which they sought to protect their children were not, in the end, escapable.

In all the groups, the girls were looking for an escape from the abiding sense of isolation they had experienced. They looked for continuity and loyalty, and unconditional acceptance.

The Turban Queens:

We got our own group, we don't need nobody else. Somebody comes to hang out with us, it's because they want to.

The Devil's Rebels (Ladies):

That's one thing, 'cos once you're in a gang, you know you got your backup and leaders, and mostly all the gangs, they stick together. 'Cos if someone pushes you from another gang, they don't care, they'll fight all of them because they pushed you. Or just say one word sometimes, like the Mafia . . . they don't like one guy, and then everyone goes after him. That's the way it is in a gang.

Shadows of Death:

Yeah, because a lot of people grew up, you know. Everybody

grew up you know, and they noticed that, you know, you don't
have a friend, you don't have any friends . . . It's like everybody's
afraid of you, and they're going to be your friend and they're going
to be nice to you and stuff like that because they know that you
might do something to them if you don't and stuff like that. And
now it's like we're all people, you know, just a certain amount of
people are together, they're organized in a certain way, a group.

Yet the brave rhetoric of the gang cracked in the face of reality time
and again. Popeye was betrayed by a member of his gang. Gino's
expressed desire for gang unity ended in gunshot wounds inflicted
by a neighboring club in retaliation for his believed betrayal.
Connie's marriage was challenged by the girls she took into the
gang. Sun-Africa watched the Puma Crew turn against one another.
Weeza finally rejected other members of the Sex Girls for never
having been true friends.

   With isolation came fear, which was present, only half hidden, in
the belligerence they voiced. "Never trust anyone" was a sentiment
expressed by each of them. And to escape the fear, came the
"tough," "crazy" bravado that they reinforced in one another. The
aggression had a preemptive quality: having a "rep" was the best
means of defense; being "crazy" had significant advantages.

   The Turban Queens:

   I'm glad I got a reputation. That way nobody will start with me,
you know. Nobody will fuck with me – they *know*, you know.
They're going to come out losing. Like all of us, we got a reputation. We're crazy, nobody wants to fight us for that reason – you
know. They say, "No man. That girl might stab me or cut my face
or something like that."
   Did other girls hear about you?
   A lot of girls heard about us. We used to walk by and they used
to move out of our way. They never stood where we walked. If we
were going to a party, they would leave.
   They still do it. When we go somewhere, like they move away.
They give us our own little spot. Like, say, if we walked into that
corner, they all move out. Nobody goes into our corner.
   Did you have to do anything to get that reputation?
   No.
   We did because we used to . . . Like if I was to see her fighting
and I see her get beat, I would cut in, you know. And once they see

one girl get in, they all get in and we beat up the girl. So like they're always scared of us – they're still that way. They know all the girls really. You talk to any girl around here and you tell them – Green Eyes, Kookie, or any of us – they know us by heart. They know we always look for a lot of fights.

There's times, yeah. When we go to fight a girl, they end up running anyway. Like the guys – they soup everything up, you know. Like they say, "No, man, don't fight that one. She's crazy, she'll cut you up." Like with those girls on 61st that happened. Boy, they were scared. They used to see me, they'd cross the avenue.

I always get nervous, even when I'm just arguing with some-body. I get nervous. There's times, yeah, when I see a real big girl, then I get scared. I think, "Damn, I'm going to hurt her or she's going to hurt me." But once you're in a fight, you just think – you've got to fuck that girl up before she does it to you. You've got to really blow off on her. You just play it crazy. That's when they get scared of you. It's true – you feel proud when you see a girl that you fucked up. Her face is all scratched or she got a black eye, you say, "Damn, I beat the shit out of that girl, you know." And it makes you feel stronger, then you want to fight more and more. Like, "I knifed this girl that means I could kick *her* ass," and you start looking for more and more fights.

Shadows of Death:

I do remember my sister, she used to get into fights with all the girls, and I remember seeing her on the corners fighting. To me it was fun, you know, I used to like it when she used to hang out and cut out of school, and she would just stay hanging out with a lot of girls.

She was tough, tough.

Right! That's my sister – you fuck me, you get your ass kicked!

Do you get a lot of status from being in a gang?

A lot of people, they don't want to mess with you.

The Devil's Rebels (Ladies):

So sometimes they know in advance that you want a fight?

Yeah, sometimes. Sometimes it's like, you know, boring. You just want some action.

Yeah, you feel bored.

They're dying to fight with somebody. Just go up to you and push you – that's it, man. They found a fight.

It was this stance of toughness more than anything else that was borrowed from the boys whose fear they shared. In the juxta-position of two recurring sentiments, "There's always someone badder than you are" turned heriocally into "The bigger they are, the harder they fall," the underlying fear was never far away.

The threat of physical violence from which the girls had sought protection in the gang remained. If anything, it became more evident because as members they were legitimate targets of attack by other gangs. They subscribed to the "jungle" view of the streets, that only the strong survive. Beneath this sentiment, however, was the persistent fear that one day they would not be strong enough.

The Devil's Rebels (Ladies):

So long as you know how to take care of yourself, you don't have nothing to worry about.

Girls around here, they see a girl that's quiet, they think that she's a little dud. Yeah – let's put it that way. They think they don't know how to fight. That's the way it is around here.

So you have to be tough?

You don't act really tough because if you act really tough, that's when a lot of girls be looking for you. You got to act calm and everything. You act tough – forget it.

It's like an invitation.

Yeah.

When you really want to, you fight. The only time you act tough is when they come up to you.

You asked if mothers encourage girls to get down? Yeah, they do. Because if they want to have a good life, they first have to learn how to survive. That's the first thing, they have to learn how to defend theirselves. Anywhere you go, you're going to come up with some fight or argument. You have to learn that first.

The Turban Queens:

So you've got to fight. Do you feel scared when you fight?

Yeah, they say the more scared you are, the more power you get. It depends on who you're fighting also.

When I'm fighting with somebody I get nervous, and that's

where you get more strength . . . The blood goes higher and higher
– you get stronger than you think.
So before the fight starts?
We'd be walking up and down, I be shaking.

The Sex Girls:

Does New York change people into fighters?
Well, over here they have to. They have to because, see, like let's
say I'm a new jack around here, right? You be going to the store –
they be taking your money. Now if you ain't going to kick their ass,
they going to keep picking on you. So before they wind up kicking
your ass, you got to get tough on them. If not, you can't even walk
the streets by yourself. They're going to wind up hurting you or
killing you or whatever they feel – they're going to start taking all
your shit. You have to be tough out here. Kick people's asses.

Shadows of Death:

So I had always tried to avoid trouble, but being hanging out
with gangs and all that kind of stuff, they don't care. At the time
they didn't care, or anything like that. Or, if you mess with their
ladies, or anything like that, they're going to get rid of you real
quick, so it's like something that grows on you. Being with these
kinds of people makes you grow that attitude with them. And with
anger even more.

The Devil's Rebels (Ladies):

Round here you have to know how to fight. If you can't fight,
they beat you up. I mean beat you up.
That's why I don't like to fight. I'm lucky I haven't killed
nobody.
Could a girl who couldn't fight manage around here?
If she can't fight, she still has to fight.
Somebody will push her. Like, if a girl can't fight, they do any
stupid thing to fight with her. Like a tough girl – I mean a girl like
us – knows that she fights with another chick that don't even know
how to fight, she beats her up, she knows she's going to come back
and get her revenge. That's why you learn how to fight. When you
fight once and you don't know, that's when you learn how to fight.
When you're scared and everything, they're always picking on

you. You have to learn to be brave. Comes to the time, when you don't know how to fight, you're so scared, you're so wild, you don't even realize you're hurting the girl. I've seen it happen.

⌜For these girls, there was no escape in the gang from the problems they faced: their female role could not be circumvented, their instability remained and was magnified, their isolation was covered by a rough veneer. The gang was no alternative life for them. It was a microcosm of the society beyond. Granted, it was one that had a public image of rebellion and excitement and offered a period of distraction (discussions of gang feuds and honor and death). But in the end, gang or no gang, the girls remained alone with their children, still trapped in poverty and in a cultural dictate of womanhood from which there was no escape.⌟

Girls have been part of gang life for over a hundred years, from social clubs through years of prohibition and corruption to the "bopping" gangs of the 1950s and through the civil disorders and the woman's movement of the 1970s. Social scientists are now more sensitive to relationships of girls with other girls, and the small amount of available research reflects a growing concern with girls beyond their sexual relationships. As they assume a more three-dimensional representation, girls appear increasingly as sisters in the gang instead of as molls. But it cannot be said that their roles have altered substantially. They exist as an annex to the male gang, and the range of possibilities open to them is dictated and controlled by the boys. Within the gang, there are still "good girls" and "bad girls," tomboys and fallen women. Girls are told how to dress, are allowed to fight, and are encouraged to be good mothers and faithful wives. Their principal source of suffering and joy is their men. And though the girls may occasionally defy them, often argue with them, and sometimes patronize them, the men remain indisputably in control.

Many social commentators might wish to find that this state of affairs has been washed away since the 1970s. Some criminologists believe that the increase in female crime is a direct result of the liberation of women. Some radical criminologists hoped to see a new revolutionary awareness springing from oppressed women and where better to look than at women in urban ghettos? Social control theorists maintain that crime results from the failure of individual ties to mainstream values, and who would be a better candidate for such alienation than urban minority women who have so little to gain by commitment to conformity?

These expectations were unrealistic. The gang is not a counter-culture but a microcosm of American society, a distorted mirror image in which power, possessions, rank, and role remain major issues but are found within a subcultural life of poverty and crime. Gangs do not represent a revolutionary vanguard rejecting the norms and values of a capitalist society that has exploited them. When gang members talk of politics, they talk of the American Dream, of pride in their country, of High School Equivalency Diplomas. They want better welfare and health benefits, they want more jobs, but they don't want revolution. Gangs exist not in an anomic vacuum where sex roles are forgotten and anything goes, but in a subculture deeply embedded within the value system of Western capitalism. Girl members as women want to be American, to be free, to be beautiful, to be loved. These girls subscribe to the new woman's dream, the new agenda: No more suffering or poverty. No more lonely, forced "independence", living alone on welfare in a shabby apartment. First, a good husband; strong but not violent, faithful but manly. Second, well-dressed children. Third, a beautiful suburban apartment. Later for the revolution.

Chapter 7

Girls in Gangs: The Sequel

Gangs are back in fashion for 1990s social science. They are the thing to study. In 1984, when this book first appeared, there was little being published on the subject. Criminology was off gangs. They had been hot in the fifties – in fact they had dominated the field to the point that theories of crime *were* theories of gangs. The prototypical criminal was the urban gang member and sociology was abuzz with debate over the role of psychopathology, blocked opportunities, group process, criminogenic lower-class value systems, and class conflict in the schools. The gang remained viable in the sixties as a wave of liberalism inspired grass-roots movements, federal programs, and academics to "turn gangs around" by extolling and exploiting their solidarity and cohesion in the service of their local communities. When liberalism failed and the programs folded, academics turned away looking for greener pastures. Through the seventies and early eighties the gangs became invisible: they disappeared from the newspapers and the academic journals. (When I was doing my research, many people seemed surprised that I had found any gangs to study.) But out on the streets of New York, Chicago, and Los Angeles, kids hooked up on street corners, put on their colors, and continued to claim their turf or their barrio just as they had been doing for years.

Through the eighties, the law and order lobby grew. Overcrowded prisons were bursting at the seams, the death penalty was effectively restored, victim services sprouted, fear of crime was the popular academic field of study, and the gun lobby managed to defend legitimate ownership of automatic weapons. A "them and us" mentality crystalized. Tom Wolfe's blockbuster *Bonfire of the*

Vanities portrayed the Kafkaesque nightmare of one of "us" entering the sordid, filthy world of "them." The hunt was on for the dangerous few who threatened the security of the prospering middle-class. Government funds were channeled into studies of "career criminals" (who used to be called recidivists). The challenge was to map out their pattern of criminal escalation so that such offenders could be identified early. Once identified they could be "selectively incapacitated," a euphemism for locking people up in prison on the basis of crimes they *might* commit in the future. It was a short step from career criminals to the reawakening of interest in gangs. If the task was to locate future serious offenders quickly and cheaply, politicians were sure that the gang was a convenient place to find them. So gang members returned to criminology, not as the politically misguided yet macho heroes of the sixties but as the villains and folk devils of the yuppie era.

Gangs have always been convenient whipping boys for any crime wave because of the lack of systematic national data on their numbers, location, and collective criminal record. Because police are not required to maintain or report such information, gangs remain ephemeral. Because we don't know where they are, who they are, and for what crimes they are arrested, they can be resuscitated at will to account for any serious crime problem that is currently afflicting the nation. Serious crime is usually a synonym for index or felony crimes and more violent offenses. But official statistics suggest that gang members account for only a small proportion of violent offenses. Estimates based on official criminal justice data suggest that about between 1 and 5 percent of all violence arrests involve street gang members.[1] In one study it was found that about 20 percent of juvenile violent offenders in Philadelphia were youth gang members.[2] Their rate of involvement in violence was between one-and-a-half and two times that of non-gang members. However, this study examined police records of crime and knowledge of the individual's gang membership may well have affected the police decision to record the crime officially as opposed to merely cautioning the offender.

One of the positive effects of the recent renewed interest is that we now have more sensitive data on gang crime than we did before (albeit on a small sample of gang members from a few cities.) This data has come from the use of self-reported delinquency questionnaires. By asking gang members (and non-gang members as a comparison group) about the crimes they have committed we can go some way toward approaching the "dark figure" of crime –

crimes for which no arrest is ever made. These questions are posed under conditions of strict anonymity to encourage informants to tell the truth. (The amount of deception is quite low, at least as indicated by validity checks of whether those questioned report crimes known to the police or for which they were arrested. Unfortunately, concealment is most prevalent among young, urban, minority males – the ones whose official crime rate is usually the highest.)[3] These studies can give us at least a tentative answer to the question of whether gang members are more criminal than other teenagers in their neighborhoods.

When gang and non-gang teenagers from Chicago, Los Angeles and San Diego were asked if they had ever been involved in twelve different offences, gang members came out higher every time.[4] But when they were asked how many times in the last year they had done each of these crimes, there were no differences between the two groups for the violent acts. As the report concludes: "Although gang members are involved in violence, the frequency of their participation apparently is no higher than non-gang youth." Studies show the presence of a "dangerous few" out there but they are not especially likely to be gang members. They probably operate in groups, since most delinquent acts are group events, but research does not indicate anything special about the "gang" that produces violent or serious offending.[5] Much of the violence that does take place in gangs is non-fatal and directed toward other gang members rather than the general public.

There has been virtually no interest in the convergence of gang membership and serious offending among girls. In part this springs from the conventional wisdom that women just do not commit felonies (a conviction that seems immovable even in the light of the fact that 20 percent of felony arrests are of women). Gang girls in particular fall victim to their traditional fate. Sometimes they are written off as organizationally marginal and therefore uninteresting. As one sociologist concisely dismissed them, "female gangs . . . were actually more similar to groupies whose identity was closely tied to that of male gang allies."[6] Sometimes they are caricatured as "good girls" incapable of serious crime or as "bad girls" inciting boys to do it for them. One government report concluded that "females are more likely to make a positive contribution toward conventionalizing male gang behavior rather than inciting male gang members to violent or criminal activity."[7]

Now let's go to the data.[8] The percentages of gang girls admitting felony assault and minor assault were 29 and 23 percent respectively, which was significantly lower than for boys. But the number of acts this group had committed in the past year was somewhat higher than for boys. Although girls may be less likely to become involved in gang-related violence, those that do are as involved as males. Because the absolute numbers of females in gangs is lower than that of boys, the amount of gang-related violence among girls is considerably lower. But to caricature gang girls as the pawns of male gang members (or the reverse) misses the point. Gang girls, like their male counterparts, have differing degrees of involvement in violence, probably related to their position in the gang and the approval they receive for it from their peers.

Another factor in the resurgence of interest in gangs has been the increasing concern with the development of an urban under-class – a class characterized not by temporary poverty but by institutionalized racism and classism, which make economic escape virtually impossible. The buoyant economy of the 1980s combined with affirmative action programs already in place, swelled the ranks of the black middle-class. Those who attended college and became professionals moved out of inner city neighborhoods to richer communities and suburbia. The flight of the best and brightest left a core of urban blacks in neighborhoods now devoid of positive role models, of those well placed to lobby for better living conditions, and of those who in an earlier age might have begun businesses and created jobs.[9] Unemployment among young black males reached astronomical proportions. Unable to find steady employment, they were forced to take temporary work whenever it was available. As even the casual labor market declined, crime became a real economic option. Since most street crime is intra-racial and directed at victims who live within a few blocks of the offender's home, a cycle of crime developed which successfully deterred new businesses or families from locating there. Neighborly trust diminished and with it the sense of community which has been shown to act as a deterrent to crime. With the neighborhoods impersonalized and fragmented, there was little social organization to exert control over the downhill slide.

It was in this context that the "new" gang was recognized by sociologists.[10] But apart from the fact that gangs have recently been noted to have a larger percentage of older members than ever before (a result of the high rates of neighborhood unemployment) there is little evidence that the new gangs look much different from the old ones. Recent studies confirm that gang members continue to engage in cafeteria-style crime, doing a little of everything. They do not specialize in the property crimes that might be expected from their marginalized economic position.

The new gang is really the same old gang. Indeed, many of its proponents explicitly note the resemblance between contemporary gangs and those described in the 1920s. What is new is the explanation that is being offered for its existence – the underclass. Gangs have existed for well over a century in spite of the fact that they are periodically "rediscovered" by the media, researchers or the Justice Department. When they are put in the spotlight, a new set of causes is proposed for their mysterious appearance. At the turn of the century it was immigration, then it was blocked opportunities, then the breakdown of the nuclear family. Today it is the urban underclass. It is as if there were some collective academic amnesia. But that is not the answer. In fact this seems to a classic case of losing sight of the forest because of the trees. The slightest alteration in appearance or organization of the gang is taken as evidence of its mutation into a new phenomenon, even though researchers should expect just such differences as a function of the method of data collection, the geographical location of the gang, the shifting availability of criminal opportunities, and the selective attention and values of the researchers.

Instead these transitory effects (which statisticians call "measurement error") are given the status of significant changes. If there is a new gang, there must be a new explanation for it (and of course more dollars spent on pursuing it). The underclass is rightly a high-priority concern of sociologists. As a source of human suffering and chronic wastage of human potential, it deserves more than just research; it deserves a political solution. But the plight of the underclass will not be helped by holding it accountable for a phenomenon which predates it by nearly a century. Poverty and gangs have always gone hand-in-hand. Neither one of them is new, though today both are more entrenched and more stigmatized. To those who remain unconvinced I present the brute fact that only one-in-ten gang members is female. Yet women are the principal victims of chronic poverty, marginalization, and unemployment. There are more women than men trapped in the underclass. If gang membership is a simple function of underclass membership, where did all the young women gang members go? We should have witnessed a massive rise in their numbers in the last decade, but none is yet apparent. Those who support the underclass–gang connection must account for the pivotal role of gender in mediating this relation.

If the form and activities of the gang have not radically changed, there is some evidence that gang membership now shows more signs of social pathology and alienation than before. The sociologist, Joan Moore, collected information from two waves of gang members in Los Angeles;[11] one group had been active in the 1940s and 1950s, while the second, younger cohort had joined during the 1960s and 1970s. The results suggest not only that the gang seems to be more central to the lives of its members now than in the past, but that involvement in serious crime has slowly become more prevalent. Drug use and violence are more frequent in the younger group.

The centrality of the gang seems to have become more evident in the lives of young women than young men, and this may be linked to the especially disadvantaged backgrounds from which they come. For example, younger women said the gang was "very important" to them and described themselves as "wild" more often than did the older women. The women were more likely than the men to find their spouses in the gang. Women gang members more often came from broken homes and from homes in which no one was employed. They more often came from families in which they had witnessed their mothers being beaten by their fathers. About one-third reported that a family member had made sexual advances toward them. More of the women had experienced a death in their family during childhood, had grown up with a heroin addict in the home, or had seen a member of their household arrested.

It seems then that social fragmentation has had a special impact upon female gang membership. The data suggest a deterioration in gang members' sources of support ouside the gang – a fact which is borne out by the finding that younger members' parents were more likely to express disapproval of the gang than in earlier generations. In Los Angeles, the gang has shifted from being an accepted and integrated part of barrio life to becoming a more alienated and autonomous youth group. In another city, Milwaukee, sociologist John Hagedorn has argued that institutionalized racism and unemployment has created a black underclass for whom the gang constitutes both a route to economic gain and a source of emotional support.[12] With little sense of pride or identity in being black and with little sense of community allegiance, gang members travel across the city to hang out with others who are equally alienated from the workplace and their own neighborhood.

As usual, concern over the impact of underclass membership has been disproportionately focused on men. Statistics on the feminization of poverty are frequently cited, but usually in connection with the spectre of an increase in male gang membership. Yet as we have seen, it is female gang members who come from some of the most impoverished, broken, and disorganized families. And it is they who will become the mainstay of their own future families when the males leave. Because of the exclusive concern with male gang members, the female members still find their lives caricatured and dismissed in a footnote or a paragraph. John Hagedorn, for example, reports that the girls' involvement with their gang "appeared to cease after the women turned eighteen or became mothers." And that apparently is the end of them. But more detailed data from Los Angeles paints a very sorry picture of gang girls' futures.[13] Although 94 percent had children, only 23 percent were raising them with their spouses. As Joan Moore notes, "the vast majority [of men] do not establish families or bring up children." In these womens' households, 22 percent included someone who was chronically ill or handicapped, 43 percent included a heroin addict, and two-thirds had a member who had been arrested.

Such statistics can only hint at the day-to-day experience of these women's lives. After the brief flowering of adolescence they become invisible again, trapped inside projects or run-down tenements, quietly raising the children which their husbands are happy to father but unable or unwilling to support and raise. Male gang members threaten to develop into the career criminals of tomorrow, so they attract our concern. But women suffer quietly, so we don't hear them – not until they publicly disgrace themselves by neglecting their children, or trading sex for crack. Then we hear them loud and clear. And we are hearing more and more about that.

It was the media that "discovered" how crack cocaine was being distributed by street gangs. In Los Angeles, local black gangs had coalesced into two factions: the Crips and the Bloods. These rival groups, identifiable by their preference for blue and red attire respectively, were heralded by the *New York Times* as "the main distributors of crack throughout the Western United States."[14] But researchers who have worked for many years with Los Angeles gangs maintain that they are not, and have never been, drug-dealing organizations. Selling drugs has been a staple economic means of survival for some gang members, but it is an individual activity, not a product of an orchestrated group enterprise.

California police data show that about 25 percent of arrests for drug sales were by individuals with gang involvement.[15] Another study concurred; only about a quarter of gang members interviewed in three major cities, including Los Angeles, were associated with gangs which could be considered well-structured criminal organizations with systematic involvement in drug sales.[16]

The media's interest in crack has not only implicated street gangs but has displayed a fascination with the involvement of women. Studies estimate that between a quarter and third of crack users are female.[17] But it is not their mere participation that sells newspapers. It is the intersection of their sexuality and their motherhood with drugs that produces the roar of indignation.[18]

The attraction of crack is that it gives an intense high without the prohibitive expense of cocaine. By heating cocaine with baking soda, cocaine "rocks" or "crack" are produced which can be sold in affordable units – usually priced between three and ten dollars. Because crack is smoked rather than injected it eliminates the intravenous fix (with its telltale tracks and risk of HIV infection) which deterred many from using hard drugs. While the pleasure of an escapist high is taken as sufficient explanation of its use by men, among women its use is said to be "intricately intertwined with negative self image. Women who perceive themselves as unattractive use drugs to feel prettier."[19] Even the motivation for crack use among women is reduced by the media to concern for sexual attractiveness.

But it is the exchange of sex for crack that has far and away caused the most alarm. One study of urban drug users indicated that female and male use is remarkably similar with respect to dosage (an average of 32 rocks per week) and dollars spent (an average of $350 per week).[20] Among women this kind of money can be earned by selling their bodies – an option that is largely unavailable to men. Moreover, although curbside sales are increasing in popularity, a considerable part of crack selling and use still takes place in "crack houses" where there is a constant stream of customers coming and going. Women who spend time there quickly find that they can use their bodies to obtain a fairly continuous supply of crack. The exchange of sex for drugs is not viewed as prostitution, since money does not usually change hands. One study of adolescent female crack users in Miami found that 27 of the 38 girls interviewed admitted trading sex for crack during the one year prior to interview.[21] These girls admitted an average of 706 tricks, or about two acts of prostitution per day.

These are shocking figures, particularly in the light of the ages of these girls, all of whom were between 14 and 17. But we need to keep a balanced view of these facts. However much prostitution is to be deplored, it is probably less antisocial than the robberies committed by many male addicts to sustain their habits. Secondly, it takes two to make an exchange. The media seems much less concerned about the morals of the men who are exploiting the girls than about the morals of the exploited. Indeed, a good deal of attention has been paid to the allegedly aphrodisiac qualities of crack, and the term "crack whores" implies an eager participation on the part of the women. Yet it is clear from the statements that these women make that the exchange is, from their point of view, purely utilitarian. As one Miami girl said, "All you want to do is get 'em up and get 'em off as quick as you can."[22]

It is also clear that many of the young women who engage in sex for crack were criminally active long before they used crack. On average the Miami girls used marijuana at age 9, cocaine and heroin at 11, and crack at 13. Their first act of prostitution was at age 11, and of robbery at age 12. They admitted to 1,620 offenses per subject during the one year prior to interview, which averages out to 4.4 criminal acts per day. Crack use sustains and encourages a pattern of antisocial behavior that began many years before. And it is the girls themselves that are likely to be the first victims of their behavior. Many of their johns are intravenous drug users. This fact, combined with failure to use condoms and the cuts and blisters on the mouth which result from crack smoking, make the possibility of contracting AIDS very real.

Another area of concern about women users has arisen from their role as mothers. "Addiction to crack can kill parental instinct," the *New York Times* announces,[23] although the story makes it quite clear that it is only maternal and not paternal instinct that is in question. The two million cases of child abuse and neglect reported annually are being largely attributed to the crack epidemic. The cost of drug use eats up the families' meager resources and the effect of the drug is to increase aggression, newspapers allege. Through their role as mothers, women are again singled out for a special kind of moral censure. The social problems of poverty, unemployment, inadequate and nonexistent child care alternatives, absent fathers, and rundown neighborhoods can all be hidden behind the "bad mother." What kind of mother can this be who would use drugs? The kind who, if she were in white suburbia might be swallowing valium or putting vodka in her morning orange juice – in short, the desperately unhappy kind. And what of the father? Most of them fled the scene before blame was being thrown around. We blame the mother because she stayed with her children and did a lousy job. The father is excused because he did not even clock in for parental work.

The line between using and selling is much less sharp for crack than for heroin and other hard drugs. The production process is both easy and cheap, and production and sales provide a convenient way for many users to sustain their habit. While heroin distribution was owned by organized crime groups, crack appeared with such speed and such availability that there were no established territorial organizations to handle it. This has had a particular impact on women. Traditionally, women have been excluded from adult organized crime except in ancillary roles. This has been attributed to the pervasive sexism of men in such groups, who are said to have a common belief that women are too physically weak and lacking in esprit de corps to be accepted. Though women may be fiercely loyal to their male partners, they cannot be trusted to hold group secrets, and so they are excluded from the planning and performance of crimes. The more structurally complex, professional, economic, and rational the organization is, the less likely women are to be given meaningful roles in it. The deprofessionalization of crack sales may have created openings for women. A New York City study of drug selling found that 24 percent of sellers were women.[24] Of these, 48 percent were low-level crack sellers. Women accounted for slightly over one-third of retail crack sellers.

But is there a connection between street gang membership and drug selling among young women? The data suggest that the link exists but is weaker than it is for men. A survey of gang members indicates that a third of male gang members, compared to less than a quarter of female members, admit to selling drugs.[25] But young men and women who do sell admit to about the same number of sales per year – an average of about 40 incidents. If we turn the question around, we get similar results. Among the New York City crack sellers, over a third of men and a quarter of women sold crack as part of a gang. The nexus of women, gangs, and drugs is likely to prove an attractive one to the media. But we would do well to remember that for many women and men in poverty crack offers a lucrative, if risky, source of income. The relatively simple conversion of cocaine to crack, which can be done in a kitchen, results in a 100-percent profit margin. One woman with five children was receiving $600 a month from welfare. Crack selling brought in about $1,000 a week. Though the gang may provide tutelage in the skills and connections needed to start up, the attraction of drug sales speaks for itself.

Although the involvement of women in the underworld of gangs and drugs presents exactly the kind of moralistic voyeurism on which much of the media thrives, it is ironically an area which women researchers have generally avoided. In recent years there has been an outpouring of work by women scholars on the male domination of social science generally, and a new attention given to feminist criminology specifically.[26] The result has been a rapid growth in our understanding of women as victims. Research has been directed toward documenting the bias of the criminal justice system in its treatment of female offenders at each stage of processing, from the police, to courts, and to corrections. Another major area of concern has been the victimization of women in their homes by their male partners. These are both important areas, but the feminist agenda has stopped short of acknowledging women as offenders. In 1975, Freda Adler's book *Sisters in Crime* suggested that women's "liberation" had caused an increase in female offending by freeing women from the home and affording them similar legitimate and illegitimate opportunities to those available to men.[27] The feminist response was immediate, heated, and well-supported by data indicating that such a thesis was wrong.[28]

The vehemence with which the idea was attacked seemed to signal to female researchers that theories about women as offenders were going to be subject to considerably more scrutiny than those of women as victims. It was much more ideologically comfortable about women academics to concentrate on the institutionalized sexism and patriarchy which oppressed poor and minority women. But such a position does disservice to women as a whole. Firstly, it encourages the traditional stereotype of women as passive and exploited. It refuses to credit women with the capacity to take action, to strike back, to find means, legal and illegal, to put bread on the table and to construct an identity for themselves. (This criticism was leveled at Marxist criminologists many years ago when they seemed determined to view the working class as passive recipients of the political and economic brutality of the establishment. Since then, left-wing academics have become more willing to acknowledge the condescension inherent in such a position.) The twin facts that women have the competence to commit crime if they choose and that the vast majority do not are both central to a full understanding of crime. Our current theories are theories of half the population because they are wholly predicated on male patterns of offending. An adequate theory must be able to explain the most universal and the most powerful fact of all and that is women's relative desistance from crime. But this can only be understood by including women who offend as well as women who do not.

The second reason why we need to broaden our horizon to include women offenders is that if women scholars will not do it, men will. And indeed male scholars have begun to examine female offending. It seems to me that two themes are emerging from their work which would be much less likely to be apparent among women researchers.

The first is a traditional acceptance of the need for distance between subject and researcher. This distance is particualarly troubling when the two do not have even gender in common. Because women are raised in a male-dominated world, they are taught to view it through male eyes by learning male history, reading the great male writers, and following male politics. The world of women is private, marginal, and ill-documented. It is particularly difficult for males to enter it without a real commitment to listening carefully to women's voices. Yet few male social scientists seem willing to do this.

Instead, the male academic sits in his office deriving predictions from a theory. These predictions are then turned into questions to which subjects can respond yes or no, true or false. Often the interviewer is someone other that the researcher, a "blind" technique to ensure that the researcher's expectations cannot influence the subject's replies. These methods may ensure "objectivity," but they also ensure that the researcher remains ignorant of the social context in which the women live, and hence liable to misunderstand the issues which seem to them to be important, and the interpretations they place upon their actions. By forcing the complexity of women's lives into checkmarks in boxes on a piece of paper, we think we are doing "pure" science and reducing "error." But what we are doing is demanding that complexity be reduced to simplicity and that women's views be translated into the response alternatives that the male researcher imposes. His choice of alternatives *defines* the alternatives. This "objectivity" is in fact merely the imposition of someone else's subjectivity.

Feminist scholars have written eloquently about women's ways of knowing, and there is much consensus around women scholars' suspicion of traditional social science methods.[29] Women are more cynical about the possibility of "value-free" science and the discovery of "universal" laws of human behavior. Women's sense of connection with others and their intimate involvement with children teach them that there are multiple perspectives on any issue. To deny the validity of alternative views, to assert that one is "objective" while another is "subjective," is both to betray the true state of things and to place oneself in the role of God. Social science must maintain its relationship with the real world and reflect the views of the people whom it studies. Error, as women see it, lies not in having a relationship with the people we study but in failing to know them at all.

This belief has paid off in rich and sensitive accounts by women of women who are living on the margins as hustlers, addicts, and gang members.[30] In these ethnographic works, twilight worlds are illuminated by a sense of the writer's connection and concern with the people whom she seeks to understand. They stand in stark contrast to the grim determination of much criminological research to wrench criminals away from polite society by finding some variable (*any* variable) that stigmatizes them as different.

Another theme that is emerging is a focus upon women as bit players in the male world of crime. Here the marginality of women in crime groups reflects not the sexism of the researcher (as it did in the bad old days) but the sexism of the male criminal underworld. Whereas the old researchers barely saw female members at all and so relegated them to footnote status, the new researcher poses the question: why are crime groups structured in sexist ways?[31] This new question is designed to explain the "facts" that female crime is individualistic rather than subcultural and that females act in support of males when they commit crime. But when it comes to juvenile crime, there is serious reason to doubt these "facts." Self report delinquency questionnaires show that girls are more, not less, likely to commit offenses in groups rather than alone.[32] Teenage girls have also been found to have closer, more loyal, and more harmonious relationships with their friends than do boys.[33] With this in mind, it should come as no surprise that studies comparing the sexes find that association with delinquent peers is the strongest predictor of delinquency for girls as well as boys.[34] Others have examined relationships between girls in delinquent groups. They report that it is relationships with and approval of delinquency by other girls, not boys, which correlates with delinquent behavior.[35] The "fact" of females as attached to the group only by virtue of their relationships with males was a byproduct of male researchers' exclusive focus on male gang members, and of their failure to obtain first-hand accounts from girls themselves.

I do not want to romanticize young women's friendships (they are filled with much of the same rivalry and ambivalence as anyone else's), nor to deny the importance of romantic and sexual relationships (which are extremely important to both sexes in adolescence, although completely absent from researchers' accounts of male gang members.) Rather I want to raise a question about the origin of our assumption that female friendships are not as solid as male friendships and that young women are led into delinquency by "bad boyfriends."[36] Wherever those ideas came from, it was not from any female delinquent or scholar that I have talked to.

For the future, I hope that women's experiences in gangs as in other arenas will be taken increasingly seriously as a topic of research. I also hope it will be examined from an insider's perspective by those with a real commitment to understanding the lived reality of these women. I hope that social science will one day accept the need to admit the complexity, contradiction, and diversity already described by many pioneering women scholars. Mostly, I hope that the lives of half the population will be included as an integral part of our understanding of human behavior, rather than as a footnote to the lives of men.

Notes

Introduction to the Second Edition

1. E. Liebow, *Tally's Corner* (Boston: Little, Brown and Co., 1967).

2. O. Lewis, *La Vida: A Puerto Rican Family in the Culture of Poverty: San Juan and New York* (New York: Vintage Books, 1965).

3. Y. S. Lincoln and E. G. Guba, *Naturalistic Inquiry* (Beverly Hills, Calif: Sage, 1985); R. Harre and P. Secord, *The Explanation of Social Behavior* (Totowa, N. J.: Littlefield, Adams and Co., 1985).

4. This brief discussion is informed by: N. Chodorow, *The Reproduction of Mothering* (Berkeley, Calif.: University of California Press, 1978); C. Gilligan, *In a Different Voice: Psychological Theory and Women's Development* (Cambridge, Mass.: Harvard University Press, 1982); J. Hagan, J. Simpson, and A. R. Gillis, "Feminist Scholarship, Relational and Instrumental Control, and a Power-control Theory of Gender and Delinquency," *British Journal of Sociology, 39* (1988): 301–36.

Chapter 1: The Praised and the Damned

1. On societal structure see A. K. Cohen, *Delinquent Boys: The Culture of the Gang* (Glencoe, Ill.: Free Press, 1955); R. K. Merton, *Social Theory and Social Structure* (Glencoe, Ill.: Free Press, 1957); R. A. Cloward and L. E. Ohlin, *Delinquency and Opportunity* (Glencoe, Ill.: Free Press, 1960). On class relations see W. B. Miller, "Lower Class Culture as a Generating Milieu of Gang Delinquency," *Journal of Social Issues, 14* (1958): 5–19; E. Stark, "Gangs and

Progress: The Contribution of Delinquency to Progressive Reform,"
in D. F. Greenberg (ed.), *Crime and Capitalism* (Palo Alto, Calif.:
Mayfield, 1981). On rites of passage see H. Block and A. Nieder-
hoffer, *The Gang: A Study of Adolescent Behavior* (New York: Philo-
sophical Library, 1958). On group cohesion see M. Klein and L.
Crawford, "Groups, Gangs and Cohesiveness," in J. F. Short (ed.),
Gang Delinquency and Delinquent Subcultures (New York: Harper &
Row, 1968). On ecological pressures see F. M. Thrasher, *The Gang*
(Chicago: University of Chicago Press, 1927); C. Shaw, *Delinquency
Areas* (Chicago: University of Chicago Press, 1929). On learning
mechanisms see E. Sutherland and D. Cressey, *Criminology* 10th ed.
(New york: Lippincott, 1978). On linguistic usage see W. Labov,
Language in the Inner City (Philadelphia: University of Pennsylvania
Press, 1970).

2. Estimating the size of gang membership generally has been a
problem. Few cities keep statistics on gang membership and those
that do use different definitions of gang, gang membership, and
gang crime. These matters and the role of the New York City media
are discussed in W. B. Miller, *Violence by Youth Gangs and Youth
Groups as a Crime Problem in Major American Cities* (Washington,
D.C.: U.S. Government Printing Office, 1975), and in W. B.
Miller, "Gangs, Groups and Serious Youth Crime," in D. Schichor
and D. Kelly (eds.), *Critical Issues in Juvenile Delinquency* (Lexington:
Lexington Books, 1980). A more recent estimate of New York gang
membership suggests that numbers have declined to 4,300 members
in 86 gangs. This decline was contemporaneous with the dis-
mantling of the Police Gang Intelligence Units in Brooklyn and the
Bronx and so may represent a less sensitive estimate. See J. A.
Needle and W. V. Stapleton, *Police Handling of Youth Gangs* (Washington, D.C.: U.S. Department of Justice, 1983).

3. Miller, *Violence by Youth Gangs and Youth Groups*.

4. This discussion of class value orientation draws upon the
work of Cohen, *Delinquent Boys*, especially his discussion of "college
boys" and "corner boys," and of Miller, "Lower Class Culture as a
Generating Milieu of Gang Delinquency." The views of these
theorists on the value systems of gang members have been considered incompatible. The literature on female gang membership
suggests that girls from the same class background differ in their
adherence to middle- versus lower-class values or focal concerns.

5. M. Wallace, *Black Macho and the Myth of Superwoman* New
York: The Dial Press, 1978).

6. W. F. Whtye, *Street Corner Society: The Social Structure of an*

Italian Slum (Chicago: University of Chicago Press, 1943).

7. H. Asbury, *The Gangs of New York* (New York: Capricorn Books, 1970). Originally published in 1927.

8. *Ibid.*

9. *Ibid.*, emphasis added.

10. *Ibid.*

11. Thrasher, *The Gang*.

12. Whyte, *Street Corner Society*.

13. W. Bernard, *Jailbait* (New York: Greenberg, 1949).

14. Cohen, *Delinquent Boys*; Cloward and Ohlin, *Delinquency and Opportunity*; Miller, "Lower Class Culture as a Generating Milieu of Gang Delinquency."

15. Welfare Council of New York City, *Working with Teenage Groups: A Report on the Central Harlem Project* (New York: Welfare Council of New York City, 1950).

16. J. F. Short and F. L. Strodtbeck, *Group Process and Gang Delinquency* (Chicago: University of Chicago Press, 1965).

17. R. Rice, "A Reporter at Large: The Persian Queens," *The New Yorker, 39* (1963): 135 ff.

18. K. Hanson, *Rebels in the Streets: The Story of New York's Girl Gangs* (Englewood Cliffs, N. J.: Prentice-Hall, 1964).

19. L. Bowker, H. Gross, and M. Klein, "Female Participation in Delinquent Gang Activities" (Paper delivered to the American Society of Criminology, San Francisco, 1979). This study is also discussed by G. Luce, "Delinquent Girl Gangs," in J. Seigel (ed.), *The Mental Health of the Child* (Washington, D.C.: U.S. Government Printing Office, 1971)

20. The Molls are discussed in W. B. Miller, "The Molls," *Society, 11* (1973): 32–35, and the Queens in E. Ackley and B. Fliegel, "A Social Work Approach to Street Corner Girls," *Social Work, 5* (1960): 29–31. A fuller account of the Queens was provided by personal communication with W. B. Miller and will appear in W. B. Miller, *City Gangs* (New York: Wiley, forthcoming).

21. W. B. Miller, "Youth Gangs in the Urban Crisis Era," in J. F. Short (ed.), *Delinquency, Crime and Society* (Chicago: University of Chicago Press, 1976); H. C. Collins, *Street Gangs: Profiles for Police* (New York: New York City Police Department, 1979). See also J. F. Short, "Gangs, Politics and the Social Order," in Short (ed.), *Delinquency, Crime and Society*.

22. For the thesis that women's liberation led to an increase in female crime see F. Adler, *Sisters in Crime: The Rise of the New Female Criminal* (New York: McGraw-Hill, 1975). Opposing positions

have been taken by other writers; see for example: P. Giordano and S. Cernkovich, "On Complicating the Relationship Between Liberation and Delinquency," *Social Problems*, *26* (1979): 467–481; C. Smart, "The New Female Criminal: Reality or Myth?" *British Journal of Criminology*, *19* (1979): 50–59; J. Gora, *The New Female Criminal: Empirical Reality or Social Myth?* (New York: Praeger, 1982).

23. Miller, *Violence by Youth Gangs and Youth Groups*.

24. W. Gale, *The Compound* (New York: Rawson, 1977).

25. J. Quicker, "The Chicana Gang: A Preliminary Description" (Paper delivered to the Pacific Sociological Association, San Jose, 1974).

26. W. Brown, "Black Female Gang Members in Philadelphia," *International Journal of Offender Therapy and Comparative Criminology, 21* (1977): 221–228.

27. Short and Strodtbeck, *Group Process and Gang Delinquency*.

28. Bowker, Gross, and Klein, "Female Participation in Delinquent Gang Activities"; Quicker, "The Chicana Gang"; P. Giordano, "Girls, Guys and Gangs: The Changing Social Context of Female Delinquency," *Journal of Criminal Law and Criminology, 69* (1978): 126–132.

29. Asbury, *The Gangs of New York*; Thrasher, *The Gang*; Ackley and Fliegel, "A Social Work Approach to Street Corner Girls."

30. R. Horowitz, "Masked Intimacy: Adult Delinquent Gangs in a Chicago Community" (Paper delivered to the American Society of Criminology, San Francisco, 1980); S. Browne, *Adult Commitments of Former Adolescent Delinquents* (Ann Arbor, Mich.: University Microfilms International, 1981).

Chapter 2: Urban Living for Girls

1. In reporting these and the following statistics, the most recently available data has been sought. Annual data is not collected for much of the information, however, so the given figures may go back as far as 1978. The following sources were used: J. Lash, H. Sigal, and D. Dudzinski, *State of the Child: New York City*, 11 (New York: Foundation for Child Development, 1980); National Puerto Rican Forum, Inc., *The Next Step Toward Equality* (New York: National Puerto Rican Forum, Inc., 1980). Recent data were also supplied by Alan Guttmacher Institute, Aspira of New York,

Bureau of the Census (Census of Population and Housing), New York City Board of Education (Profile Division), New York City Department of Health (Bureau of Health Statistics and Analysis), New York State Department of Education (Bureau of Statistical Services), New York State Department of Social Services (Public Information Office), Planned Parenthood of New York City, Inc.

2. D. P. Moynihan, *The Negro Family: The Case for National Action* (Washington, D.C.: U.S. Department of Labor, 1965).

3. L. Rainwater and W. Yancey, *The Moynihan Report and the Politics of Controversy* (Cambridge, Mass.: M.I.T. Press, 1967); J. Ladner, *Tomorrow's Tomorrow: The Black Woman* (New York: Doubleday, 1972); M. Wallace, *Black Macho and the Myth of Superwoman* (New York: The Dial Press, 1978); J. Hale, "The Black Woman and Child Rearing," in L. F. Rodgers-Rose (ed.), *The Black Woman* (Beverly Hills, Calif.: Sage Publications, 1980).

4. U. Hannerz, *Soulside: Inquiries into Ghetto Culture and Community* (New York: Columbia University Press, 1969). See also R. Staples, *The Black Woman in America* (Chicago: Nelson-Hall, 1973).

5. Wallace, *Black Macho and the Myth of Superwoman*; Hale, "The Black Woman and Child Rearing"; E. Engram, "Role Transition in Early Adulthood: Orientations of Young Black Women," in Rodgers-Rose (ed.), *The Black Woman*.

6. E. Herzog, "Is There a Culture of Poverty?" in H. H. Meisner (ed.), *Poverty and the Affluent Society* (New York: Harper & Row, 1966); Wallace, *Black Macho and the Myth of Superwoman*. See also E. Liebow, *Tally's Corner* (Boston: Little, Brown and Co., 1967), and B. Dill, "The Means to Put My Children Through: Child Rearing Goals and Strategies Among Black Female Domestic Servants," in Rodgers-Rose (ed.), *The Black Woman*.

7. L. Rainwater, "The Problem of Lower Class Culture and Poverty-War Strategy," in D. P. Moynihan (ed.), *On Understanding Poverty* (New York: Basic Books, 1968).

8. *Ibid.*; Hannerz, *Soulside*; Liebow, *Tally's Corner*. See also L. Myers, "On Marital Relations: Perceptions of Black Women," in Rodgers-Rose (ed.), *The Black Woman*.

9. Wallace, *Black Macho and the Myth of Superwoman*. Different interpretations of this male-female relationship have been given by R. Hill, *The Strengths of Black Families* (New York: National Urban League, 1972), and by L. F. Rodgers-Rose, "The Black Woman: A Historical Overview," in Rodgers-Rose (ed.), *The Black Woman*. On female support networks see C. Stack, *All Our Kin: Strategies for Survival in a Black Community* (New York: Harper & Row, 1974).

10. D. Schulz, *Coming Up Black: Patterns of Ghetto Socialization* (Englewood Cliffs, N.J.; Prentice-Hall, 1969).

11. L. Rainwater, *And the Poor Get Children: Sex, Contraception and Family Planning in the Working Class* (Chicago: Quadrangle, 1960). On the role of mothers and grandmothers in absorbing children who are not their own see R. Hill, *Informal Adoption Among Black Families* (Washington, D.C.: National Urban League Research Department, 1977). See also R. Bell, "The Relative Importance of Mother and Wife Roles Among Negro Lower Class Women," in R. Staples (ed.), *The Black Family: Essays and Studies* (Belmont, Calif.: Wadsworth, 1971).

12. L. Rainwater, "Crucible of Identity: The Negro Lower Class Family." *Daedalus, 95* (1966): 172–216.

13. J. Fitzpatrick, *Puerto Rican Americans: The Meaning of Migration to the Mainland* (Englewood Cliffs, N.J.: Prentice-Hall, 1971); E. Acosta-Belen and E. H. Christenson, *The Puerto Rican Woman* (New York: Praeger, 1979).

14. E. B. Massara, "Que Gordita! A Study of Weight Among Women in a Puerto Rican Community" (Doctoral thesis, Bryn Mawr, 1979).

15. A. Pescatello, *Female and Male in Latin America* (Pittsburgh: University of Pittsburgh Press, 1973).

16. M. Lopez-Garriga, "Strategies of Self-Assertion: The Puerto Rican Woman" (Doctoral thesis, City University of New York, 1976).

17. H. Sofa, *The Urban Poor of Puerto Rico: A Study in Development* (New York: Holt, Rinehart and Winston, 1974).

18. O. McCauley, "A Study of Social Class and Assimilation in Relation to Puerto Rican Family Patterns" (Doctoral thesis, Fordham University, 1972). See also N. Glazer, "The Puerto Ricans in New York," in H. Meisner (ed.), *Poverty in the Affluent Society* (New York: Harper & Row, 1966); Fitzpatrick, *Puerto Rican Americans*; N. Glazer and D. P. Moynihan, *Beyond The Melting Pot*, 2nd ed. (Cambridge, Mass.: M.I.T. Press).

19. M. Abramson and the Young Lords Party, *Palante! Young Lords Party* (New York: McGraw-Hill, 1974).

20. O. Lewis, *La Vida: A Puerto Rican Family in the Culture of Poverty: San Juan and New York.* (New York: Vintage Books, 1965). See also S. Sheehan, *A Welfare Mother* (Boston: Houghton Mifflin, 1976).

21. Massara, *Que Gordita!* See also P. Cooper, *Growing Up Puerto Rican* (New York: Arbor House, 1972).

Chapter 6: No Escape

1. For data on gang membership and gang crime see J. Hargrove, *Annual Report of Gang Activity in Brooklyn South and North* (Internal Memo, New York City Police Department, 1976–1978); H. Collins, *Street Gangs: Profiles for Police* (New York: New York City Police Department, 1979); W. B. Miller, *Violence by Youth Gangs and Youth Groups as a Crime Problem in Major American Cities* (Washington, D.C.: U.S. Government Printing Office, 1975); J. A.Needle and W. V. Stapleton, *Police Handling of Youth Gangs* (Washington, D.C.: U.S. Department of Justice, 1983).

2. Miller, *Violence by Youth Gangs and Youth Groups*.

3. M. Klein, *Street Gangs and Street Workers* (Englewood Cliffs, N.J.: Prentice-Hall, 1971); J. W. Moore, *Homeboys: Gangs, Drugs and Prison in the Barrios of Los Angeles* (Philadelphia: Temple University Press, 1978).

4. W. B. Miller, "Violent Crimes by City Gangs," *Annals of the American Academy of Political and Social Sciences, 364* (1966): 96–112.

5. J. B. Mays, *Growing Up in the City* (London: Macmillan, 1954); P. Scott, "Gangs and Delinquent Groups in London," *British Journal of Delinquency, 7* (1956): 4–24; D. Downes, *The Delinquent Solution* (London: Routledge and Kegan Paul, 1966); S. Cohen, *Folk Devils and Moral Panic* (London: MacGibbon and Kee, 1972).

6. J. Higham, *Strangers in the Land* (New York: Atheneum, 1973).

7. J. Bell and T. Gurr, "Terrorism and Revolution in America," in H. Graham and T. Gurr (eds.) *Violence in America: Historical and Comparative Perspectives* (Beverly Hills, Calif.: Sage Publications, 1979).

8. R. Brown, "The American Vigilante Tradition," in Graham and Gurr (eds.) *Violence in America*.

9. D. Jacobs, "Street Gangs Behind Bars," *Social Problems, 21* (1974): 395–409.

10. W. Gale, *The Compound* (New York: Rawson, 1977).

11. W. B. Miller, "Lower Class Culture as a Generating Milieu of Gang Delinquency," *Journal of Social Issues, 14* (1958): 5–19.

12. H. Thompson, *Hell's Angels* (New York: Random House, 1966).

13. Gale, *The Compound*.

14. A. Riess, "The Social Integration of Queers and Peers," *Social Problems, 9* (1961): 102–120; D. Lockwood, *Prison Sexual Violence* (New York: Elsevier, 1980).

15. O. Lewis, *La Vida: A Puerto Rican Family in the Culture of Poverty: San Juan and New York* (New York: Vintage Books, 1965).

Chapter 7: Girls in Gangs: The Sequel

1. S. Pennell and C. Curtis, "Juvenile Violence and Gang Related Crime." (San Diego Association of Governments/Criminal Justice Evaluation Unit, San Diego, Calif., 1982); I. Spergel, "Violent Gangs in Chicago: In Search of Social Policy," *Social Services Review*, *58* (1989): 199–226.

2. P. E. Tracy and E. S. Piper, "Gang Membership and Violent Offending: Preliminary Results from the 1958 Cohort Study (Center for Studies in Criminology and Criminal Law, University of Pennsylvania, 1982).

3. M. Hindelang, T. Hirschi, and J. G. Weis, *Measuring Delinquency* (Beverly Hills, Calif.: Sage, 1981).

4. J. Fagan, "Social Processes of Delinquency and Drug Use among Urban Gangs," in C. R. Huff (ed.), *Gangs in America* (Beverly Hills, Calif.: Sage, 1990).

5. M. Morash, "Gangs, Groups and Delinquency," *British Journal of Criminology*, *23* (1983), 309–31.

6. C. R. Huff, "Youth Gangs and Public Policy," *Crime and Delinquency*, *35* (1989), 524–37.

7. I. A. Spergel, "Youth Gangs: Problem and Response: A Review of the Literature" (Executive summary: Paper prepared for the National Youth Gang Suppression and Intervention Project, 1989).

8. Fagan, "Social Processes of Delinquency."

9. W. J. Wilson, *The Truly Disadvantaged* (Chicago: University of Chicago Press, 1987).

10. M. W. Klein, "Thoughts on Street Gangs, Neighborhoods and the Urban Underclass" (SSRC Meeting on Communities and Neighborhoods, Santa Fe, New Mexico, January 1989); J. W. Moore, "Isolation and Stigmatization in the development of an Underclass: The Case of Chicano Gangs in East Los Angeles," *Social Problems*, *33* (1985), 1–30.

11. J. Moore, "Changing Chicano Gangs: Acculturation, Generational Changes, Evolution of Deviance or Emerging Underclass," in J. H. Johnson Jr. and M. L. Oliver (eds), *Proceedings at the Conference on Comparative Ethnicity* (Los Angeles, Calif.: UCLA Institute for Social Science Research, 1988).

12. J. M. Hagedorn, *People and Folks: Gangs, Crime and the Underclass in a Rustbelt City* (Chicago: Lake View Press, 1988).

13. J. Moore, "Changing Chicano Gangs."

14. "In the Middle of L.A.'s Gang Warfare," *New York Times*

Color Magazine (May 22, 1988), p. 30.

15. M. Klein, C. L. Maxson, and L. Cunningham, "Gang Involvement in Cocaine 'Rock' Trafficking" (Los Angeles, Calif.: Center for Research on Crime and Social Control, Social Science Research Institute, 1988).

16. J. Fagan, "The Social Organization of Drug Use and Drug Dealing among Urban Gangs, (1989)" *Criminology*, *27* 633–69.

17. J. Fagan and K. Chin "Violence as Regulation and Social Control in the Distribution of Crack" (Paper presented to the National Institute of Drug Abuse, Rockville, Maryland, 1989); B. Frank, W. Hopkins, and D. S. Lipton "Current Drug Use Trends in New York City" (Albany: New York State Division of Substance Abuse Services, 1987); T. Mieczkowski, "Crack Distribution in Detroit," *Contemporary Drug Problems*, *17* (1990), 9–30.

18. I am indebted to Lisa Maher for many of these thoughts on women, crack, and sexual control. Her interpretation of these issues can be found in her forthcoming doctoral dissertation, available from Rutgers University, School of Criminal Justice.

19. J. Nelson, "Back from Crack," *Essence* (January 1990), 57ff.

20. Mieczkowski, "Crack Distribution in Detroit."

21. J. A. Inciardi, "Trading Sex for Crack among Juvenile Drug Users: A Research Note," *Contemporary Drug Problems*, *16* (1989), 689–97.

22. Ibid.

23. "Addiction to Crack can Kill Parental Instinct, *New York Times* March 17, 1990), p. A1. New York Times (1989) Drug Arrests Jailing Many Mothers. *New York Times*, April 17, 1989, p. A1.

24. L. Maher, and J. Fagan "The Political Economy of Female Participation in Illicit Drug Markets" (Rutgers University, School of Criminal Justice, forthcoming).

25. Fagan, "Social Processes of Delinquency."

26. S. Simpson, "Feminist Theory, Crime and Justice," *Criminology*, *27* 605–31; K. Daly, and M. Chesney-Lind, "Feminism and Criminology," *Justice Quarterly*, *5*, (1988) 497–538.

27. F. Adler, *Sisters in Crime: The Rise of the New Female Criminal* (New York: McGraw-Hill, 1975).

28. C. Smart "The New Female Criminal: Reality or Myth?" *British Journal of Criminology*, *19* (1979), 50–9; F. M. Heidensohn, *Women and Crime: The Life of the Female Offender* (New York: New York University Press, 1985); D. J. Steffensmeier, "Sex Differences in Patterns of Adult Crime 1965–1977," *Social Forces*, *58* (1980), 1080–109.

29. C. Gilligan, *In a Differnt Voice: Psychological Theory and Women's Development* (Cambridge, Mass.: Harvard University Press, 1982); E. F. Keller, *Reflections on Gender and Science,* (New Haven, Conn.: Yale University Press, 1989); S. Ruddick, *Maternal Thinking: Toward a Politics of Peace* (Boston, Mass.: Beacon Press, 1989).

30. E. Miller, *Street Woman* Philadelphia: Temple University Press, 1986); M. Rosenbaum, *Women on Heroin* (New Brunswick, N.J.: Rugers University Press, 1981); M. G. Harris *Cholas: Latino Girls and Gangs* (New York: AMS Press, 1988).

31. D. J. Steffensmeier, "Organizational Properties and Sex-segregation in the Underworld: Building a Sociological Theory of Sex Differences in Crime," *Social Forces, 61* (1983), 1010–22.

32. N. Emler, S. Reicher, and A. Ross "The Social Context of Delinquent Conduct," *Journal of Child Psychology and Psychiatry and Allied Discipline, 28* (1987) 99–109.

33. P. Giordano, S. A. Cernkovich, and M. D. Pugh, "Friendships and Delinquency," *American Journal of Sociology, 91* (1986), 1170–202.

34. J. Figueria-McDonough, W. H. Barton, and R. C. Sarri "Normal Deviance: Gender Simlarities in Adolescent Subcultures," in M. Q. Warren (ed.) *Comparing Female and Male Offenders* (Beverly Hills, Calif.: Sage, 1981).

35. P. Giordano, "Girls, Guys and Gangs: The Changing Social Context of Female Delinquency," *Journal of Criminal Law and Criminology, 69* (1978), 126–32; L. H. Bowker, and M. W. Klein, "The Etiology of Female Juvenile Delinquency and Gang Membership: A Test of Psychological and Social Structural Explanations," *Adolescence, 18* (1983), 740–51.

36. A. Campbell "Female Participation in Gangs" in R. Huff (ed.), *Gangs in America* (Beverly Hills, Calif.: Sage, 1990).

Index

292

Gangs as...

① a sense of escape
② an
③
④

why men join gangs
↓
why women join gangs
① escape
② protection
③ boredom